D1328532

The
Italian
Cinema
Pierre Leprohon

Lucia Bosè in *Cronaca di un Amore* (Antonioni, 1950)

THE
ITALIAN CINEMA

Pierre Leprohon

Translated from the French by
Roger Greaves and Oliver Stallybrass

Praeger Publishers
New York · Washington

Visual Studies Workshop
Research Center
Rochester, N.Y.

BOOKS THAT MATTER

Published in the United States of America in 1972
by Praeger Publishers, Inc., 111 Fourth Avenue,
New York, N.Y. 10003

Le Cinéma Italien by Pierre Leprohon
Copyright © 1966, by Editions Seghers, Paris

This translation, which contains revisions and
expansions of the original French text
Copyright © 1972, Secker & Warburg, London

Designed by Michael Farrell

Library of Congress Catalog Card Number: 70–99314

Printed in Great Britain

Contents

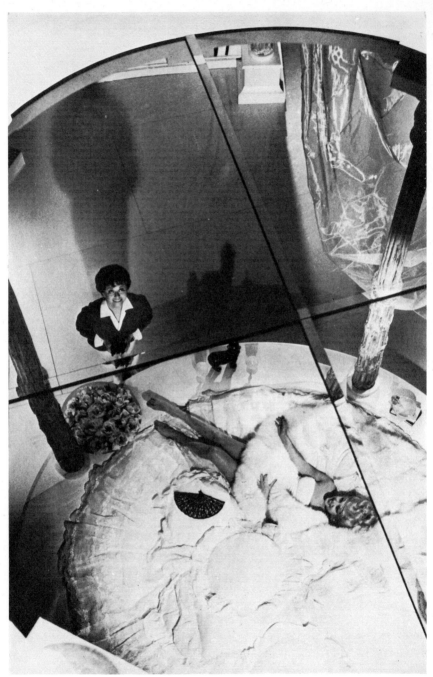

Giulietta Masina, Sandra Milo in *Giulietta degli Spiriti* (Fellini, 1965)

1. The Early Years (1895–1908)

Italy's long-term contribution to the invention of cinematography was a notable one. It was Leonardo da Vinci who devised and described the camera obscura. Early experiments with this device were performed in the 17th century by another Italian, the Neapolitan Giambattista Della Porta; and, also in Italy, Father Athanasius Kircher, a German Jesuit who died in Rome in 1680, took these experiments a stage further and developed the 'magic lantern' described in his treatise *Ars magna lucis et umbrae*. But strictly speaking the invention to which these experiments led was photography; cinematography did not see the light of day until 1895, when patents were taken out in both Italy and France. On 11 November of that year Filoteo Alberini patented a device, the Kinetografo Alberini, for taking, printing and projecting films.

Two months earlier, Italy had celebrated her twenty-fifth anniversary. During the long period in Italian history known as the Risorgimento (1815–70), social and political thinking had centred on the notion of a united Italy; and unity had been achieved on 20 September 1870 when King Victor Emmanuel's army had marched into pontifical Rome. Significantly, this historical event was the subject of the first Italian film worthy of a place in the annals, *La Presa di Roma* (also known as *La Breccia di Porta Pia*), made in Rome in 1905 by Filoteo Alberini. From the very outset, therefore, the Italian cinema (like the American, Russian and German cinemas) was bound up with its country's political history – and with the general trend in social thinking, which was to determine the main stages in its development. It seems indispensable, then, to begin this discussion with a cursory look at the internal situation of Italy at the time the cinematograph was beginning its career.

'We have made Italy,' said Massimo D'Azeglio at the time; 'now we have to make the Italians.' Paul Guichonnet has defined the social state of the country as follows:

The life of the nation was severely compromised from the outset by two grave handicaps. The first of these was the disequilibrium between the North and the South, which unification did nothing to redress; indeed, the situation deteriorated as a result of the concentration of wealth and activity in the Po valley. Secondly, all business was in the hands of a tiny élite, which became even more select as a result of Pius IX's ban on Catholic participation in the legislative elections. This ban was not withdrawn until 1904.[1]

Despite the Law of Guarantees of 1871, the Pope, proclaiming himself a 'voluntary prisoner' in the Vatican, brought about the refusal of a large section of the population to support the new state. Following the example of the old continental nations, the Italian government, faced with the growing problem of overpopulation, led the country into a megalomaniac policy of nationalism, armament and colonialism that bore no relation to its real possibilities and diverted capital and energy from the equipment of the home sector.

Eritrea and Somaliland were in Italian hands. A conflict with Abyssinia broke out in 1893. Only a few years after its unification, Italy let itself be drawn into a policy of vainglorious conquest, when at home the country was oppressed by the poverty, illiteracy and insanitation that hampered its growth for half a century.

At the time Filoteo Alberini was perfecting his *kinetografo*, in December 1895 and early 1896, the conquerors were encountering serious difficulties in Abyssinia. On 1 March, 25,000 men were defeated at Adowa. Crispi, whose ambition was to crown Humbert Emperor of Abyssinia, was swept from power and peace was hastily concluded with Abyssinia.

But the defeat at Adowa, the downfall of Crispi, and the assassination of Humbert in 1900 did not prevent Italy from relapsing into this insane urge to repeat the feats of ancient Rome. The historian Mack Smith has shown that Humbert's kingdom in 1870 already bore the germ of Fascism, with its overriding insistence on the idea of nationalism, its barriers to popular participation in government, and the enthusiasm of its masses for Garibaldi-type leaders of men.

'*Risorgimento*, unfinished revolution. . . .' It is with this motto that Carlo Lizzani begins his *Cinema italiano*.[2] And Nino Frank writes:

The end of that century and the beginning of this one constituted the painful era when Italy was attempting to absorb its over-rapid unification. After fifteen centuries of fragmentation, political unity had been acquired in the space of twenty years. With a South of starving peasants and fishermen, a North that was discovering the joys of capitalism and forming an industrial proletariat, a Centre that desired nothing more than the emergence of a petty bourgeoisie of bureaucrats and freemasons . . . these were years of poverty and social unrest. . . .[3]

Unfinished revolution. If the moral reawakening of the élite was reflected in the monumental work of the idealist philosopher Benedetto Croce (1866– 1952), it was undoubtedly the nationalistic rhetoric of Gabriele D'Annunzio (1863–1938) that reflected the sensibility of the average Italian and fore-shadowed the crisis of Italian culture under Fascism.

D'Annunzio's false eloquence got him cast in the role of one of the 'leaders of men' which the period demanded; with his capture of Fiume in 1919, it attracted the Italian people to the dangerous notions of Fascism. 'It is impossible not to mention D'Annunzio here,' writes Nino Frank:

He was the product of the illusions of his day and age, which sought escape through the sublime – and a very ordinary 'sublime' it was too! He was typical of the aristocratic intellectuals of his day; he won a popularity that is in direct contradiction with the nature of his work. His grandiloquence, his swagger, and his 'common touch' . . . reached every level of society, including the cinema. . . . D'Annunzio is one of the key figures of this period.

With this famous name, then, the history of the Italian cinema overlaps with the history of Italy. Even in this very brief survey of the political scene we can detect the main characteristics and contradictions of the whole Italian cinema down to the present day – the cinema of Rossellini or De Sica as much as that of Blasetti or Riccardo Freda, and the silent despair of *Ladri di Biciclette* (*Bicycle Thieves*) as much as the heroic sweep of *Scipione l'Africano*, or *La Regina delle Amazzoni*. This disparity, if we may call it that, belongs thus both to a race and to its history.

Ten years elapsed between the date of Alberini's patent and what may be called the birth of the Italian cinema: *La Presa di Roma* in 1905. In Italy there was no expansion of the cinema comparable to the boom that occurred in France. Why was this? It is true that the attendant political and economic circumstances were hardly favourable; but equally, of the many devices patented at that time, Alberini's among them, only one really worked – the

Lumières'. We can conclude, therefore, that Alberini's crude invention was rapidly ousted by the imported *cinématographe*. Lumière's first delegate to Italy was Eugène Promio, who trained Vittorio Calcina (1847–1916) as the Lumière representative in Italy. While Promio continued his round of Europe, Calcina recorded events and royal visits and helped to enrich Lumière's general catalogue. This catalogue, which has been unearthed by Georges Sadoul, contains some twenty-five views of Italy – towns and famous people, notably the marriage of the Prince of Naples – and above all the shots of Venice filmed by Promio, whose panorama of Saint Mark's Square shot from a boat is our earliest example of a tracking shot.[4]

According to one authority, the first movie camera in the capital was brought there by Baron Kanzler, son of the General Kanzler who had defended Rome in 1870.

Assisted by young Carlo Respighi – the future Prefect of Ceremonies at the Vatican – Kanzler successfully used this device for his research on Christian archaeology, with particular reference to the architecture of the catacombs. A considerable number of films were produced in this way. One of them, *The Tomb of the Martyr*, can still be projected today owing to the excellent state of preservation of the print.[5]

Dilettanti apart, however, there is every reason to believe that the Italian public's first encounters with this new form were provided by Lumière's *cinématographe*. In 1896, a Lumière imitator, Italo Pacchioni (1872–1940), shot the inevitable arrival of a train in Milan railway station and 'comic views' including *La Gabbia dei Matti* (*Madhouse*), *Il Finto Storpio* (*The Sham Cripple*), and *La Battaglia di Neve* (*Snowfight*), titles which suggest that these scenes were not staged for the camera but filmed from life, as were Promio's productions.

In 1896, Leopoldo Fregoli (1867–1936), a famous music-hall impersonator, met Louis Lumière in Lyons and arranged for a few of the latter's films to be projected as part of his act. The success of these film shows encouraged him to film his own music-hall numbers: Fregoli at the restaurant, Fregoli at the seaside, Fregoli the hairdresser, Fregoli and the lady at the restaurant, Fregoli in the Army, Fregoli the conjuror, and so forth. Prints of these short films from the 'Fregoligraph' are still in existence at the Cineteca Italiana.[6] Fregoli used many trick shots and even hit on the idea of projecting his films in reverse; later he gave them a vocal accompaniment from the wings, imitating the voices of the characters on the screen.

So moving pictures had, almost certainly, already made their appearance in Rome when a Frenchwoman, Mme Lelieur, got together with several friends, among them Luigi Topi and Ezio Cristofari, to found a Franco-Italian company for presenting moving picture shows with the Edison Kinetoscope. The novelty was so successful that soon afterwards Luigi Topi opened another hall on the via Nazionale. It was here that he hit on the idea of making a film of his own for the Easter holidays of 1900: a 'passion play' in ten tableaux for which he hired a music-hall artiste, Fremo, as Christ, and a singer, La Belle Otéro, as Mary. This film, an adaptation of *tableaux vivants*, was the first example in Italy of what became a flourishing genre.

However, if Fregoli and Topi merit recognition as pioneers of the Italian cinema, the cinematograph, as they used it, remained a mere recording device, with no autonomy whatsoever.

The first real sign of concerted activity came in Turin, the capital of the house of Savoy and, significantly, the starting-point of Italian unity. To this lively, enterprising city of northern Italy Edoardo Di Sambuy, a member of the Photo-Club, had brought a camera back with him from France.[7] He passed it on to a dealer in optical and photographic equipment, Arturo Ambrosio, under whose aegis Roberto Omegna (1876–1948) shot the first Italian newsreels. These were of two local events: the first automobile race from Susa to Moncenisio and manœuvres at the Colle della Ranzola. Each film was 98 metres in length. A year later, in 1905, Omegna continued his experiments, with the mounted manœuvres of the Lancers, the opening of a mountain refuge, another race from Susa to Moncenisio, and the earthquake that occurred in September in Calabria and Sicily. Omegna then turned to the documentary, the field in which he was to win fame a few years later; but the advent of the first production companies, coupled with the emulation of foreign models, resulted in a preference for the romantic vein that was to ensure the success of screen entertainment. (By this time, remember, Méliès had been reigning supreme for seven or eight years; he was already on the verge of his decline.)

In June 1904, Alberini the inventor branched out into showmanship, founding the Cinema Moderno in Rome. In 1905 he went further still, launching his 'Primo stabilimento italiano di Manufattura Cinematografica Alberini e Santoni'. At the end of that year, Alberini and Santoni built in the via Appia nuova a studio which the prospectus claimed to have all the latest equipment imported from France and Germany. 'Novel and interesting subjects' would be treated, with no expense spared as regards staging, sets or cast. And the partners made no bones about their aim of moving into the front rank.

In line with this declaration of policy, Alberini produced in 1905 *La Presa di Roma*. This film (seven scenes, 250 metres) had the collaboration of a famous actor, Carlo Rosaspina, and, more important still, the co-operation of the Ministry of War 'for the uniforms, artillery, and weaponry'. At a stroke the Italian cinema had jumped the fairground era and was starting as an industry, the profitability of which was rapidly confirmed. On the technical level its lack of experience brought both difficulties (hence the call on foreign technicians) and freedom. The latter was very rightly stressed by Henri Langlois in an enthusiastic article written after the Italian Exhibition at the Cinémathèque Française in 1954:

Being completely inexperienced, the Italian cinema of the years 1906–9 was able to assimilate all the discoveries made in France, Great Britain and the U.S.A. without exhausting its creative genius.

Having no tradition, no fixed prejudices, having learned their technique beforehand, by watching other people's films, without being troubled or cramped by established routine, the Italian directors of the years preceding the First World War took to the camera like ducks to water, educated by the effort of others, unhampered by fixed modes of procedure.[8]

In 1905, Alberini and Ambrosio distinguished themselves as pioneers in yet another respect, since they were the first to bring together the entrepreneur and the technician, the producer and the director. By early 1906, less than a year after it had been founded, the firm of Alberini and Santoni had become a joint-stock company, Cines, headed by Baron Alberto Frassini as secretary and the French engineer Pouchain as chairman, with Alberini as technical director. Cines was floated by a Vatican financier, Ernesto Pacelli, the uncle of Pius XII; but technically and artistically the enterprise escaped the founder's intentions almost immediately.

Hence the new industry was controlled by men who had nothing in common with the fairground showmen who launched the cinema in France, and this fact explains the tremendously rapid rise of the cinema in Italy. In 1907, the country already had 500 picture houses with a total annual receipt of 18 million lire.

With the exception of *La Presa di Roma*, however, activity in 1905–6 seems still to have been cautious in both Rome and Turin. Alberini's output barely exceeded a monthly print footage of 500 metres, comprising a few dramas and comedies. Ambrosio tried his hand at directing in the garden of his villa, with Giovanni Vitrotti as his cameraman: drama, comedy, comic sketches including 'piquant scenes' in a Parisian vein: *Paravento* (*The Folding Screen*), *Primi Calori* (*The First Hot Spell*), etc.

As early as 1906, about sixty films were produced, along with some thirty documentaries or newsreels. The success of a national prestige film, *Cavalleria Infernale* (also known as *I Centauri*; 102 metres), on the Rome Riding School, and a sequel on the same theme, *Tor di Quinto*, made Ambrosio decide to found his company and extend his production. In the space of a few months he sold 857 prints of his *Cavalleria Infernale*.

Cines was less active but, it seems, more ambitious, with an adaptation of the famous Lysis Girls' number, a pantomime-ballet called *Malia dell'Oro*, with a musical accompaniment by Romolo Bacchini, who also wrote the music for a drama scripted by Turchi, *Pierrot Innamorato*, filmed in twelve scenes. But if its management and finance were fully equal to its ambitions, Cines lacked technicians; realizing this, it imported them from abroad as it had already done its equipment. The success of Pathé – whom just about all the early Italian film-makers blatantly plagiarized – led Cines to make an offer to one of the French firm's best technicians, Gaston Velle. Velle accepted and left for Rome, taking several assistants with him. He gave Cines the benefit of his experience – and the very subjects he had just been filming in Vincennes for Pathé. *Viaggio in una Stella*, for instance, was filmed in Rome in July 1906 just a few weeks after Velle had filmed *Voyage dans une Etoile* in Paris, and before it had been shown there. Charles Pathé was angry and struck back – not at Velle, but at another *émigré*.

With Gaston Velle as their artistic director, Cines produced a great many films in every genre: costume films, drama (*Otello*), ballet (*Il Fauno*; *The Faun*), and even a 95-metre colour film, *Japonaiseries*. At the end of the financial year, Cines had net profits amounting to 500,000 lire, when its registered capital was only 300,000 lire.

Ambrosio's success in Turin with the early costume films of Luigi Maggi earned him a competitor, Carlo Rossi. Rossi's partnership with the Prussian financier Remmert in a wireless telegraphy venture was giving poor returns, and this led him to seek another outlet for his ambitions. Tempted by the example of Cines and Ambrosio, he formed the firm of Carlo Rossi with his partner Remmert, the latter's son-in-law Sciamengo, and a young man just out of technical school who first served as office boy, then took charge of the accounts. Six months later, Giovanni Pastrone, the future director of *Cabiria*, was company secretary of what had become Sciamengo and Pastrone. Interviewed in 1949, Pastrone said:

At that time, the Italian film industry had still to get off the mark. Rossi and Remmert were thus obliged to call in technicians from France. In late 1906 they hired five 'traitors' from Pathé's at Vincennes, who arrived in Turin at the beginning of 1907. Their leader was Lépine, who had been general manager of the Pathé studios. He was accompanied by his two sons-in-law (the cameramen Caillaud and Comte), a technician, Zollinger, who was Swiss, and a third cameraman, Eugène Planchat.[9]

In hiring technicians from Pathé, Rossi was following the profitable example set by Alberini. But Charles Pathé had already contrived (perhaps with a threat of legal action) to get Velle back to Vincennes in that same year of 1907, and he resolved to hit back at these 'traitors'. He accused Lépine of stealing industrial secrets, and indeed appears to have proved his accusation. The team had taken with them plans of equipment, which they apparently then had executed for Rossi. Lépine was sent to prison in Turin for several months. Some of the Frenchmen left Rossi for Ambrosio.[10]

The partners quarrelled and the company was sequestered before it could make representations. Sciamengo and Pastrone reorganized it as Itala, while Rossi got himself taken on by Baron Fassini at Cines and ultimately became the active head of that firm.

Itala made its début with romantic and costume films shot on location: a rehash of Richepin's novel *La Glu*, a film about Napoleon on Elba, and so on. But young Pastrone realized that total success would depend on improvements in filming and projection; he tried to eliminate flickering, with partial success. The year 1908 was to mark in every field a great step forward in Italian production.

The success of the first 'film factories' in Turin and Rome soon attracted attention elsewhere in northern Italy, which was then making great efforts to develop its industry and organize its economy. Competitors were not long in appearing, notably in Milan, where several firms were founded in 1908. S.A.F.F.I. (later Milano Film) was headed by a former photographer, the cameraman Luca Comerio, who had made his début the year before with documentaries on the Army and the royal visit to Greece; this firm made 300-metre costume films and adaptations of literary works. Two other companies were founded in Milan, those of Bonetti and of Croce. But Turin, with the hundred or so films produced by Ambrosio, remained the chief production centre. Aquila was founded there by Otto Lenghi, who produced an adaptation of *Le campane di Corneville* (*The Bells of Corneville*), while Pasquali, journalist and scriptwriter, left Ambrosio to found a company under his own name. Lastly, in Rome, the Azaglio brothers and Lamberto Pineschi were building up a production company which in 1909 became Latium. Other firms, more or less short-lived, were founded for the purpose of filming local events in Venice, Florence, Velletri, Naples and even Palermo. All this activity shows the interest aroused by the infant industry; but its significance for the history of the cinema is small. For that reason it does not seem necessary to go into detail here. Also, the three firms that had given rise to much of this proliferation remained the most important ones, and it was they that set the trends in Italian production.

Ambrosio had the largest output and the most consistent success at the box-office, sweeping the board with *Gli Ultimi Giorni di Pompei* (*The Last Days of Pompeii*). Itala also made a hit with *Il Conte Ugolino*, adapted from Dante, and did very well out of comedy. By the end of 1908 it was shooting three or four films a week, with a total footage of 500 to 600 metres. Cines, for its part, had increased its capital to 3 million lire. Reorganized by Carlo Rossi, who had left Turin to become its art director, the young firm went from strength to strength.

After 1908–9, however, the general advance was of such proportions that we must now turn from the history of the individual firms to more general considerations, and attempt to define in terms of the early personalities the trends and genres that were to stamp this cinema with its particular impress and thereby determine its subsequent development.

But before doing so I should mention the fact – neither economic nor artistic but, significantly, aesthetic – that the Italian cinema was the first to give rise to theoretical and critical studies. Some of these studies, indeed, anticipated future developments: those published in the Turin *Stampa* in May 1907 by the writer Giovanni Papini on the philosophy of the cinema and in *L'Illustrazione Italiana* in December of the same year by Edmondo De Amicis ('Cinematografo cerebrale', which Mario Verdone has called 'a frenzied insight, an uncannily accurate prophecy of everything that was to come').[11]

In the same year Ricciotto Canudo was writing from Paris (*Vita d'Arte*, Siena, January 1908): 'Fantasy has had its day in the theatre, and a new variety of the marvellous, imposed by science, will inspire the artists of tomorrow.'

From the outset, therefore (and throughout its career), the Italian cinema was defined, encouraged and guided by a particularly numerous and active band of critics.

The intellectuals' early interest in the new art was another consequence of the lack of any real fairground era in the Italian cinema. The discredit attached to the early cinema in other countries was non-existent in Italy, where the cinema attracted attention from the élite at a much earlier stage. The first film criticism in the Italian press began appearing as early as 1910. Neither among writers nor in the theatrical world, with one odd exception that I shall discuss later, do we find any of the disdain which the cinema aroused for many years elsewhere. No other country can boast as large an output of cinema literature; and books and magazines on the subject still abound in Italy today.

2. The Golden Age (1909–16)

With the popular success of the historical novel and drama in the 19th century, it is hardly surprising that from the start moving pictures should have been expected not merely to record the present, but also to re-create the past. Barely a year after *L'Arrivée du Train en Gare de La Ciotat*, Georges Hatot was filming for Lumière such titles as *Robespierre, Marat, Charles XII,* etc.; and the first deliberate move from artists and writers to take the French cinema out of the fairground was *L'Assassinat du Duc de Guise*. Italian film-makers also turned to the past for their first subjects. The historical genre was not an Italian speciality; it was virtually universal in a Europe weighed down by its past. But the persistence of the genre in Italy led to the emergence of a peculiarly Italian style of historical film.

The tremendous boom that began in 1908 was marked by an early blossoming, virtually unique to Italy, of the costume film. Rehashes of history or period literature, the first creative attempts of the Italian cinema, proliferated for several years. Some subjects, indeed, were filmed several times over by competing producers or rival stars. Nero, Napoleon, Monte Cristo, Garibaldi, Julius Caesar and Manon Lescaut were the big attractions in this first year, and formed the nucleus around which the Italian silent cinema developed.

Producers drew the subjects of their films from literature or history, and even at that early date hired professional actors to interpret them. The Italian cinema began, in fact, at the stage of Calmettes's and Le Bargy's *film d'art*.

Very early on, therefore, it became necessary to bring in a third person to complete the original production team of producer and cameraman. Plots and actors called for a director, and as early as 1908 several emerged who were to leave their mark on the history of the Italian cinema. Some of them, such as Ernesto Pasquali, who in 1909 filmed *Teodora Imperatrice di Bisanzio, Cirano de Bergerac, Capitan Fracassa*, and a version of *Ettore Fieramosca* featuring large numbers of mounted extras, or Luca Comerio, who was responsible for the first adaptation of Manzoni's *I Promessi Sposi*, were producers who combined both functions. But most of them were actors who became interested in the new art form and, without abandoning their first profession, undertook to adapt themselves to the film and it to them. Such were Luigi Maggi, mentioned in the previous chapter; Giuseppe De Liguoro, who directed and acted in *Il Conte Ugolino, Oedipus Rex*, and other films; and Emilio Ghione, who was to turn to directing after making his name as an actor. But in this early phase other interesting figures came to the fore: Giovanni Pastrone who filmed *Giordano Bruno* under the pseudonym Piero Fosco; Mario Caserini who, after *Otello* and *Garibaldi* (1907), directed *Romeo e Giulietta* (*Romeo and Juliet*, 1908), and with *I Tre Moschettieri* (*The Three Musketeers*, 1909) made an international hit that ensured the prosperity of Cines; Enrico Guazzoni, a former interior decorator discovered by Alberini, who made his début in 1910 with *Brutus, Messalina* and *Agrippina*; Nino Oxilia, who joined Pasquali some time later and is cited as the director of *Giovanna d'Arco* (1913) starring Maria Jacobini, but died four years later aged twenty-nine; and Lucio D'Ambra, playwright and journalist, later to specialize in light comedy.

These were the men who, in the space of a few years, were to bring the Italian cinema to unrivalled supremacy.

Charles Pathé's concern about Italian competition was fully justified. After stopping the emigration of his technicians, he now had to face competition in this important market from indigenous producers. He decided to fight them on their own ground, and founded a subsidiary which he christened F.A.I. (Film d'Arte Italiano). He appointed three highly competent personalities to lead it: Riccardi, Lo Savio and Ugo Falena. The last two were well known in the theatre world; Lo Savio was appointed director and Ugo Falena scriptwriter. This triumvirate hired the famous actors Ermete Novelli, Ruggero Ruggeri, Cesare Dondini and Ferrucio Caravaglia, and introduced two young actresses, Francesca Bertini and Maria Jacobini, who were to become two of the most famous *dive* – 'goddesses', or stars – of the Italian

Brutus (Guazzoni, 1910)

golden age. By 1909, this French-controlled Italian company was attracting attention with three films as ambitious as its intentions: *Otello, La Signora delle Camelie* (*The Lady of the Camelias*) and *Carmen*. Well-tried subjects such as these could not fail to succeed, even though they were produced in accordance with the theatrical tradition of Le Bargy's *film d'art*. Nonetheless, F.A.I. continued in the same successful vein with *Lucrezia Borgia, Salome, Rigoletto, Il Re Lear* (*King Lear*), *Lorenzaccio*, etc. To enumerate all these films seems unnecessary; most of them have no more than historic value, and the few prints that have come down to us are not readily accessible.[1]

The main works of the Italian film pioneers are listed in the biographical section of this book. But most of these films, 'historical' in more senses than one, do not stand scrutiny any better than do many commercial films today. It seems more profitable to examine a few key films and their contribution to the evolution of the cinema as a whole.

Contemporary reactions to *Il Conte Ugolino* were enthusiastic:

Dante filmed? It sounds like a wager. Yet it has been done, and the result is truly artistic. In Pisa, near Ugolino's *palazzo*, a poster announces *Il conte Ugolino*. Where once was history now are ghosts . . . the ghosts of the cinema. . . .

'A Dantean vision,' says the poster, and the poster is right. No theatre could render this scene of horror with such frightful intensity. Gustave Doré attempted to do this at his peril. (What has become of his picture now?) Here the cinema triumphs over painting and the stage. The medium contrives to convey the poetry itself (and what poetry!), which the skills of the painter and actor could not do.

. . . One must admit, with enthusiasm and a little soul-searching, that the cinema is entering a new era in its development. . . . Witnessing the crowds besieging the film theatres, large or small, I am convinced that here, without a shadow of doubt, is the theatre of the future and that the future, alas, will be content with it.[2]

There is a wealth of meaning in that 'alas'. This apart, however, we may suppose that the author of this piece was struck as much by the power of the Italian productions as by the enthusiasm of the audiences. By then, the *film d'art* in Paris had brought to the cinema some of the prestige and several of the big names of the theatre. What struck this observer in Pisa and Florence was thus something quite different. 'Where once was history now are ghosts.' In that same year of 1909, the actress playing Beatrice Cenci mimed her anguish on the terrace of the very castle where Beatrice was actually sentenced to death. And Caserini, the director of *Beatrice Cenci*, subsequently filmed other productions in their true historical setting.

We may suppose that this created a kind of symbiosis between the audience and the artistic illusion and was responsible for the immediate success of the cinema in Italy, for the producers' enthusiasm for this kind of film, and for the prestige that soon devolved on the genre. 'Life as it is lived' was Lumière's motto. The Italian cinema went one better: life as it *was* lived – the ancient heroes resuscitated on the scene of their exploits. This faculty for introducing dramatic fiction into a framework of reality is peculiar to the cinema.

In this respect alone, then, the Italian films were quite different from, say, the *films d'art*, whose conventions were merely transpositions of the age-old techniques of the theatre, less dialogue. But by going on location the cinema freed itself from the limitations of the stage and showed a breadth of approach which very soon obliged it to invent a technique. A parallel can be drawn between the early Italian cinema and its American counterpart. What the latter sought in movement, the former sought in breadth of staging; and owing to the necessity for constantly changing the visual field in order to pass from the general to the particular, and vice versa, it used and perfected a technique peculiar to itself. Like shooting on location, which was also favoured by the Italian climate and the quality of the natural light, 'big' staging in fact tended to increase the impact and realism of the illusion, and helped to free the film from the limitations imposed on it by Le Bargy and Calmettes.

This characteristic is conspicuously apparent in *Gli Ultimi Giorni di*

'Realism of the illusion': unidentified early Italian costume film

Pompei (*The Last Days of Pompeii*), made in 1908 for Ambrosio by Luigi Maggi. In the words of a contemporary critic, 'the theme of this drama is splendidly rendered in the arena scene, when the great historical episode of the eruption of Vesuvius begins, with the terror of the fleeing spectators suffocated by the terrible effects of molten lava.'

Here, too, there were 'Dantean visions'. The theatre is totally surpassed by the frenzied crowds of Italian costume films, as it is by the careering horses of early American westerns. In both Hollywood and Turin, indeed, history, recent or otherwise, was the means to self-discovery, and through its agency the laws of the new art form were formulated.

It is clear, moreover, that the Italian public's ready acceptance of the *cinema dell'arte* was due, in part at least, to the national character itself, with its natural exuberance and its passion for entertainments of all kinds. For better or worse, the early Italian film discloses a major virtue: it is the expression of a *national* cinema.

A few films from the period 1908–12 stand out from this plethora of costume films. Their reputation has no doubt been enhanced by the stir they created abroad. The film by Luigi Maggi had shown the way. In the following year

Caius Julius Caesar (Guazzoni, 1914)

(1909), Giuseppe De Liguoro made for Milano Film a version of Dante's *Inferno* in which he played Count Ugolino – a more ambitious and quite stylish remake of *Il Conte Ugolino*. A thousand metres in length, containing many trick shots, its hand-tinted images were inspired by the engravings of Gustave Doré. Giuseppe De Liguoro's lyrical approach to the spectacular was strikingly original, well ahead of anything made anywhere else in the world at that time.

The 'big scene' continued to be the hub of such films as *La Caduta di Troia* (*The Fall of Troy*), one of the first productions of Giovanni Pastrone, with gigantic sets and 800 extras, or *La Gerusalemme Liberata* (1911) by Guazzoni, who was also to make a name for himself in this genre. On *The Fall of Troy*, Frederick Talbot wrote in 1912:

At the time of its production the films of the establishment were shut out from the American market, but the sensation created by it caused a demand among moving-picture enthusiasts in the United States, who saw no reason why they should be denied a film which was to be seen in every other part of the world. The Trust was compelled under public pressure to admit the film into the country – it forced its way into a rigorously protected territory sheerly by force of merit.[3]

Luigi Maggi's *Il Granatiere Rolland* (1910), with its 2,000 extras, was more than just a spectacular. Arrigo Frusta's scenario portrays a collective drama, Napoleon's Russian campaign, as seen through the experiences of one character; and Maggi added to the impact and verisimilitude of his film by shooting the retreat scenes in the Piedmont Alps. The natural setting is an integral part of the action and gives the cameraman, Vitrotti, scope for images which, in Georges Sadoul's words, 'opened the way to Thomas Ince and the Swedish cinema'.

With these few films whose success confirmed the quality of the art form and laid the foundations of Italian supremacy, there were others showing a desire to be original in theme and treatment. Among them was the justly famous *Nozze d'Oro*, also by Luigi Maggi (1911), which dealt with very recent historical events, those of the Risorgimento. The story is told by an old couple who witnessed the events and is expressed in a series of flashbacks. This technique, which had as yet seldom been used, here tended to give a contemporary dimension to history, thereby increasing its impact on the audience.

A year later, in 1912, there was another film by the same director, *Satana*, remarkable mainly for its scenario by the poet Guido Volante (1876–1916). *Satana* can be regarded as the prototype of the genre of Griffith's *Intolerance* and Ince's *Civilization*, and prefigures the modern episode film, with several plots on a single theme. In *Satana*, this theme is the problem of evil: the Devil is depicted in three episodes, biblical, medieval and modern. In the final episode the Devil appears in the guise of a steel magnate. With this film we find the young Italian cinema tackling problems of ethics and social theory. The naïveté of the plots ought not to obscure the intention inspiring them. Luigi Maggi occupies an important place in this early period. His use of narrative breaks new ground and takes on psychological overtones. Other directors sought merely to portray characters from a fantastic past – whether truly historical or purely imaginary.

It is also true to say that, in its response to the current taste for history, the early cinema was largely dependent on the literature that created that taste: these really were *costume* films; and Monte Cristo or the giant Ursus seemed as real to their audiences as Nero or Joan of Arc. Dante, Tasso, Shakespeare, Victor Hugo, the elder Dumas and Manzoni furnished Caserini, Guazzoni and their imitators with an inexhaustible fund of material. The literary emphasis was also fostered by the interest among Italian writers in this new medium of expression. The romantic vein which D'Annunzio exploited in his dramas was to involve closer and closer collaboration between the cinema and literature, thus preparing the way for another subject-area, that of middle-class life.

D'Annunzio, with his Latin exuberance, his facile lyricism, and his fond-

Ida Rubinstein in *La Nave* (Gabriellino D'Annunzio, 1912)

ness for éclat and pathos, was the missing link between the two art forms; not unaware of the fact, he became interested in the cinema from the start. In 1911, the ex-lawyer Arrigo Frusta, a prolific scriptwriter, adapted several of D'Annunzio's works for Ambrosio: *La Nave, La Figlia di Iorio, Gioconda, Fiaccola sotto il Moggio, Il Sogno di un Tramonto d'Autunno.* D'Annunzio's son, Gabriellino, became an actor at Pathé's Film d'Arte before turning to direction. D'Annunzio's interest in the cinema was mainly a financial one. Each film based on his works brought him in 40,000 lire. Apparently he only saw one of them, *La Leda senza Cigno*, which made him burst out laughing and declare that it was 'childish and grotesque'.[4] Elsewhere he stated that the cinema, for him, was just a means of buying meat for his dogs.

Nonetheless, D'Annunzio had an enormous influence on the Italian cinema of his day, an influence due more to his prestige than to any contribution he may have made to the new art form. It was an influence which helped to steer the Italian film towards grandiloquence and empty lyricism.

In 1909, Italian production amounted to 500 films with an average length of 200 metres. This level was maintained until 1915, with the average length rising to 1,000 metres. Not all the films made were 'historical'. A proportion of the production in 1908–15 was composed of comedies, dramas, sketches and documentary items.

The early comics were completely French in style; even when they contained a few native features, they aimed merely at imitating Paris. The stimulus for this boom in comedy came from Itala, which hired an ex-Pathé comic, André Deed, just as, two years previously, Cines had signed up the technician Gaston Velle. André Deed had been a singer and acrobat at the Folies Bergère and the Châtelet before moving into films at the instigation of Méliès. His weekly screen appearances as the clown Boireau were highly successful. He left Pathé and on 1 January 1909 began working in Rome, with a contract that provided for a film a week. Known to the Italian public as Cretinetti (Little Cretin), he was rechristened Gribouille for export to France.

Giovanni Pastrone, then a powerful figure in Cines, later gave Georges Sadoul his recollections of André Deed's début in Italy:

We had begun negotiating with Pathé's two best comics, Max Linder and André Deed. There was keen rivalry between these two actors at Vincennes. Both accepted our offer. We had to choose. We decided on André Deed, who was the more famous of the two. This actor arrived in Turin in late 1908. . . . He directed his own films, occasionally helped by his brother. Between us we put the finishing touches to his scenarios. I also suggested some of the tricks which contributed to his success.

This success, and doubtless the comparatively low cost of these comic films, attracted the attention of other producers. Ambrosio launched another French comic, Marcel Fabre, who became popular under the pseudonym Robinet. Cines hired a famous clown, Fernand Guillaume, a direct competitor for Cretinetti under the pseudonym Tontolini (Little Silly); but Guillaume won greater fame in Turin when he created the character Polidor for Pasquali. Emile Verdannes became Toto. The enthusiasm for French comedy was so great that several Italian comics made names for themselves – or tried to do so – under frenchified pseudonyms: Max Jolicœur (Armando Gelsomini), Fricot (Ernesto Vaser), Kri-Kri (Giuseppe Gambardella), and the rest.

The originality found in some of their films – for example, the trick shots used by André Deed – was inspired by Zecca or Méliès. So there is little justification for crediting the Italian cinema with this imported comedy, despite a few *trouvailles* in which Mario Verdone detects a foretaste of surrealism.

Strangely enough, the cinema, based as it was on pantomime, did not at that time attract the exponents of the *commedia dell'arte*. Nino Frank, in his book *Commedia dell'Arte*, defines the Italian sense of the comic as follows: 'The Italian likes pure play: accidents, fights, somersaults, falls, disguises, slaps, confusion, situations, happenings, thing-people, estrangements – a precisely visual comedy, Bergsonian laughter.'

This, in fact, is what we find in the comedy – Anglo-Saxon but perhaps Latin also – of Chaplin. This comedy that Italy was unable to create should have stemmed directly from the *commedia dell'arte* and its guignol characters – or from buffoonery, which is also a specifically Italian art. How are we to account for this deficiency? Doubtless imitations of the French comedians prevented the development of an inherently Italian comic vein. The immigrants from France reached the peak of their success around 1911, then went into rapid decline. André Deed returned to Paris at the end of 1911, and the genre began to wane the very next year before fading out entirely around 1915.

An interesting study of the Italian cinema by the French director Victorin Jasset was published by *Ciné Journal* from 21 October to 25 November 1911;[5] a few extracts are given below. Though the opinions may seem rather blunt, they are an accurate reflection of the facts.

Italy had some marvellous material to work with: light that was exceptionally favourable for photography, making it possible to work whatever the weather; splendid heads; lower production and labour costs; and unlimited capital.

She represented a tremendous potential rival for France, which until then had held a virtual monopoly of the industry she had created.

Despite these advantages, the Italians fumbled for many years. They had to call in French experts to help them.

Eventually they began to specialize.

Their temperament predisposed them to exaggeration and grandiloquence. This predisposition, together with the comparatively insignificant cost of labour, led them to specialize in big scenes with extras and costumes.

Italy monopolized the costume film.

A school emerged.

It aimed at impact rather than nuance, and delighted in shock tactics: its masses of sets and crowds of extras were directed with zest, often to great effect; but the costumes and settings were not always as accurate as they should have been. The Italian School seemed to have a marked predilection for episodes from French history and literature; but occasionally it translated those episodes a little haphazardly and without having studied them. Though no one noticed this elsewhere, it shocked public taste in France, where people were accustomed to much greater accuracy in such details.

... The Italians' popular success was greater than that met with by the French. Though their productions were imperfect from a purely artistic point of view, they were entertaining and often astonishingly original as well as being grandiose and lively. The Italians' originality lay in what the French considered to be their faults. They dared to do what the French school would never have had the courage to attempt. The French believed that certain subjects were impossible to film; the Italians filmed them nonetheless, after their own fashion.

If the result turned out to be full of anachronisms or mistakes, it was often entertaining – and it sold.

The innovators' commercial success proved them right, and the French market reacted accordingly. But there could be no question of competing with the Italians on their own terms: costs in France did not allow our firms such lavish use of equipment and personnel.

The comic productions of the Italian film industry were often excellent, but their origin was French and they used French actors.

The Italian producers constantly imitated developments in the French school, but with a lavishness of staging that we never attained.

Thus Italy became one of our most redoubtable competitors.

Another view – English this time – is found in the article by Frederick Talbot published in 1912 from which we have already quoted:

The experience of the Cines Company appears to confirm the theory that historical subjects make the strongest appeal. . . . Moreover, Italy is especially rich in beautiful landscape and historical sites, where the scenes can be re-enacted in their original setting – an advantage which the large companies realize to the uttermost.

The Cines Company . . . has three studios devoted to the staging of picture-plays, the premises in Rome having an area exceeding 128,000 square feet.[6]

Rome and (especially) Turin were then important production centres. In 1914, the Ambrosio and Itala studios already foreshadowed those of Hollywood and Babelsberg, with their set warehouses, property departments, carpenters' shops, large outdoor lots, editing rooms, and processing laboratories.[7] The position that the Italian film was to win on the world market was undeniably due to the resources that it had at its disposal; but none of this would have sufficed for its hegemony had it not produced works that were truly spectacular and already contained the elements of a new style of expression.

Every country writes history in its own way. In the article already quoted, the Frenchman Victorin Jasset, while acknowledging the value of *Gli Ultimi Giorni di Pompei*, concludes:

When all is said and done, the Italian school did not further the development of the art of the cinema. It followed closely the French school, magnifying the latter's faults, which were considerable to begin with.

The Italian critic Vinicio Marinucci,[8] on the other hand, has only a word or two about French influence on the Italian comics and nothing at all about Gaston Velle and his rivals from Pathé, whose contribution to the development of the art was no doubt small but who paved the way for the pioneers.

Antonio Pietrangeli, for his part, deplores the almost universal disdain for the work of the Italian pioneers, complaining that all the historians, 'including our own, virtually ignore the contribution of our early *auteurs* to the discovery of the techniques of the cinema – researches and results that were so precisely cinematographic in nature (the close-up, montage, the panning shot, the dolly . . .)'.[9] He notes as examples the details cited by his compatriot Umberto Barbaro: 'the close-ups of Lyda Borelli in *Malombra* (1913); the detail in *Cabiria* (1913) or Baldassare Negroni's close-ups of Hesperia in *L' Ereditiera* (1914); the camera movements in *Ma l'Amor Mio non Muore* (1913) by Mario Caserini, *Cabiria*, and Negroni's *Histoire d'un Pierrot* (1913); the contrasts in the editing of *Sperduti nel Buio* (1914) by Nino Martoglio. . . .'

No doubt all this is perfectly correct, but in the same period, and even before, we could point to identical discoveries made in England, America and France, since the same problems of expression gave rise to the same technical solutions – the discovery of which, in any case, was less important than the use they were put to. Invention alone has never been an absolute criterion.

The truly original contribution of the first Italian films seems to have been their feeling for space, their enlargement of the framework in which the life of crowds could express itself; fundamentally, despite the theatricality of the conception and execution, it was their quest for greater verisimilitude.

The innovatory importance of this 'conquest of space' has been ably stressed by the Neapolitan historian of the cinema Roberto Paolella. Discussing *Quo Vadis?* (taken over by Guazzoni after Caserini's departure from Cines), he writes:

In this film, for the first time, the architectonic genius of the Italians imposed the problem of perspective on the new art and resolved it with the limited means at its disposal, thereby achieving the first conquest of space, which even today is one of the undeniable skills of the Italian school.

. . . The quest for perspective is one of the essential problems of the Italian artist: from Giotto, whose re-creation of the third dimension took him beyond the stage of Byzantine painting, to the first maladroit perspective of Paolo Uccello which disconcerted the Florentines. . . .

The early Italian masters moved in the same direction with their religious films. Having mastered two dimensions, like their painters, they sought to create the third. Thus Enrico Guazzoni, in his creations of ancient Rome, was the first to place great volumes of luminous space between the camera and his sets, which were no longer erected in the studio, but outdoors. He used more architecture and curves in his compositions and filled the intervening space with pompous chariots of triumph, potbellied amphorae, and cumbersome triclinia; these spectacular masses on different planes and the wealth of detail expressed the supreme majesty of space. In the history of the cinema, this discovery has the same importance as that of perspective in the chapter of art history dealing with Paolo Uccello and Piero della Francesca.[10]

The fame that Henryk Sienkiewicz's novel was enjoying at the time had prepared the public's interest, but the success of the film exceeded the author's wildest hopes and lasted for several years on both sides of the Atlantic. Such lavishness of staging was completely new: the Roman crowds, the tortured Christians, the lions in the arena, the violent characterization, the burning of Rome while Nero looked on – these images quivering with life enthralled audiences in every country, including even such men as Rodin.

In Paris, the Gaumont Palace, the largest cinema in the world at the time, commissioned Jean Noguès to write a special musical accompaniment, which included a choir of 150 voices. In London, the promoters hired the Albert Hall, which could hold 20,000 spectators at each sitting, and the film was presented to George V and Queen Mary (as were some of the actors). *Quo Vadis?* was indubitably the first great hit of the new form of entertainment. It lasted two hours. Critics ascribed its success to the scale of the thing, without really detecting the new qualities inherent in the form itself, in the visual narrative which Guazzoni interpreted with lyricism and a remarkable sense of crowd movement. The director understood perfectly the importance of the setting within which he brought these crowds to life. Later, before tackling *Marcantonio e Cleopatra*, he stated: 'I was offered the chance to show spectators the most characteristic places in ancient Rome and Egypt, places we may all have dreamt of as children. . . .' And he intended to direct his film 'in such a way that the smallest detail will be in conformity with the strictest historical truth'.

Italian directors were not always to be so scrupulous about accuracy, but the taste for spectacle and the architectural gifts of this nation could not have found a better outlet than in the depiction of antiquity, a field in which America and Germany were soon to attempt to follow their example.

The success of *Quo Vadis?* was the consecration of the genre. The appearance of competitors, the hope for further financial triumphs (*Quo Vadis?* had brought in 150,000 dollars in America alone), and the producers' personal ambitions steered Italy towards the lavish spectacular. In 1913, reviving the first best-seller, Ambrosio and Pasquali both presented versions of *Gli Ultimi Giorni di Pompei* (*The Last Days of Pompeii*). Ambrosio's was written by Arrigo Frusta and directed by Mario Caserini; Pasquali's was directed by the actor Enrico Vidali.

Caserini duly left Ambrosio as he had already left Cines, and founded a company of his own. He is supposed to have announced yet another *Last Days of Pompeii*, 3,000 metres in length, with '30 lions, 50 horses, 1,000 players . . . a great regatta, an imperial trireme, the destruction of Pompeii' and more besides – all filmed on the slopes of Vesuvius. But his ambitious scheme never saw the light of day, since the two previous versions had not

Gli Ultimi Giorni di Pompei (Caserini, 1913)

done as well as expected. Caserini's *Nerone e Agrippina* (1913) was laughed off the screen in Paris, mainly, one conjectures, because of the extravagant acting of his star, Maria Caserini Gasperini.

However, the success of the spectacular as such was not affected, as Giovanni Pastrone showed by undertaking his famous *Cabiria* in the same year.

This work is one of the most important films in the early period of world cinema; its influence was even greater than that of *Quo Vadis?* It set a trend that was to culminate in Griffith and play a capital role in the development of the American cinema, which alone had the resources necessary to continue the genre. For the worldwide triumph of the Italian film was due to its impact; and impact, even when considered in terms of the artistry of its creator, is ultimately a quantity that can be measured in terms of finance. None of Pastrone's technical and artistic achievements in this film would have been possible without the money to pay for them. Hence with this triumph the Italian cinema exposed itself to emulation and eventually usurpation by a richer competitor. From then on what counted was not the national background or the natural setting but the magnitude of the sets and the impact of the big scenes. Pastrone's influence went beyond Griffith to Cecil B. DeMille and his imitators. 'Grandiloquence, megalomania, gigantism: the Italians did not really need D'Annunzio to put them on *that* track!' says Nino Frank. In fact, the importance of *Cabiria* has nothing to do with the D'Annunzio vein; it lies in what Georges Sadoul has called 'a conscious artistic intention' in a field where so many successes were due to chance.

Pastrone's plan had been formed in 1913. As then conceived, his film was to be called *Il Romanzo delle Fiamme* and take place during the period of the Punic Wars. This choice was inspired by the war against the Turks in Tripolitania (1911–12), which had aroused much passionate interest in Italy; the Nationalists invoked Scipio's conquest of Africa and excused the setbacks of the colonial expedition to Libya by pointing to the inconsequential victories of Hannibal. Italian imperialism, hotheaded and confused because young and insecure, spoke loftily of transforming the Mediterranean once more into a Mare Nostrum.[11]

This aspect came to the fore in the Fascist cinema of the 1930s. Did Pastrone deliberately stress it? Henri Langlois prefers to see the crux of the film in its other aspect and says, addressing the Italians:

When will you understand that the key to this film is Maciste, the Breaker of Chains, and not Scipio, the lymphatic general? When will you understand that the only reason Pastrone covered his Turin hillside with temples, steps, columns, statues, extras and engines of war was in order to crush the life out of the past more effectively?[12]

Giovanni Pastrone was shrewd and intelligent. If this was indeed his intention, it did not stop him stressing the Scipio side of his story, thereby giving the film everything it needed to be a guaranteed success. Realizing what the risks were, he wanted to hold all the trump cards; instead of depicting the life of a great man, therefore, he used history as the backdrop to an invented intrigue. This enabled him to pander to the romantic vein with the idyllic adventures of a pure young heroine protected by an invincible protagonist (both obviously borrowed from *Quo Vadis?*): Cabiria and Maciste – the 'Breaker of Chains' whose progeny was equalled only by that of Tarzan.

Pastrone also realized that he needed to back his story with a famous name. So he decided to take a back seat, not merely by using his usual pseudonym of Piero Fosco as director, but by inviting the illustrious Gabriele D'Annunzio to accept the authorship of the film, 'an undertaking of the greatest profit with the least bother, and which would not harm his reputation in any way'. D'Annunzio accepted the offer, for a consideration, and blithely informed all and sundry that he was the author of this 'Greco-Roman-Punic drama . . . an experiment in popular art on an original theme'. According to Pastrone's own statement, however, to Georges Sadoul in 1949, D'Annunzio merely added his signature to the thirty-page synopsis that he, Pastrone, had prepared, and added the sub-titles after the film had been shot. At that time D'Annunzio had fled from his creditors to France, and Pastrone's offer must have struck him as an easy way of paying off his debts. And the prestige of his name was undoubtedly a boost for the film.

Soon after joining Itala, as we have seen, Giovanni Pastrone had realized that technique was all-important if the cinema was to become a fully valid art form. Two years earlier he had installed the first gantry in the Itala studio and had just taken out a patent for a *carrello* or dolly. For *Cabiria* he decided to go all out after technical innovation. While huge sets were being built in Turin, he hired four cameramen and went on location: Hannibal crossed the Alps above Lanzo, while the Carthaginian campaign was filmed in Tunisia and other parts of the action were shot in Sicily. Pastrone did not use *trompe-l'œil* sets; for the depth that Guazzoni had attempted to achieve before him, Pastrone relied on his dolly – which by transferring the movement of the subject to the camera opened up infinite possibilities for the cinema as a whole. Once again we find the value of a film residing in the lavishness of the staging, which necessitated the use of a new technique.

Pastrone shot 20,000 metres of negative when his film could not possibly go beyond 4,500 metres or three hours' showing. This gave him a considerable margin of choice at the editing stage and allowed him to improvise to some extent during the shooting – a method which was soon imitated and gave editing its proper role in the composition of the film. The resultant intercutting meets the requirements of the scenario, which skilfully exploited one of the cinema's major assets, though at that time it was seldom used: its ubiquity. Lastly the dramatic use of artificial light (notably in the temple scenes and the burning of the fleet) was another original contribution which the silent cinema was to use again and again.

It is for these crucial innovations that *Cabiria* must be judged today, and not for the glaring faults of its grandiloquence and dramatic naïveté. Pastrone has said:

I have been criticized for the exaggerated miming – silent declamation, as it were. But remember when the film was made. This was the heyday of Sarah Bernhardt – overdone make-up, grandiloquent gesticulation and all. My film would never have been accepted as a work of art if I hadn't paid tribute to Sarah Bernhardt (rather as I had used the name of D'Annunzio), notably in the miming of Itala Almirante Manzini.

Having made this concession to the 'élite' among the audience I strove to obtain austere, unsophisticated acting from the rest of the cast. See, for example, the character of Maciste, who was largely responsible for the film's success. I trained that actor myself. Bartolomeo Pagano was not a professional; he was a docker in Genoa when I hired him.

That, too, was an innovatory stroke, repeated by the neo-realists later on. It is said that Griffith owned a pirate print of *Cabiria*, which he scrutinized

Cabiria (Pastrone, 1914)

before filming *Intolerance*. Whether this is true or false, Pastrone's film had enormous influence in its day.

The Italian costume film never equalled this success. The following year, 1915, Count Giulio Antamoro filmed *Christus!* (2,000 metres), partly in Palestine and Egypt. This film in five acts had quite a successful run abroad. Guazzoni had recently directed a much publicized *Caius Julius Caesar*. But *Cabiria* had been a consummation of the genre and interests were turning to other things. Tail coats and evening gowns were to take the place of the peplums and togas. Another style had already begun to make its mark on the youthful Italian cinema.

As we have seen, the influence of D'Annunzio had at a very early date made its mark on the new form of dramatic expression. By 1911 most of his works had been adapted for the screen by Arrigo Frusta. D'Annunzio's output was not limited to historical subjects, however. He was also fashionable as a playwright, in which role he wrote modern dramas dealing with the fatal passions so loved by the bourgeoisie of his day. Hence D'Annunzio was the originator of the modern drama that from 1910–11 onwards determined another important trend in the Italian cinema.

Cabiria (Pastrone, 1914)

Attached as he was to his country's history, the Italian filmgoer was also fond of finding in the new art form his own image, his own problems, the echo of his own emotions or pleasures. The bourgeois drama was almost bound to succeed, considering the middle-class birth of the Italian cinema and the fact that the middle classes were its best customers. The characters of the 'modern' Italian film were not Zecca's or Jasset's French *flics*, shopgirls, or tough guys, but passionate countesses, playboy aristocrats, and ambitious industrialists – the bourgeoisie which was building industrial fortunes and empires of pleasure in the Lombardy plain and the valleys of Piedmont.

At that time, according to Maria Adriana Prolo, Italian high society was passionately interested in the cinema. In Milan, Turin and Rome, aristocrats and noblemen were attracted to the cinema in the first instance by the beautiful women who appeared on the screen. Duke Caracciola d'Aquana set the tone of the drama in a scenario filmed by F.A.I. in 1913,[11] about the passionate affair of a duke and an actress. Milano Film, very active, had been reorganized under the direction of Baron Pier Gaetano Venino and Paolo Acroldi di Robbiate; one of its directors, Giuseppe De Liguoro, when filming *Gioacchino Murat* (or *Dalla Locanda al Trono*), was able to ask the Milanese nobility to come and act as extras in his film. They answered his request with the same eagerness as did their counterparts fifty years later for Antonioni's *La Notte*. But the Italian cinema lacked scriptwriters to meet this demand for bourgeois drama, and the national literature seemed to give it little to draw on. It was mainly from the French novel and theatre of the day – which likewise were essentially bourgeois – that Italy borrowed the motifs of the new genre: the works of Octave Feuillet, Georges Ohnet, Henri Bataille and leading exponents of what was then called the *feuilleton*, the popular novel, appearing in parts.

High society – women dripping jewels and men in tail coats – appeared on the screen. This bourgeois drama arose directly from a society then in its heyday, the industrial bourgeoisie.

Hence a new genre sprang up alongside the costume film. This change of direction was doubtless favoured by the adaptations of some of D'Annunzio's works on modern subjects, but equally it was influenced by the vogue for Danish films and by the melodrama which had developed in the French cinema. Caserini seems to have been one of the first to adopt the new genre (soon followed by his imitator Pasquali), though without abandoning the costume film.

Among the films Caserini made in 1911 is *L'Ultimo dei Frontignac* (*The Last of the Frontignacs*), which is none other than *Le Roman d'un Jeune Homme Pauvre* by Octave Feuillet, the prototype, and a fair representative, of the bourgeois drama found in France and elsewhere. In his *Histoire générale du cinéma* Georges Sadoul gives a few film scenarios dating from this period. The love plot is often based on social differences and problems of class. The awareness of social injustice comes across in most of these melodramatic and often fantastic adventures in which we see girls seduced, unmarried mothers abandoned, orphans restored to their parents, innocent men found guilty, spectacular acts of revenge, factories in flames, and crimes receiving their long-delayed punishment. But this aspect was European rather than purely national, an aspect reflecting the development of industry and social evolution. The same stories were filmed in Paris, Copenhagen, Berlin and Saint Petersburg. Yet the Italian cinema made a speciality of this modern drama, expressing the violent passion peculiar to the national character. Once again it was Caserini who successfully provided a prototype in 1913 with *Ma l'Amor Mio non Muore*, featuring a young beginner, Lyda Borelli, 'the first *diva* of the cinema'.

With this film by Mario Caserini we reach 'the triumph of the *femmes fatales* with their languorous poses, their rapacious glances and their jerky movements, stifled by anguish and the imminence of catastrophe, like flowers strewn over the living and the dead'.[13]

The genre had already been successful for some time, since the previous year, 1912, we find three different versions of Teobaldo Ciconi's drama *La Statua di Carne*, the first with Baldanello, the second with Pina Fabbri, the third with Clara Vendone. But Caserini's achievement is important in that it also marks the birth of the *diva*.

The costume film seemed to have submerged the actors beneath an ever-increasing flood of extras. With the modern drama, the actor – *il commediante*, a typically Italian product – returned to the fore, imposed himself on the action and dominated events. The drama generally resided in the passionate love engineered by a *femme fatale*, of whom Nino Frank has given this alluring portrait:

Woman on a pedestal, woman the bringer of dreams and the breaker of hearts, woman the cause of men's ruin and her own, the *femme fatale* – the Italians were the first to take this series of steps in characterization, giving the final product an original form. So doing, they abolished the frontiers between fiction and reality, and created that mythological figure, the star.[14]

Nino Frank shrewdly contrasts the *femme fatale* with the vamp invented in the Nordic countries, more deliberately devastating, the woman who lives off her victims' misfortunes, a kind of vampire. The fate of the Italian *femme fatale* is often as dreadful as that of her lovers, and this makes her even more appealing. She takes the form of a force against which one is powerless, since she herself is dominated by something stronger than herself. This may well be the reason for the name given to her in awe, which also defines her: *diva*, or goddess. The man whom she touches and condemns becomes the victim of a kind of holocaust; he is sacrificed to a mysterious superior power. There is something almost religious in the audiences' worship of the *dive*.

This phenomenon of the *diva* is perhaps peculiar to the national character. It explains and partly justifies a style of acting whose exaggeration tends to make modern audiences laugh. Historically, it partook more of ritual than of fashion: the *diva* was at once goddess and priestess. What she simulated on the screen was not a representation of human acts, but the performance of a liturgy necessary for the rehearsal of a form of worship, and first and foremost for the bewitchment of her victims. 'Exaggerated movements of the hips and arms, with the head thrown back, her hair suddenly spilling down her back, contortions, rolling eyes. . . .' Her miming, Georges Sadoul continues, is

very contrived, but also precise and powerful. A sudden arm gesture stops in exactly the right place. Her passionate gesticulation is expressive and forceful like the sacred Japanese dance.

Our modern sense of realism does not equip us to judge stage conventions which are probably as justifiable as those of the Nō theatre. At all events, it is in the light of this deliberate stylization that we must consider the acting of the *dive*, which consciously followed a dramatic tradition. It is almost certain

Francesca Bertini in *Avarizzia* (*Avarice*, Serena, 1919)

that the acting of Sarah Bernhardt, Talma or Mounet Sully would seem as ridiculous to us as that of Lyda Borelli or Pina Menichelli.

Caserini's discovery Lyda Borelli was a former stage actress; her style surprised some contemporary Italian critics who already felt the need for a return to realism. But these few discordant voices went unheard in the storm of success; and the vogue of the modern drama resulted in the emergence of other *dive*, some of whose names are still well known today. Francesca Bertini, Pina Menichelli, Hesperia, Maria Jacobini, Leda Gys, Lina Cavalieri and many others became household names and squandered fortunes, inaugurating the era of the stars and filling the gap left by the royal favourites and courtesans of earlier times. Some of them, such as Clelia Antici-Maffei, belonged to the aristocracy; others – Gianna Terribili-Gonzales, Italia Almirante Manzini, Giulia Cassini Rizzotto, Lina Millefleurs – have bequeathed to posterity only their names or picturesque pseudonyms.

Once again it would be pointless to give a list of titles belonging to films that have been forgotten or lost. But it is important to understand that this mythical phenomenon was to influence the evolution of the cinema and more particularly its economy.

Francesca Bertini, Gustavo Serena in *Assunta Spina* (Serena, 1915)

The ten years from 1910 to 1920 were the heyday of 'divism'. Pretty young actresses from heaven knows where, rarely from the legitimate theatre, attracted by the silent variety, captivated the public – and not merely the public at large. Inevitably, divism bred fat fees or royalties and created a fashion unknown elsewhere. A new style emerged: the miming of Borelli, the fantastic contortions of the magnificent Menichelli, were undeniably stylish. The divine creature took precedence over mere mortals working on the film; her personality and style of acting overshadowed every other factor. Dominating everything – the scenario, the directing, the lighting, the photography – the *diva* went in front of the camera for a solo performance which everything had to enhance, down to the smallest detail.[15]

This over-emphasis on a single element of any given film was to have its repercussions on technique, as close-ups became increasingly necessary to give the *diva*'s attitudes and facial expressions their full effect. Reconstructed history gave way to passion – to psychology, even. The development of this new genre in the Italian cinema was favoured at the outset by financial considerations: it was thought that the modern drama would be less costly to produce than costume films, the budgets for which had become so swollen by competition that it had become impossible to break even with them on the home market alone. In 1912, Italian production dominated the world market, but it was at the mercy of its exports at a time when the cinema in several foreign countries was developing rapidly. The day when this supremacy would be threatened was clearly not far off.

A few years were enough to smash the illusion that the modern drama would effect savings. Competition for the biggest stars became as fierce as for the biggest crowds in the costume films, and it was soon realized that a single *diva* cost more than an army of mercenaries or a herd of elephants. Francesca Bertini earned a million lire a year, Maria Jacobini 36,000 a month – payable in coins of gold. From then on the threat of bankruptcy hung over production, and production had become dependent on what the Americans were later to call the star system.

As generally happens when the actor's importance becomes overstressed, the other creative elements were diminished. The director became the servant of the *diva*; and the film seemed to be less his work than that of the star. Yet some new directors did make their appearance in this genre, so reminiscent of the theatre: Bencivenga, in 1911, with an adaptation of a play by D'Annunzio, *La Figlia di Iorio*; and Count Baldassare Negroni in 1912, with *Idillio Tragico, Lagrime e Sorrisi* – and above all *Histoire d'un Pierrot* (1913) featuring Francesca Bertini, the adaptation of a pantomime which successfully alloyed the conventions of the genre with realism in the outdoor scenes and skilful editing. Negroni soon joined the ranks of the best directors along with Nino Oxilia, a playwright originally hired by Pastrone to do a screen adaptation of one of his plays, *Addio Giovinezza!* (1913), featuring Lydia Quaranta. Oxilia also directed costume films, including a *Giovanna d'Arco* (1914) with Maria Jacobini and *Rapsodia Satanica* in which Lyda Borelli had full scope for her silent eloquence and perverse charm.

Others who made their début shortly before the outbreak of war included Gennaro Righelli, Carmine Gallone and Augusto Genina; their careers were destined to be longer than that of Oxilia, who was killed at the front in 1917.

Of the actors, men like Amleto Novelli, Febo Mari, Alberto Capozzi, Alberto Collo and Bartolomeo Pagano – better known as Maciste – were successful enough, but their fame was nothing compared with that of the *dive*. Several of them turned to directing, where they did quite well: in particular, Febo Mari, who was to direct *Cenere* (featuring Eleonora Duse), Mario Bonnard who made his début some time later, and Emilio Ghione, who partnered Francesca Bertini and other *dive* before directing them himself, while continuing to practise his career as an actor from time to time.

Alongside the mainstream of costume films and the bourgeois drama, other genres sprang up in Italy in the course of this glittering period. But the so-called *commedia brillante* (light comedy) was no more productive of characteristic works than was comedy *tout court*; it too imitated French models, at least as regards its themes, which it borrowed from the *comédie du boulevard*. Once again it was Caserini who set the fashion, with *Santarellina* (1911, 811 metres), an adaptation of *Mam'zelle Nitouche*, featuring a young comedy heroine, Gigetta Morano, who is also found in other comedies by Arrigo Frusta and Luigi Maggi. The actor Eleuterio Rodolfi, who had been Gigetta's partner in comic sketches, turned to directing also, with comedies by himself (*Il Cappello di Papa*, 1914) or borrowed from Labiche (*Il Cappello di Paglia di Firenze*).

But the greatest revelation of the *commedia brillante* was Lucio D'Ambra, scriptwriter turned director, whose most highly esteemed work seems to have been *Il Re, le Torri, gli Alfieri* (1916). This was an operetta for the screen, whose lively humour was praised by Vinicio Marinucci and which featured, alongside professional actors, a countess, a marquis and a member of parliament. Critics also detected in it traces of futurism, which we shall be discussing later. Oxilia, Genina and Gallone also worked in this field, which persisted up to the talkies and beyond, and to which *dive* such as Pina Menichelli, Lydia and Laetizia Quaranta and Hesperia occasionally lent their names.

Lucio D'Ambra's silent operetta was not as paradoxical as all that in the homeland of *bel canto*. Right at the start of the Italian cinema, the producers drew on the lyric repertory, and in 1908–9 films were made of *Il Trovatore*, *Manon Lescaut* and *Lucia di Lammermoor*. The opera score gave the orchestra ready-made material. In 1912, Wagner followed Donizetti and Verdi with *Siegfried* and *Parsifal*, filmed by Caserini. The success of opera in Italy made these adaptations inevitable. Even at this early date technicians investigated the possibility of combining the camera and the gramophone. But they never got beyond vague experiments such as the ballet *Excelsior* by Luigi Manzotti, with music by Romualdo Marenco, billed as a 'ciné-phono-choreographic spectacle'. Another significant fact is that even at this early date musicians composed original scores for these silent films. Played by the orchestra during projection, the music was always billed as a special feature. This was the case with *Lo Schiavo di Cartagine* by Frusta (1910), provided with a 'musical commentary' by Osvaldo Brunetti, with *La Legenda della Passiflora*, produced by a firm in Naples with music by Mazzuchi, and many other films leading up to *Cabiria*, for which Pizzetti wrote a *Sinfonia del Fuoco* to accompany the tragic pictures of Carthage and the Roman fleet in flames. In France, after the experimental *film d'art* in 1908, fifteen years went by before a few films such as *La Roue* (1923) and *Le Miracle des Loups* (1924) benefited from such adornments.

Nonetheless, it is on a quite different aspect that we must linger, at the moment when the Italian cinema, just before the First World War, had reached its apogee – the least-known and least obvious aspect of the cinema of this period, and yet the one containing the most promise for the future.

The baroque exuberance of the costume film and the bourgeois drama could not help provoking a reaction, and by their very grandiloquence inviting a return to everyday life. As early as 1913 a current of realism was setting in. It might have drawn inspiration from something as disputed and misunderstood, wilfully or not, as itself – *verismo*, a form of naturalism practised by the 'verist' school, and in particular by Giovanni Verga (1840–1922), whose influence was to be felt so keenly at the birth pangs of neo-realism. The Sicilian novelist was not responsible for the first Italian neo-realist theme. Yet it came from Naples, from the South, from the South of poverty and unemployment which already formed a tragic contrast with the productive North.

In 1914, Nino Martoglio, a Sicilian who had made his début in Rome, went back to his island and founded a production company in Catania. For this company he filmed in Naples *Sperduti nel Buio* (*Lost in Darkness*), adapted from a play by Roberto Bracco. This film is now considered a classic.

Critics have seen the premises of neo-realism in certain details in the great films of this period, *Cabiria* and *Histoire d'un Pierrot*. Pietrangeli refers to 'those ropes of onions and those dried fishes hanging in a cellar, which are more gripping than any of D'Annunzio's commentaries', and underlines in the second film 'highly developed awareness of crowd behaviour, from the children running after marching soldiers to the departure of the washerwomen', and the authenticity and unselfconsciousness of these crowd scenes.

A certain tendency of the bourgeois drama to stray in the direction of the class struggle has also been held to be the start of this realist trend, with films such as *Sangue Siciliano* (1911), *La Zolfara* (1912), *Lo Scomparso* (1912), and above all *Padre* (1912), made by Dante Testa for Pastrone, the drama of a man who, sentenced for a crime he has not committed, abstains from revenge to preserve the happiness of his daughter. The hero was played by the great Ermete Zacconi. The style of actors such as Zacconi and Giovanni Grasso (himself a Sicilian) in these realist dramas may also have been a reaction against the extravagance of the *dive* and their partners; it prepared, so far as the acting was concerned, for the return to human truths.

But it was *Sperduti nel Buio*, with its dramatic theme, its character, its style and its acting, which really marks a decisive turning-point in Italian production at a time when its ambitions, inflated by success, were leading it towards disaster.

Once again the heroine is a daughter of the people, seduced by a hateful marquis and abandoned on the birth of her child. This melodramatic theme *par excellence* is a good illustration, in hindsight, of the importance then

Sperduti nel Buio (Martoglio, 1914)

accorded to what would nowadays be called a social problem. The choice of subject, then, is revealing, though the story told in the film concerns the child herself, entrusted to a blind beggar, while her mother indulges in high-class debauchery in search of a way to get her revenge on the wretched marquis.

The film was shot in the slums of Naples, whose sunlit splendour contrasts with the luxury of the palace; to underline this contrast, Martoglio cut from one to the other, a technique which Soviet film-makers were to put to such telling effect. (The latter acknowledged their debt to the Italian cinema of this period.) As a social document, *Sperduti nel Buio* undoubtedly belongs to the origins of neo-realism; it is neo-realist also in its scrupulous attention to detail, with its cracked walls, its unhealthy streets, its worn steps, its suffering people. In addition, as Henri Langlois stresses, 'the striking, the overwhelming thing about *Sperduti nel Buio* that will make it one of the greatest cinema achievements of all time, is that all this is bathed in a light, a natural light that we have never seen in any film since, not even in Buñuel.'[16]

Sadoul, for his part, stresses something else:

Martoglio's vision is austere, bare, true. Stroheim's slips easily into aesthetic refinement, scepticism, cruelty. . . . In Martoglio, there is an obvious confidence in human nature, whenever the slums are being depicted. And the scenario that he chose surpasses the naturalism of *Greed*. Frank Norris and Stroheim confined the depravity of their poverty-stricken heroes to an innate vice, rapacity. Whereas *Sperduti nel Buio*, with its portrayal of the very rich and the very poor, explains the former in terms of the latter and vice versa. In this way the drama moves from the psychology of the individual to an analysis of society – incomplete, no doubt, and grandiloquent, but possessing at least the merit of having been touched on, and perhaps put more explicitly than in Griffith.

It was in this humanity and this fellow-feeling, over and above the social message and the aesthetic revolution, that the real value of neo-realism lay. Another quality – also found in the films dating from 1945 – is paramount in Nino Martoglio: his themes are determined by a contemporary problem, but they are also placed in a precise environment. Among the torrent of re-constituted ancient history and the eternal mundanities, *Sperduti nel Buio* offers an image of truth, the face of a town, Naples, whose reality has been distorted beyond measure by shortsighted bourgeois novelists.

The work was not entirely free from the kind of crude schematization which was virtually inevitable in those days; but its virtues make it a signpost in the evolution of the Italian film. Even before the fall of Fascism, Umberto Barbaro drew attention to its importance, and presented it to his pupils at the Centro Sperimentale in Rome. It had a definite influence on the postwar Italian film-makers.

The path opened up by this film was to lead further. Martoglio himself made a *Teresa Raquin* the following year – this film is now lost, as is *Sperduti nel Buio* – which displayed the same qualities in the quasi-psychological evocation of setting and the studied composition of the frame.

Two other directors, Gustavo Serena and Febo Mari – both former actors – specialized in the same kind of realism, notably with adaptations from the poet Salvatore Di Giacomo, who was currently defending the educational, social and artistic value of the cinema. Gustavo Serena directed *Assunta Spina*, starring Francesca Bertini, then *A San Francisco* by the same author, which, while continuing to serve the cult of the *dive*, also introduced verist elements.

Febo Mari went to Sardinia to direct and act in a film which was the sole cinematic venture of the great Eleonora Duse: *Cenere* (1916), adapted from a novel by Grazia Deledda. The experiment came too late to be significant or even repeatable, but it was enough to allow this actress of genius to grasp immediately the very essence of this new art form. 'If I were twenty years younger,' she said,

I would start all over again in the cinema; no doubt I would achieve very great results, something like the discovery of an absolutely new art. I would first have to forget completely everything belonging to the theatre and express myself in the language, which is as yet non-existent, of the film.[17]

Eleonora Duse in *Cenere* (Mari, 1916)

In *Cenere* the quality of her acting was enhanced by outstandingly beautiful photography, which Sadoul compares to the images that Figueroa was to give to the Mexican cinema thirty years later.

Another film by Febo Mari, *Fauno*, aroused the interest of Delluc, but Mari seems already to have been heading towards another movement which we shall discuss later: futuristic aestheticism.

Italian production was at its height in 1914; it had conquered the European market and overcome American protectionism. If this success was not due to the low level of output in other countries, as some critics would have us believe, there can be no doubt that 'the beginning of the war helped Italy greatly in the conquest of the foreign markets, for France, Germany and Russia halted their output, and America had still not realized what cinema was about; hence Italy was the cinematic ruler of the world.'

This opinion is taken from a study of the Italian cinema by Emilio Ghione, actor and director.[18] Here are some further extracts from this study:

It has been reckoned that between 1914 and 1919 there were up to twenty-two production companies in Italy, filming night and day. Each of these firms employed complete troupes on a yearly basis. Tiber in particular had five such troupes: those of Baldassare

Negroni and Hesperia, Gennaro Righelli and Maria Jacobini, Emilio Ghione and Kally Sambucini, André Habay and Matilde Di Marzio, and lastly Polidor's, which had a monopoly of comedy.

In 1914, the public elected its idols. The crowds packed in to see the new stars of the screen: Francesca Bertini, Hesperia, Pina Menichelli, Gianna Terribili-Gonzales, Kally Sambucini, Diomira and Maria Jacobini, Italia Almirante Manzini, Diana Karenne, Maria Carmi, and so on.

Among the actors were Amleto Novelli, Alberto Capozzi, Tullio Carminati, Luigi Serventi, Alberto Collo, Mario Bonnard, Gustavo Serena and myself.

The directors had their share of success. We may mention, among the more important ones: Augusto Genina, Carmine Gallone, Enrico Guazzoni, Baldassare Negroni, Gennaro Righelli, Campogalliani, Luciano Doria, Umberto Paradini, Gabriellino D'Annunzio and Piero Fosco.

But success and prosperity were soon to have effects which foreshadowed what was to happen again later on, for the same reasons, in Hollywood and elsewhere.

In the grandiose edifice which the Italian cinema was building, cracks suddenly appeared. The first was the craze for stars.

Front-ranking artists such as Francesca Bertini, Hesperia and Pina Menichelli, aware of their commercial value, increased their demands. By continually dangling the threat of production stoppages over the industrialists' heads, they got their own way in everything. The star could be seen criticizing the script, giving advice to the director, and complaining if she learned that a rival's film had run for a fortnight, when hers had made only ten days. All this led to enormous losses, as will be seen from the following example.

One day, in a studio in Rome, at half past eight in the morning, 200 extras were ready and waiting for the arrival of the star. At a quarter to twelve, the star telephoned to say that she had guests at her house and could not go to work. Net result: 200 people to pay and a day wasted. And all through lack of a professional conscience!

Star warfare in Rome grew to unprecedented proportions. The most memorable duel was that between Francesca Bertini and Hesperia. The former was the star of Caesar, belonging to the lawyer Giuseppe Barattolo; the latter of Tiber, belonging to another lawyer, Gioacchino Mecheri.

Their muted rivalry soon broke out into the open. Hesperia filmed *La Signora delle Camelie*. Immediately afterwards, Francesca Bertini did the same.

The bad example was communicated to the male stars. Febo Mari, while shooting *Attila, il Flagello di Dio* [*Attila, the Scourge of God*], refused to wear a beard and a wig. Alberto Capozzi in his turn refused the role of Saint Paul so as not to have to wear a beard.

In spite of everything, output continued to grow. Several industrialists who had set out with little in the way of capital soon found themselves with fortunes; two of them in particular, the lawyers Mecheri and Barattolo, enjoyed the confidence of the large banks and produced film upon film, each seeking to outdo the other. The competition between these two men was later to sign the death warrant of the Italian cinema.

Other events, graver ones than the star system or the producers' ambitions, were to put an abrupt halt to this tremendous boom.

The privileged position of Italian production was to last for only a few months. On 23 May 1915 Italy entered the war alongside the Allies, and its films were thereby subjected to the same conditions as those of the other belligerent countries: loss of the central European market, isolation, lower resources, and a shortage of directors and technicians.

For a time, nonetheless, production carried on under its former momentum. The largest annual footage of new productions to date was achieved in 1915. The country was reckoned to have 1,500 picture houses and eighty production companies, many more than the figure given by Ghione, which doubtless included only the main firms. The two major genres still gave signs of vitality: the costume film, the older of the two, seems to have remained the speciality of Guazzoni (*Madame Tallien*), while the bourgeois drama gained ground with the films of Caserini, Negroni, Genina, and Gallone (who adapted Henri Bataille), and with new adaptations of D'Annunzio, notably *Il Fuoco* in which the new *diva* Pina Menichelli made her mark, and the director Giovanni Pastrone made several interesting technical innovations in the shooting.

The Neapolitan school gained ground with Martoglio and Serena; Emilio Ghione, following the example of Gasnier in New York and Feuillade in Paris, launched the detective series for which he created Za la Mort, a kind of romantic apache, played by himself. War-happy films also made their appearance, of course; they were as mediocre as their counterparts elsewhere, some of them starring the *dive*: *Colpa Altrui* (Francesca Bertini), *Sempre nel Cor la Patria* (Leda Gys), *Pro Patria Mori* (Gianna Terribili-Gonzales), and others. The genre soon died out.

The effectual reign of the *dive* continued. Lyda Borelli appeared, more sophisticated than ever, in an experiment by a newcomer, A. G. Bragaglia, *Perfido Incanto* (1916), with expressionist sets. This film has been seen as a forerunner of *Caligari*. But it indicates a new urge towards aestheticism in accordance with the spirit of the times. Lucio D'Ambra also used stylized costumes and sets in *Il Re, le Torri, gli Alfieri*. Two years earlier, Aldo Molinari had presented *Mondo Baldoria* as 'the first futurist subject in the cinema', but it was not recognized by the high priest of the movement, Marinetti, who launched his manifesto of futurist cinematography on 11 September of the same year, 1916. Mario Verdone has drawn attention to the references to 'visual analogies, the simultaneity and interpenetration of different filmed times and places, object-dramas, and disproportions'.[19] But this obscure terminology is a gloss on discoveries which had already been made, notably in *Cabiria*. As for the experiments of Arnoldo Ginna – blurring and distortion effects – it seems unlikely that they were known to the French *avant-garde* (as Mario Verdone supposes they were) when directors such as

Gance and L'Herbier were to use them to such telling effect.

Henri Langlois examines the intellectualist tendency of the cinema of this period from another angle:

The whole *avant-garde* movement at the end of the 19th century found its expression in the cinema, thanks to the Italians.

The symbolists, the Pre-Raphaelites, and even the futurists were to influence this art.

Pathé, Gaumont and Eclair were completely ignorant of the Russian ballet and Diaghilev. The Italians were not long in taking their inspiration from them and eventually called in Ida Rubinstein. . . . S.C.A.G.L.[20] swore by Maurice Donnay, Italy by Henri Bataille; this distinction is a clear indication of the time-gap between the two.

It was in Turin and Venice that Max Reinhardt shot, in 1913 and 1914, the film which pre-dated German expressionism by five years. Paris knew nothing of Saint Petersburg and Moscow and the men of the theatre with whom Turin collaborated, and Antoine's first film was not a French film but an Italian one, four years ahead of those he was to make for S.C.A.G.L.

In short, when historians want to know, not how a period lived, but how it thought, when they want to know what the main trends of the 19th century were, even what academism looked like, there is only one cinema between 1909 and 1915 to which they can refer: the Italian cinema.

Henri Langlois also stresses the quasi-innate culture of the Italian directors (unlike so many French or American film-makers) – their ability to see the world 'with the eyes of habitués of museums and opera houses'.

But did not this culture itself (like that of the creators of the French *film d'art*) result in the Italians' applying to the film the rules of other art forms, and neglecting its own requirements? Italian innovations always concerned the objects being filmed, and never (except in Pastrone) the apparatus used for filming them. But we shall return to this question later.

3. The Period of Decline (1917–29)

The reign of the *dive* was a necessary stage in the artistic evolution of the Italian cinema, but it was also a reflection of the way of life of a particular social class and of the film world itself, as if the actors had taken themselves for the roles they were playing. The lure of the stars was not confined to the screen. Together with the prosperity of this new industry, it attracted into the studios a great many members of the Piedmontese, Lombard and Roman nobility. Neither before nor since has there been anything like the array of dukes, counts and marquises that the Italian cinema could muster in the decade from 1910 to 1920.

While the captains of industry were building their frequently insecure fortunes, part of the nobility was attempting to restore its prestige with these sham glories and presenting to itself and to the public the spectacle of its decadence in a kind of masochistic romanticism. The upper-class drama to which the Italian film devoted itself so wholeheartedly was almost never to the credit of its heroes; like the character of the *diva* herself, it expressed rather an obsession with self-destruction. And the rising bourgeoisie seems to have been so fascinated by the decadent prestige of the doomed class that it fondly imagined that to ape it was to resemble it. Lawyers and bankers turned actors to play counts and dukes, sacrificing themselves vicariously to fickle Woman.

Hence, what might seem at first sight to have been merely an aesthetic trend, inherent in Italian extravagance, was in fact a social trait the very outrageousness of which is particularly revealing – of a certain class rather than a period or country.

While the northern aristocracy got rich, went bankrupt, and committed suicide, all in the name of the *dive*, the southern masses sank under the weight of poverty which the realist movement of Martoglio and the Neapolitan school had attempted to expose.

The grandiloquent self-portrait presented by the Italian cinema, this complacency in catastrophe, became reality with the entry into the arena of the lawyers Giuseppe Barattolo and Gioacchino Mecheri. The artisans of the early days, the Ambrosios and Pasqualis, together with the innovators such as Pastrone, Guazzoni, and Caserini, had all had their day. Big business took control, and the directors became the minions of the *dive* or their impresarios. Art cannot survive that kind of contract. But the industry itself was doomed, though its dangerous narcissism blinded it to the death agonies that were taking place.

Carlo Lizzani writes:

> The leaders of the Italian film industry do not seem to have realized that the war was playing havoc with the economic, social and intellectual structure of every nation, that the new fashions and tastes would require new forms of art to satisfy them.

Between the developing French cinema, the nascent Danish and German cinemas, and the triumphant Italian cinema there existed a kind of dramatic kinship which prevented the occurrence of any head-on collision of interests. It was quite the opposite with the massive importation of American westerns and comedies which took the old world by storm from 1916–17 onwards. The American film made the Italian style, above all the style of its *dive*, look antiquated and grotesque.

But the people concerned remained blithely unaware of the sarcasm of the critics and the hoots of the public. Lizzani rightly stresses 'the increasing lack of receptivity in the Italian cinema, the utter blindness by which those responsible for it seemed to have been stricken as the country crept towards the profound historical crisis precipitated by the war'.

The year 1917 was a dark one for warring Europe as the great illusions yielded to lassitude. In Italy, the Austrians had broken through at Caporetto and were threatening the Po valley. When victory came the following year, Italy was left with more bitterness than joy, as in the post-Risorgimento period, and had to cope with increasingly urgent internal problems.

Maria Jacobini in *La Casa sotto la Neve* (Righelli, 1921)

In the cinema, there seems to have been little realization among producers that they had lost their hegemony. The exaltation of passion and the high-lighting of adultery in Italian films had closed the Anglo-Saxon markets, and a blasé France had laughed them off the screen. The war and the Russian Revolution had eliminated the important outlets of Central and Eastern Europe. And America had conquered a world market which it intended to hold.

Despite this changed situation, the Italian cinema attempted to carry on as before. The year 1916 saw new attempts at the costume film: Guazzoni, the past master of the genre, filmed *Fabiola*, an edifying drama of Christian Rome; Caserini, a *Resurrezione* full of local colour; Negroni, *La Principessa di Bagdad*; and Febo Mari, after the realism of *Cenere* and the aestheticism of *Fauno*, filmed an ambitious *Attila*, followed by a *Judas*, in 1917. A recently founded company, Tespi of Rome, produced, also in 1917, *Frate Sole* by Mario Corsi, a good new version of the Franciscan legend already filmed by Antamoro. Among the founders of Tespi was the dramatist Pirandello, who had several of his works turned into films. But he came too late to stem the deluge.

Tosca was a great success and a personal triumph for Francesca Bertini.

Partnered by the indefatigable Febo Mari, Pina Menichelli was the heroine of *Tigre Reale*, an incredible and cliché-ridden story of a *femme fatale* adapted by Pastrone from an early novel by Verga.

Upper-class drama and light comedy proliferated under the direction of the habitués Ghione, Caserini, Lucio D'Ambra, and the newcomers Brignone, Gallone and Genina. Yet the dangers of this stagnation were beginning to strike the professionals who had some experience of the cinema and were not dazzled by the brilliance of the *dive*. Arturo Ambrosio, the pioneer, wrote in 1919: 'The Italian cinema has had its head turned by its success and has remained content with these facile victories. . . .' Plot and interpretation should 'respect order and moderation'. With less ceremony, a trade journal, *La Vita Cinematografica*, puts its finger on the weakness:

Consider the Americans, who present real actresses and not professional hysterics as we invariably do. Hitherto Italian films have been made for the *dive*; the rest have no importance. Even the scenario is subordinated to the demands of the ham actress of the moment who, puffed up with pride, usurps the place of the director, the producer, and the shareholders. This mistress is a tyrant. . . . Enough of this rivalry, we need to industrialize.

The rivalry referred to by Emilio Ghione had indeed reached a sorry pitch. The lawyer Mecheri had bought up Itala and at that time headed eleven different companies. The industrialization propounded by the Italian journal came about in the form of the trust, with backing from the world of finance, but without any renewal of technique or policy.

Emilio Ghione says:

A powerful bank which had kept a professional watch on the boom in the cinema industry put up several million lire to float a trust of large production companies, the Unione Cinematografica Italiana [U.C.I.].

Thereupon the two lawyers began squabbling about who was going to be the managing director: Barattolo won when Mecheri backed down, his rival having promised to buy his two production companies, Itala and Tiber. And the deal was soon concluded.

In any case, U.C.I. hoped to gain a monopoly by buying up all or almost all the Italian studios, even if it meant paying much more than they were worth. It paid 13 million lire for a studio that had cost slightly less than two million a year before; a cinema worth 600,000 lire was sold for 1,800,000 lire. The artists too were bought up one after the other; U.C.I. hired anyone and everyone, at any price. It was the beginning of the end.

There was better – or worse – to come. Technicians and actors were brought to Rome from abroad, especially from France, but they continued to churn out the same old rubbish. Alexandre Devarennes transposed Balzac's *Vautrin* to Italy; after him came Antoine, who adapted Bernstein; Gaston Ravelle, who filmed Paul Bourget; André Deed, who had turned director; and Georges Lacroix, who died in Turin in 1920 aged forty. Even Musidora, the heroine of Feuillade's *Les Vampires*, came to work in Italy; and Americans, notably Herbert Brenon, moved into the studios in Rome.

But [Emilio Ghione continues] people had gradually lost confidence in U.C.I. The outworn techniques and styles were incapable of reconquering the world markets. To cope with this state of affairs, a few financiers got together, and founded an independent production company that welcomed all those dissatisfied with U.C.I. . . . This new firm was created in Turin under the name of Fert; its head was Enrico Fiori. Stefane Pittaluga, the owner of a circuit of 300 cinemas, irritated by U.C.I.'s distribution policy, soon gave his backing to the new company. Pittaluga countered Barattolo's announced intention of introducing the American block-booking system – films sold by tens – by joining Fert as a producer, thereby hastening the crash of the U.C.I. trust. The Italian cinema became the arena of financial conflicts which the circumstances barely warranted in either camp.

Emilio Ghione joined Fert along with Righelli, Genina, Almirante and a few actors. Some partiality is evident in his optimism as regards the new firm, whose activity was to be very short-lived. In a few years the total production of Italy fell by more than half – to 220 films in 1920. But it saw all the less reason to change its style since Germany had become a competitor, with the costume films of Lubitsch, Eichberg, and Buchowetzky, *Madame Du Barry*, *Anna Boleyn*, etc.

The industry continued blindly to believe that its salvation depended on lavish staging. This error of judgement was to be as fatal as the *dive* had been, whose day was already over. Like his colleagues of those days, Emilio Ghione was mistaken when he wrote: 'In an attempt to restore, to rebuild all that U.C.I. had systematically destroyed, Caramba, that brilliant exponent of costume, immediately accepted responsibility for the direction of the great historical film *I Borgi*.'

Even if this courtly drama was, as we learn from Ghione, hailed by the Italians as a masterpiece, it was not sufficient to ensure the prestige of Fert; nor were other historical dramas directed by Mario Almirante, or Ghione's own attempt to revive his popular Za la Mort series.

The Italian cinema was collapsing on every front. Its prosperity had depended on its exports, and the end of foreign sales was the end of prosperity. The system of three- and six-month bills merely drove the declining industry nearer to the wall. The drop in production worsened every year: from 220 films in 1920, it fell to 100 in 1921, 50 in 1922, 20–30 in 1923, 15–20 in 1924, and dwindled to around 15 in 1925–6, and less than a dozen in 1927–8.

As early as 1923, Robert Florey, then a young cinema columnist, had occasion to write after a trip to Italy: 'We have got used to saying that the Italian cinema industry is going through a crisis. . . . What I have seen allows me to be more categorical: the Italian cinema industry has ceased to exist.'[1]

Maria Jacobini in *Oriente* (*Daughters of the Desert*, Righelli, 1924)

Artistically, in fact, the Italian cinema had been dead for several years already. Its death throes were spectacular, as desperate efforts were made to avoid the inevitable demise; but they were made, not with new methods or resources, but with the usual stupid insistence on the old unwanted formulas. Thus, *Gli Ultimi Giorni di Pompei* and *Quo Vadis?*, which marked the rise and triumph of Italian production, were to be the essential reasons for its decline and fall.

What became of the directors? Before Fert's attempt to redress the situation, Ernesto Pasquali died while working on a film. Giovanni Pastrone retired out of dissatisfaction with the methods of U.C.I., which had bought up Itala. Baldassare Negroni also retired – for a time at least – while Guazzoni filmed yet another *Sacco di Roma* (192.) and a *Messalina* (1923), and Ambrosio made *Teodora* and lent the prestige of his name to the ultimate *Quo Vadis?* As for the younger generation – Genina, Gallone, Righelli, Palermi – after the closure of Fert, they put forward the idea of a consortium to bring some life back into Italian production. In June 1923 Genina declared: 'We want contacts with other countries. We want to know what is happening abroad and collaborate more closely with our French and English colleagues.'

But in fact they went to work abroad.

Rina De Liguoro in *Messalina* (Guazzoni, 1923)

The cinema was not the only thing that was in a bad way. Emilio Ghione summarizes the situation as follows:

In 1921, the cinema was in jeopardy. The political situation at home had been very serious for two years, with the Communists in complete control of the country and declaring strike upon strike up to the sudden appearance of the Black Shirts. In the meantime, all this had gradually brought the Italian cinema to a state of total ruin.

This is to over-simplify history. Italy soon felt that it had been cheated by the peace treaty, despite its 'reunification' with Trent and Trieste. In Villat's words:

Allied resistance exasperated the Italian nationalists, for whom these external objectives were an attempt to divert the unrest at home. (The men back from the trenches were sickened by the lack of social justice, and the countryside was in the clutch of profiteers.) The high cost of living led to disturbances both in the towns (where there were riots in July 1919) and in the country. . . .
[On 12 September of the same year] the poet D'Annunzio entered Fiume; presenting the Peace Conference with a *fait accompli*, he occupied the palace of government. This heroic adventure was a foretaste of the techniques of Fascism.[2]

53

This successful expedition must have influenced Mussolini, who was planning to do at home what D'Annunzio – the 'John the Baptist of Fascism' as he has been called – had dared to do abroad. Returned as deputy for Milan in May 1921, Mussolini organized a Fascist Party congress in Naples on 24 October 1922, and on 28 October marched on Rome.

The unrest was greater than ever; the government's failure to cope with events allowed Mussolini to win the malcontents to his cause. On 6 April 1924 the elections gave him a majority of four million votes, as against a Socialist, Catholic and Liberal opposition of two and a half million. Villat writes:

Mussolini struck back at the opposition immediately; Matteotti was assassinated on 10 June 1924, press censorship was introduced, and the assassination attempts of 1925 and 1926 led to special police measures; Italy gradually came round to the conception of totalitarian power, whereby the Fascist Party became synonymous with the State.

This was the climate in which the Italian cinema, already threatened by so many other factors, was struggling to stay alive. In such an explosive political situation, there was no hope of a renewal of Martoglio's realist trend which might have put the Italian film on the right track. That was not to happen for another twenty years.

On the contrary, in those days of grandiloquence, Italy pinned its hopes on antiquity. As early as 1921, U.C.I., still clinging on, announced its decision to remake *Quo Vadis?* on such an enormous scale that two years went by before filming commenced. But, Ghione tells us, the first version, in 1912, had cost 50,000 lire and had earned several million; the second time round, in spite of much higher costs, the operation had also brought in considerable profits. The producers naïvely thought that a third version, with still higher costs, would bring in even more and lead to a recovery. However, realizing that he needed to give his venture foreign appeal, Barattolo decided that Nerò should be played by Emil Jannings, whose fame would sell the film abroad. The same considerations led Barattolo to employ a German distributor as a kind of superviser; he seems to have had little confidence in the ability of Gabriellino D'Annunzio, who was to direct under Ambrosio's artistic eye.

This triumvirate did not rule without disagreement, which, says Ghione, sometimes turned into violent arguments; and the extravagance of the big scenes was such that a slave girl got badly burned and another unfortunate extra was eaten by a lion.

The financial problems were no less troublesome. German finance having stepped in to keep the cameras turning, the film was finally completed and shown in 1925. Jannings's presence was insufficient to save the film, which lacked both the impact and the feeling of Guazzoni's version. For the producers, it was a disaster: the U.C.I. studios closed and the firm went bankrupt.

Its directors were forced to find their own capital in order to carry on working. Ghione, starting from the principle that costs, actors' fees in particular, should be kept to a minimum, made *La Nostra Patria* in the country around Rome for a mere 100,000 lire. Gallone, whether more ambitious or merely more fortunate, found backing to the tune of one and a half million, and filmed the epic of Garibaldi as *La Cavalcata Ardente*. Patriotic exaltation was the order of the day; the film was a success. But the Italian cinema's successes seemed merely to have hastened its fall. Genina, who had had a success for a small outlay with *L'Ultimo Lord*, featuring his wife Carmen Boni, unhesitatingly accepted offers made to him by Berlin. Carmine Gallone was signed up in his turn, as had already been Guido Brignone, Maria Jacobini, the intrepid Albertini, and even the valiant Maciste, who had just appeared in a particularly spectacular *Maciste all'Inferno* and who a few years before had been making mincemeat of enemy Austrians in *Maciste Alpino*.

Before leaving for Babelsberg, Carmine Gallone gave a helping hand to his colleague Amleto Palermi who was repeating the disastrous mistake of the producers of *Quo Vadis?* It is Emilio Ghione who relates this final episode in the fall of the Italian cinema. The year is 1926:

Amleto Palermi got all the papers to announce that he was shortly to direct a monumental historical film called *Gli Ultimi Giorni di Pompei* (*The Last Days of Pompeii*). He hired, at enormous expense, the largest studio at Cines where no film had been made for years, hired the cameramen Donelli and Armenise for the fabulous fee of 6,000 francs a month each, signed up Diomira Jacobini, Maria's sister, to play Cicca, and Lido Menetti (who was to die in 1929, in North America, following a motor-car accident) to play Glauco, filled the sports stadium with 5,000 extras dressed as ancient Romans, and in this improvised arena shot some remarkable scenes with gladiators, lions, etc., and took an enormous amount of stills, which he immediately had enlarged. Then he put these enlargements in a trunk and disappeared to Vienna (leaving his brother Lamberto holding the baby in Rome), with the aim of selling the film that he had barely commenced. Since the negative would cost a total of three million lire, and since all that he had been able to raise up to then was 500,000 francs, he needed the rest, or part at least, to continue working.

But the buyers in Vienna, despite the photographs that Amleto Palermi showed them, were not easily convinced. They didn't like the names of Diomira Jacobini and Lido Menetti as the stars. But they agreed to co-operate if Palermi replaced them with Maria Korda and Victor Varconi. Palermi had no choice but to accept.

In their turn the buyers in Berlin accepted the names of Maria Korda and Victor Varconi, but in addition they demanded that Goetzke should play Arbace. Once again, Amleto Palermi complied with their wishes.

On his return to Rome, Palermi had some difficulty in getting back to work. Diomira Jacobini demanded an indemnity of 25,000 lire and Lido Menetti 15,000. Both had to be paid. Worst of all, Maria Korda demanded 6,000 lire a day and Varconi 1,500. Each

Bartolomeo Pagano in *Maciste Alpino* (Pastrone, Borgnetto and Maggi, 1916)

worked for exactly 100 days and the director paid them 600,000 and 150,000 lire respectively. This, together with the fee paid to Goetzke, brought the cost of the three main artists to close on one million lire. Half way through the film, Amleto Palermi found he had already spent the three million. So he begged his friend Carmine Gallone to delay his departure to Berlin and take over the direction of the other half of the film while he, Palermi, went in search of capital. All in all, the film cost seven million lire.

This was the last important film to be shot in Italy. Instead of *The Last Days of Pompeii* it could almost have been called *The Last Days of the Italian Cinema*.

The time had not yet come when Mussolini would call the cinema his 'most powerful weapon'. Yet the government was beginning to feel concerned at all the bankruptcies and emigrations. On 2 April 1926 a royal decree set up a committee of inquiry at the Ministry of National Economy. Production was virtually non-existent, and the 3,227 cinemas in Italy at that time could only get hold of foreign films, an intolerable situation in a state whose declared aim was autonomy. The first legislative measure taken on the advice of the committee of inquiry was a mere gesture intended to encourage home production by making it obligatory for the cinemas to include at least one Italian film in every ten they showed.

This decree was powerless to change the situation, or to support an industry that had practically gone out of existence. But Pittaluga, who was virtually alone in continuing to turn out a few films, saw this measure as a promise of future backing. Already the owner of a circuit of 150 cinemas, and controlling several hundred more, he bought up the failing companies – Cines, Itala, Caesar, Palatina – increased his capital from 50 to 150 million lire, and thus gained control of the entire Italian cinema. In March 1927 Mussolini gave him the job of getting production under way again and distributing the films of L.U.C.E. (L'Unione Cinematografica Educativa), which had just been set up following a report by Senator Corrado Ricci. In the words of the report:

Our schools, public festivals and cinemas require films of an essentially scientific, historical and patriotic nature; we must oblige the cinema-owners to include one or several of these films in their programmes, and attempt to correct public taste, which has been corrupted by films whose moral and aesthetic qualities have all too often left much to be desired.

This, then, was the first significant – but, according to Nino Frank, unpopular – manifestation of State intrusion in the Italian cinema. The making of scientific films was favoured by the inauguration in Rome, that same year, of the International Educational Cinematographic Institute, founded under the aegis of the League of Nations.

But from *La Vita delle Api* (*The Life of the Bees*) and *Circolazione del Sangue* (*Circulation of the Blood*) L.U.C.E. soon moved on to documentaries of a different kind, intended to sing the praises of the regime and serve as propaganda, starting with *Il Duce* – the saga (in three parts) of the Black Shirts and their chief, Mussolini.

This first government measure was soon followed by the nomination of a controlling body for the cinema (Ente Nazionale per la Cinematografia) attached to the Ministry of the Press and Propaganda; the man chosen to head this body was Luigi Freddi. The censor's office was also reorganized: it examined scenarios, commissioned new films, and distributed the finished products.

Pending the recovery of home production, Pittaluga signed agreements with firms in Germany and America. The protectionist quota was increased from 10 to 25 per cent in 1928, inciting a few small firms to go back into production despite the powerful influence of Pittaluga. Thus, some ten films were made by such survivors from the golden age as Camerini, Almirante, Negroni and Antamoro, who directed a second *Frate Francesco* featuring the French actor Romuald Joubé, or from newcomers who blithely mounted the same old hacks: Manzoni's *I Promessi Sposi*, directed by V. M. Del Colle, and *Garibaldi*, filmed by the playwright Aldo De Benedetti.

Seven years after the march on Rome, the Italian cinema had not recovered. It continued to ebb slowly away at a time when elsewhere the silent cinema had become a thing of the past, thanks to the invention of a new dimension: sound.

Having reached this point of double hiatus – in the art as a whole, and in the formerly flourishing Italian industry – we must pause for a moment. On the threshold of the 1930s the Italian film industry was in utter ruin. Not surprisingly, therefore, few of the early cinema historians had anything but scorn for it.

The early historians may have had great difficulty in discovering source material at a time when the Italian cinema had been more or less out of existence for several years; but later historians continue to repeat the same old clichés, with the result that the discussions, though less dismissive than they were, are still inexact and superficial.[3]

What, then, by way of recapitulation, were the positive results achieved by the Italian film to date?

Well before *Cabiria*, the great historical reconstructions had brought to the cinema a breadth of approach which, artistically, was as important as movement in the American cinema. This distinctive characteristic was a product of Italy's wealth of history and its taste for grand opera. The use, not to say the discovery, of the technical procedures that had made the fame of *Cabiria* stemmed directly from this national characteristic.

But as soon as it passed from the general to the particular, from the past to the present, from the historical film to the upper-class drama, the Italian cinema relapsed into the theatricality that it had driven from the screen; and it perished. The promise of the realist movement is of considerable importance; but in an evaluation of the Italian silent cinema it remains a mere indication of what was to come. The misunderstanding deplored by Pietrangeli extends even to the famous *dive*, who are remembered with none of the affection that we have for Mack Sennett's bathing beauties or the blonde teen-age Mary Pickford. The baroque side of Lyda Borelli discussed by Georges Sadoul and admired by Salvador Dali has little value outside its context; and this is why the Italian *dive* will never be more than period pieces. The legacy of all those melodramas full of tears and passion is a social document – the self-portrait, willed or not, of an era, a world as devoted to extravagance and cynicism as ours is to eroticism and violence. So, paradoxically enough, it is the basis of reality in the masquerade of the upper-class drama that gives it its historical value. It is interesting to bear this in mind along with the handling of crowds in *Quo Vadis?* or *Cabiria*.

Nino Frank is another defender of the Italian film:

Eisenstein often declared that the film-makers to whom he owed most were the pre-1917 Italians. At the other end of the scale, Griffith never admitted quite so much, but the influence of the Italian films can be detected beneath the surface in *Intolerance* – just as it guided, *mutatis mutandis*, the satirical wit of Lubitsch (compare the success in Germany between 1919 and 1921 of the zany comedies produced in the studios of Turin).[4]

The sudden demise of the Italian cinema certainly helped to cause this critical neglect of its recent past.

And there is another extremely important point. As we have seen, the Italian cinema came into being ten years after that of Lumière and Méliès. It thus sidestepped the formative period and, when the time came, got off to a flying start thanks to the existence of a sum of experience to which its contribution had been nil.

The same thing is happening again today. From 1916–17 to 1932–3, Italian films produced nothing of original value. Yet this was the period when the 'silent art' grew, flowered, and died its beautiful death, and when, from 1927–8 onwards, a promising yet dangerous technique tried its paces, stumbled, went astray, but by its very mistakes opened the way to the future. That is to say that for fifteen years or so, for the whole duration of a crucial period in the art of the cinema, Italy was absent, and played no part in developments from which, when the time came, as in 1908, it would merely draw the benefits.

This negative fact has to be borne in mind when we attempt an assessment or rehabilitation of the Italian cinema. While the German cinema expressed the fantastic contemporary social scene, while America discovered the poetry of the wide open spaces and the comic possibilities of the absurd, while Sweden charmed us with its legends, while the infant U.S.S.R. burst the screen with its faith in the Revolution, and while the French *avant-garde* indulged in perilous innovations and experiments, Italy tried to sew the sequins back on its fancy dress, without realizing that the days of fancy dress were over.

The history of the Italian silent cinema is rich as regards industrial organization, oddity, human interest, and perhaps even documentary value; but we must admit that its aesthetic contribution is negligible, and its technical contribution nil. All that we can find in its favour are the crowds of *Pompei* or the dolly used for *Cabiria* – hardly sufficient to compensate for the dearth of good Italian films during the magnificent classical period of the silent cinema. Italy produced nothing comparable to *The Docks of New York, The Crowd, La Passion de Jeanne d'Arc, The Circus, Napoléon, La Glace à Trois Faces, Metropolis.* Nothing to compare, either, with *Le Million, The Blue Angel, Die Drei von der Tankstelle, Broadway Melody, Hallelujah.* In the development of the cinema, she seems to have been a forerunner, but she took no part in the struggle for technical mastery; if she helped to compose the silent image, she made little contribution to the formation of a language.

The contribution of the Italian cinema to the new art form has to be sought elsewhere.

4. The Cinema Under Fascism (1930–43)

In Italy the renewal of the cinema was not the dramatic affair that it was elsewhere – for the simple reason that its teams had split up and production had practically ceased to exist.

The bankruptcy of the producers and the retirement or emigration of the directors did not, of course, fail to produce reactions. These reactions stemmed from the daily press and from periodicals, in which young intellectuals – Luigi Chiarini, Francesco Pasinetti and others – demanded a new approach to the cinema; and they aroused the enthusiasm of a young columnist who founded a series of little magazines in which he denounced the inertia of the Pittaluga company and demonstrated the need for a national cinema. His name was Alessandro Blasetti. Not content with polemics, he founded a co-operative production company called Augustus. Among its leaders were Aldo Vergano, Umberto Barbaro, Goffredo Alessandrini, Mario Serandrei and Libero Solaroli. With these new names, and with Genina, Gallone and others whose careers had taken them abroad, the Italian cinema entered a new era, a slow process of development that reached maturity twelve years later. *Sole* (*Sun*), directed by Blasetti in 1929, handles a topical theme, the draining of the Pontine marshes put in hand by Mussolini.

In this, his first film, which seemed to fit the requirements of government propaganda, the young director laid the foundations of neo-realism. Abandoning the costume film and the archaic sentimental drama, he tackled a contemporary social problem to illustrate the triumph of young ideas in the face of conservative hostility to national progress.

'Without deliberately setting out to produce Fascist propaganda,' writes Carlo Lizzani, 'Blasetti happened to be in agreement with the slogans of the regime.'[1]

This was to be a common position among Italian film-makers up to the fall of Fascism. But, if the subject and the setting reveal the presence of a new approach, the form has been held to be too deliberately paramount. Lizzani writes:

The tight editing, the audacious framings, and his tendency to consider bodies and faces as a form of still life, as beautiful objects rather than as centres of emotion, passion and suffering, shifted the centre of interest to the form, to the composition, and away from the scrutiny and discovery of human nature.

These lines are quoted because they also introduced, as early as 1929, one of the contentious issues of the Italian cinema, to which we shall return: the issue of formalism. Hence Blasetti's *Sole*, besides being a forerunner of neo-realism, appears to have been the first example of the 'calligraphy' which the anti-Fascist critics were to attack in the early work of some of the great directors of the future. Thus, despite what today seems to be a somewhat ponderous style, and a tendency to preach, Blasetti's first film is important historically. It marked the first glimmer of a revival; its success gave new heart to Italian producers.

The same year saw the appearance of *Rotaie* (*Rails*) by Mario Camerini, who had made a modest début six years earlier. The sober, concrete titles of Blasetti's and Camerini's films form an eloquent contrast to the *Gipsy Passions* and *Satanic Rhapsodies* of the previous period. And the names of these two directors were to dominate the period that saw a timid recovery in the Italian film and a renewal of its themes.

These last silent films are in the realistic tradition of the Neapolitan school. Blasetti's heroes, like those of *Terra Madre* in 1930, are peasants; Camerini's are two young men in search of work in a world of squalor and poverty.

As time went on [writes Lizzani] Blasetti emerged as the preacher of the honest middle classes, while Camerini became their discreet confessor. The former portrayed with ever-increasing warmth the myths, dreams and illusions of his flock, while the latter scrutinized with ever-increasing prudence the hearts of his congregation to discover their modest sins. For many years other directors merely repeated, with less artistry, the admonitions of Blasetti or the whisperings of Camerini.

The hope placed in the protectionism introduced by the government encouraged Cines to equip its studios for sound, and the Pittaluga company installed sound projectors in its cinemas. To cope with the ban on films in foreign languages, Pittaluga organized a dubbing department. In 1930 only nine films were made – the lowest output ever recorded in Italy; this was due in part to uncertainty about how sound could best be exploited, and in part to the shortcomings of the technical equipment. However, an Italian sound film was undertaken by Gennaro Righelli, *La Canzone dell'Amore*, which was filmed in three versions.

All the companies, however, were in the red. The following year, Pittaluga's death exposed the true financial situation of the trust: a deficit of four million lire. These were hardly the ideal conditions for entering a period that seemed to require a renewal of leadership and plant. The first requirement, however, had already been met; the second was in hand. Gradually, with moral and financial support from the government (including a tax on the dubbing of foreign films, the revenue being ploughed back into the industry), the Italian cinema was reborn. Bolstered by the government, Cines started up again, with, as artistic director, the talented writer and journalist Emilio Cecchi, just back from a trip to the United States, who pinned his hopes on a cosmopolitan production policy. He encouraged the interest in the cinema shown by Luigi Pirandello, the only Italian author of the day who could boast a European reputation, and called in German directors, notably Walter Ruttmann to direct Pirandello's novella *Il Silenzio*, adapted for the screen by Emilio Cecchi, Soldati and Ruttmann, and set in the Terni steelworks; whence its title, *Acciaio* (*Steel*), and the predominance of documentary characteristics over the dramatic theme.

Cecchi's initiatives were unable to stave off the bankruptcy of Cines in 1933. Gradually, however, output increased: 13 films in 1931, 22 in 1932, 36 in 1933.

Barattolo returned to work at Caesar. On the initiative of Count Volpi de Misurata, the first Exhibition of Cinematographic Art opened at the 18th Venice Biennale in 1932. The same year, a film by Gioacchino Forzano, *Camicia Nera*, celebrated the tenth anniversary of the march on Rome. Fascism had discovered its 'most powerful weapon'. But first the weapon had to be forged. The Direzione Generale per lo Spettacolo was founded in 1934 as a department of the Ministero per la Cultura Popolare, while in the Gruppi dei Fascisti Universitarî (G.U.F.) film departments were formed which were to be the nurseries for the Italian cinema of the future. For the time being it was sufficient to restore confidence among the professionals, and to assist the industry's recovery. This was the course adopted in the early 1930s, when several survivors of the golden age – Guazzoni, Negroni, Almirante, Campogalliani – returned to the studios; the most important of the new-comers were Blasetti and Camerini.

Nino Frank has called Blasetti 'the Don Quixote of the Italian cinema, the least naïve and the canniest Don Quixote of them all'. Blasetti's first volte-face – there were to be many others – was a return, in *Resurrectio*, to the old, outworn traditions. Then, still according to Nino Frank, he first 'took a vehement stand against the talkies, but immediately filmed the two most famous music-hall patterers of the day, the Roman Petrolini (in *Nerone*), and the Neapolitan Viviani (*La Tavola dei Poveri*; *The Table of the Poor*). *Nerone* is a parody. Yet both films can be safely forgotten.

With *Terra Madre* (1930) Blasetti returned to the real world of peasants. But this theme needs to be handled carefully if it is not to lapse into post-romantic sentimentality; and Blasetti did not manage to avoid all the clichés. However, the young director's sense of epic composition was confirmed in scenes such as the Mass in the fields and the flocks grazing in the Campagna. *Terra Madre* got a few good reviews; it would be interesting to see it again today.

Two years later Blasetti brought out the film Lizzani considers to be his masterpiece: *1860*. This skilful and intelligent piece of work seems to combine the two aspects which the Italian cinema would henceforth tend to emphasize: the perennially resilient costume film and the realist trend. The subject is historical: an episode in Garibaldi's campaign for the liberation of the Bourbon kingdom of the Two Sicilies. But the subject is treated realistically. To quote Lizzani again:

The fact that Garibaldi appears only incidentally and that the main thread is provided by the humble doings of a Sicilian mountain peasant and his young wife seems to suggest a polemical intention. . . . The facts, the characters and the landscape form the basis of a patriotic passion at its simplest: a Sicilian peasant's desire for revolt and liberty.

This distortion of the usual historical perspective served Blasetti's artistic and perhaps even his political aims. It shifted the centre of interest from historical facts to the aspirations of the people, to the point of eclipsing the national hero with a couple played by genuine peasants. His firm adoption of a popular standpoint and a humble authenticity indicate an equivocal attitude towards the imperatives of the regime. The film prudently went no further than Garibaldi's first victory at Calatafimi, thereby avoiding the delicate problems of the hero's struggle against the Papacy. Thus, consciously or unconsciously, Blasetti sidestepped the more or less avowed directives of the dictatorship in order to express what he and most people felt. This cry for liberty, this peasant revolt, must have sounded strangely in the ears of Fascists, even in the context of national unity. Blasetti, writes Lizzani,

was continually on the point of going out on a limb. The more seriously he took Fascism in the years that followed, the further his warm and generous nature took him from the paths of conformism. This was the case even with *Vecchia Guardia*, which was supposed to be a piece of overt Fascist propaganda, a film to affirm Blasetti's loyalty to the regime, but which failed to live up to what the Fascists expected of it.

Yet it was the story of a young Fascist in the days of the march on Rome.

This underlines the discrepancy between the director's intentions – or those foisted upon him – and their results. Blasetti's films are notable for their reserve, which in itself was enough to steer him away from what Lizzani calls 'the imperial bugles'. Even Bardèche and Brasillach praise this reserve, while regretting the absence of

the furious beauty of the Russian films. . . . They are so reticent about themselves that they seem almost too discreet, too polished, too preoccupied with avoiding the inflated style of yesterday.[2]

We may suppose that Blasetti was reticent less about himself than about the regime for which he worked. What interests him in the story of his Sicilian shepherd or his peasants who join the militia for the march on Rome is the people – depicted in silhouettes that combine tenderness and irony, or in frequently admirable scenes of rural life, composed in a way that succeeds in marrying realism and poetry. Blasetti remained true to his early ambition of giving his country a cinema peculiar to itself. He was not always successful in minimizing the banality imposed upon him by circumstances. An instance of this was *Aldebaran* (1935), glorifying the Italian navy, a hackneyed theme whose equivalent has been trotted out in every country of the world, whatever the regime – in Great Britain, in America, in Japan, by John Ford and by Marcel L'Herbier.

Confronted with the same problems as Blasetti, Mario Camerini resolved them in accordance with his own temperament, which inclined him towards the comedy of character. His discretion and sensitivity were in direct opposition to the grandiloquence of the past decades and to the swagger that was soon to bring the cinema in line with the political system.

He was made famous, mainly abroad, by a single film: *Gli Uomini, che Mascalzoni!*, a pleasant comedy in which the humour makes up for the sentimentality, and which has clearly been influenced by the French silent film, notably by René Clair and Jean Epstein. This assimilation of French style is an example of the ease with which Italian film-makers bridged the gap still existing between the two styles. Filmed on location in natural settings (the Milan fair), and using a mobile camera, this is a lively little film whose technique has worn extremely well.

Vittorio De Sica, Lia Franca in *Gli Uomini, che Mascalzoni!* (Camerini, 1932)

It was followed by other minor successes, remarkable for their finesse: *T'amerò Sempre* (*I'll Love You Always*), *Il Cappello a Tre Punte*, and above all *Darò un Millione* (*I'd Give a Million*, 1935), the story of a millionaire who dreams of giving all his money away. This film brought together for the first time that fruitful pair Cesare Zavattini, as scriptwriter, and Vittorio De Sica, in the lead. Camerini returned to a similar theme two years later with his *Il Signor Max*, more overtly satirical, but just as sympathetic towards the poor.

But the political scene had changed; Fascism had gained control. The days were over when it had to court the favours of the petty bourgeoisie or crow about the draining of the Pontine marshes. By 1930 Mussolini was bombarding the Kufra Oasis in Libya, dispatching (against six villages and 500 natives) 3,800 soldiers, 5,000 camels, 400 motor vehicles, and twenty aeroplanes, and proclaiming after this famous victory 'Italy's invincible power in Africa'. In 1935 came the invasion of Abyssinia; in 1939, that of Albania. This era of conquests, this renaissance of Imperial Rome, needed a cinema worthy of them. In 1935, the Duce ordered the construction near Rome of a magnificent group of studios fitted out with all the latest equipment, and founded the C.S.C. (Centro Sperimentale di Cinematografia) as a

Fosco Giachetti, Antonio Centa in *Squadrone Bianco* (*The White Squadron*, Genina, 1936)

training-centre for young technicians. Cinecittà was officially opened on 21 April 1937; but Pittaluga's Cines, put back on its feet by government money, had already resumed work, the deserters of the lean years had returned to the eternal city, and newcomers answered the call of the Duce. Genina turned Joseph Peyré's *L'Escadron Blanc* into *Squadrone Bianco* (*The White Squadron*). Camerini had to direct the party-glorifying *Il Grande Appello*; but this kind of greatness was thrust upon him, and he immediately returned to his unpretentious little comedies. Blasetti taught directing at the C.S.C. and belonged to its board of governors. Lizzani writes:

Blasetti's *Vecchia Guardia* had furnished proof of his loyalty to the governing regime. How is it, then, that, whether as volunteer or as conscript, he never joined the ranks of direct propagandists? And why, indeed, did he turn his energetic hand to formalism?

In the same connection, Bardèche and Brasillach profess their surprise at the fact that

the only director with a genuine epic feeling wasted his time on a series of insignificant trifles, as he did when he returned to the spectacular in the early Italian manner.

Alessandro Blasetti was doing in Fascist Italy what most of the great French directors were to do in occupied France. He sidestepped the present and fled towards the past, towards preciosity, towards the baroque, towards the polished manner and formal qualities through which he could reveal his skill in widely differing genres. It was in this spirit that he directed, one after the other, *La Contessa di Parma*, a lively fantasy, *Ettore Fieramosca*, *Retroscena* and *Un'Avventura di Salvator Rosa*, scripted by the young Renato Castellani, who was soon to make a name for himself. Finally, in 1940, Blasetti directed *La Corona di Ferro* (*The Iron Crown*), as delirious a pseudo-historical fantasy as any of those so dear to the hearts of Italian film-makers in the days of D'Annunzio. The film cost 40 million lire, a huge sum in those days, and mobilized a host of extras, 7,000 horses, an entire zoo – in short, the resources of *Ben Hur, Tarzan, Robin Hood, Cabiria* and *Quo Vadis?* rolled into one. Massimo Girotti played with appropriate energy a cross between a mythological hero and a superman involved in the most extravagant adventures. The film won the Grand Prix at the Venice Biennale in 1941 – which was not much more than the festival of the Rome-Berlin axis. We shall probably never know what was in Blasetti's mind when he performed these antics, whose very excesses were a cause for admiration and which, in occupied France, had an unwittingly hilarious success. There is reason to believe that Blasetti himself had his tongue in his cheek while making this film. Lizzani tells us that the author intended his film as a message of peace, and Blasetti himself has confirmed this. In France it was seen above all, in the words of Bardèche and Brasillach, as 'the epitome of artificiality and bric-à-brac: ladies in wimples met Florentine lords in front of a Greek temple, and people in togas greeted people with Russian tiaras, or Byzantine athletes, in front of Gothic mosques' – with everything swept along at a fantastic pace through a series of combats, tournaments, fires and miracles. The film should remain as a model of the genre. It was revived a few years ago and was greeted with some warmth by younger critics, who found its mad nightmare world in keeping with the pace of their period. *The Iron Crown* can be considered as a major stepping-stone to the 'neo-mythologism' of the 1960s.

Blasetti continued with *La Cena delle Beffe* (*The Jester's Supper*, 1941), based on a play by Sem Benelli (*La Beffa*), a romantic story of revenge in 15th century Florence.

Blasetti's career – the original *Sole* and *1860* followed by this relapse into outmoded traditions – is to say the least unusual. External circumstances and his own shortcomings were no doubt equally responsible for these meanderings. Nino Frank was right to call him a Don Quixote: throughout his career, Blasetti continued to go from one extreme to the other.

There is nothing to stop the propaganda film producing a masterpiece like

La Corona di Ferro (*The Iron Crown*, Blasetti, 1940)

any other genre; for proof we need go no further than *Potemkin*. The geometric designs in Leni Riefenstahl's *Triumph des Willens* (*Triumph of the Will*, 1935) and the rancorous hatred in Steinhoff's *Hitlerjunge Quex* (1938) were undeniable qualities. If the Italian Fascist film has little to show, it is because it lacked men of sufficient talent. Another reason is that it was motivated by *folie de grandeur*, a vain attempt to emulate Germany. Nazism was a diabolic force; Mussolini's Fascism – at least in its pretensions to greatness – was never more than a façade.

Yet it is difficult to pass judgement on the Fascist cinema, for the simple reason that we know virtually nothing about it. It would be interesting to reconsider these films in a non-political context; yet they are frowned upon much as the Soviet films were forty years ago. It is unlikely that the Fascist cinema has many surprises in store for us; but we should not condemn it out of hand. If the monument of the genre, *Scipione l'Africano* (1937) by Carmine Gallone, was indeed, as Lizzani writes, 'clumsy and overblown', the Venice retrospective of 1959 enabled Yves Boisset to rehabilitate in very enthusiastic terms *L'Assedio dell'Alcazar* (*The Siege of Alcazar*, 1940), by Augusto Genina, filmed in Spain shortly after Franco's victory in the Civil War. 'Convinced, passionate and grandiose, the film assumes a heroic style to extol

Isa Miranda in *Scipione l'Africano* (Gallone, 1937)

the fierce resistance put up by a small group of Falangists who take refuge with their wives and children in the Alcazar at Toledo. . . . The appalling suffering of the besieged families is communicated with moving restraint.'

With *Bengasi*, Genina subsequently turned his hand to what Vittorio Marinucci has called 'the cinema of Africitis', a genre in which we also find films by Romolo Marcellini (*Sentinelli di Bronzo*) and Goffredo Alessandrini (*Giarabub* and *Abuna Messias*). The German mountaineer-director Luis Trenker filmed *Le Condottiere*, a paean to Fascism set in 15th-century Florence.

Prior to his Fascist films, Alessandrini had had a notable success in 1931 with *La Segretaria Privata* (*Private Secretary*), a mediocre musical comedy (remade from a German comedy) whose popular tunes could be heard all over Rome in 1932. Thereafter he filmed *Cavalleria*, which made the name of Amedeo Nazzari and introduced Anna Magnani, followed by *Luciano Serra, Pilota*, a film about the Air Force during the Abyssinian War, scripted in part by a young director of short films, Roberto Rossellini, and purportedly directed by Vittorio Mussolini.

From the foundation of C.S.C. and Cinecittà the Duce had given his son various titles in the official hierarchy of the Italian cinema. Already 'director' of the journal *Cinema*, he became a film director at Alessandrini's expense, much as Gabriellino D'Annunzio had done in Jacoby's *Quo Vadis?*, merely by having his name included in the titles.

All in all, the achievements of the Fascist cinema did not amount to much; though more films were produced, they were mainly trifles in the style invented by Camerini, who continued to lead this field; some of these films, such as *Ore 9 Lezione di Chimica* by Mario Mattoli, *Rose Scarlatte* by Vittorio De Sica (who had progressed from acting to directing), or Camerini's *Una Romantica Avventura*, had a modest success in France a few years later. Carlo Lizzani dismisses these films uncompromisingly:

Dutiful camp followers such as Bragaglia, Mattoli, Brignone, Gallone and so on blurred the direct onslaught of the out-and-out propaganda films with a smokescreen of white telephones and mawkish romance. . . . It seems unbelievable today that at a time of worldwide suffering there was such a proliferation of films as non-existent, as empty and as alien to the national mentality as our 'commercial' films of those years. . . . They were full of gesticulating, soulless shadows speaking a language which would be quite incomprehensible today. These shadows regularly dressed up in evening dress, fed on costly dishes, and bellowed opera or whispered sweet nothings, depending on whether they featured famous singers or those gallant pomaded juvenile leads made to measure at Cinecittà for the entertainment of the Italian provinces. . . .

These twin currents of noisy propaganda and escapist charm seemed to answer the Party's wishes, for the time being at least. The Venice festival, by now almost entirely an Italian and German affair, nourished enthusiasm for the cause, and there was much self-congratulation over production figures. 'We made 109 films in 1939, we'll make 120 in 1940,' Vittorio Mussolini declared officially. The real figures were one-third lower; nonetheless, the Italian film industry had indeed made a spectacular recovery. As in the golden age, the studios in Rome attracted directors and stars from abroad. The Rome-Berlin axis facilitated exchanges with Germany, but several French directors also went to work with the Italians. After Max Ophüls, Jean de Limur, Jeff Musso and Pierre Chenal, Marcel L'Herbier (*La Comédie du Bonheur*) and Jean Renoir (*La Tosca*) were in Italy in 1940. They could not fail to be impressed, as all visitors were, by the contrast between the antiquated arrangements at Billancourt or the decrepit studios at Courbevoie and the 150-acre site at Cinecittà with its twelve shooting-stages, its set warehouses, its workshops, its luxurious dressing-rooms, its restaurants, and its bar opening onto lawns and flowerbeds.

The Centro Sperimentale, founded five years earlier, was now in possession of the huge buildings which still house it today, opposite Cinecittà, having been opened with great ceremony by Mussolini in January 1940.

The interest aroused by the Venice festival, at least in the pre-war years, and the seminal influence of Pirandello were other factors which contributed to the international prestige of the Italian cinema.

However, the Fascist government's reorganization of the national cinema was to result in the emergence of a talented young generation with little inclination to follow official directives and soon secretly in revolt against those objectives. Technicians, writers and journalists were discovering and discussing the great works of the Soviet, American and French cinema, and the theories of Eisenstein, Pudovkin and Béla Balász. Political ferment went hand in hand with an aesthetic revolution which tended to reject outright the swaggering bluster of the Fascist cinema and the artistic mediocrity of the bourgeois comedies. Luigi Chiarini founded the review *Bianco e Nero*. *Cinema*, the official journal directed by the Duce's son, was itself turned surreptitiously into a vehicle for the new ideas. 'Shielded by this prestigious puppet, two young columnists from *Cinema*, Gianni Puccini and Domenico Purificato, contrived to give the review an anti-Fascist orientation, with the complicity of Francesco Pasinetti, teacher of cinema history at the Centro Sperimentale.'[3]

Many of these young men were later to become important critics or directors: Giuseppe De Santis, Guido Aristarco, Glauco Viazzi, Carlo Lizzani, Ugo Casiraghi, Michelangelo Antonioni and others.

This underground movement spread to the North. In Milan one of the young intellectuals connected with the review *Corrente*, Alberto Lattuada, laid the foundations of the Cineteca Italiana with two friends belonging to the Fascist university groups (G.U.F.), Luigi Comencini and Mario Ferrari – the latter died soon afterwards – and for the seventh Milan Triennale they organized a cinema exhibition with an international retrospective festival. The time was May 1940, just before the attack on France. In spite of threats, Renoir's *La Grande Illusion* was included in the programme. Its showing was a memorable event. At the point where the characters sing the Marseillaise, the audience applauded and joined in the singing; fighting broke out, the police intervened, and Lattuada avoided arrest by escaping through a skylight in the projection room. An inquiry was ordered, but since the performance had been given under the aegis of the G.U.F. the affair was finally swept under the carpet to avoid compromising more important personages. Lattuada settled in Rome, where he began his career as a technician.

On 10 June 1940, while the German Army moved on Paris, Mussolini declared war on France.

If the wars in Africa and Spain had clearly impressed on many Italians how adventurous and shaky were the foundations of Mussolini's policy, and if the dictatorship, the racial laws, and the bows to Hitler had disaffected wide sectors of public opinion, the decision to enter the war alongside Germany came as a great shock to all Italians and produced nationwide fears that tragedy was imminent.[4]

Yet political events did nothing to halt the new boom taking place in the Italian cinema. Output went up from 78 films in 1939 to 119 in 1942. But this sudden proliferation included a good many of the old war horses. Mario Mattoli made another *Ultimi Giorni di Pompei* in 1937, and the following year Blasetti directed *Ettore Fieramosca*, not to mention *Cesar Borgia*, *Fedora* and *Fra Diavolo*, precursors of the astonishing *Iron Crown*. But a new kind of sensibility also became apparent. In this respect the moving austerity of some of the war films and the romantic refinement of the films by the young directors known as 'calligraphers', though very different, are equally revealing.

The Second World War was particularly unpopular in Italy, and as in France it completely failed to mobilize the patriotic enthusiasm so abundant in 1914. On the contrary, a plea for tolerance is what we find in a number of films made on the initiative of a naval officer, Francesco De Robertis, a dramatist drafted to lead the cinema service of the Italian Navy. His assistant at that time was a director of documentary films from the Istituto L.U.C.E., Roberto Rossellini (who, it may be recalled, had also worked as a scriptwriter with Alessandrini). The two men worked together on the script of *Uomini sul Fondo*, which De Robertis directed on board a submarine before the outbreak of war. This film, writes Mario Verdone, attains 'the dimensions of an epic without the least overstatement'. With this treatment of a human theme in an authentic setting, and using non-professional actors, Francesco De Robertis blazed a trail that was later to be followed by neo-realism. For several years this currently neglected director was regarded as the leader of a new school. *Uomini sul Fondo* was followed in succession by *La Nave Bianca* (*The Hospital Ship*), scripted by De Robertis and directed by Rossellini, *Alfa-tau*, about the Submarine Branch, *Marinai senza Stelle* and *Uomini e Ciele*, dating from 1943.

I was shown this last film, which remained unfinished, in Rome in 1947, when it was still considered to be exceptional. There can be no doubt that De Robertis was as much a precursor of the new Italian cinema as Blasetti and Camerini were. His official position and his unequivocal adherence to Fascism must not be allowed to detract from his stylistic contribution, even though he never again achieved the high quality of *Uomini sul Fondo*. There is also reason to believe that his influence on Rossellini was profound; it is certainly clear in *The Hospital Ship*, a peaceful propaganda film, the first full-length film Rossellini was allowed to direct. Unfortunately, the script was weighed down with a wartime romance. But, following his master's example, Rossellini shot the film at sea with a cast of officers, doctors, nurses and casualties.

Rossellini was to direct two other films for Mussolini's propaganda service, though their outlook was nationalistic rather than purely Fascist. *Un Pilota Ritorna* (*A Pilot Returns*) was an extravagant tale about an Italian pilot who, having been captured in Greece, manages to escape by boarding an enemy plane and flying it back to his home base, almost getting shot down in the process. There was a sub-plot in the form of a sentimental love story. The film ended in a flight of lyricism, with the pilot looking down from his plane over all the landscapes of Italy at once. *L'Uomo della Croce* (1943) was, according to Sadoul, no improvement; its hero was an Italian padre on the Russian front, who promptly swapped his cross for a rifle and fought alongside the Black Shirts against the Reds. In Rome the film got a savage review from the young critic Giuseppe De Santis, who called it pointless and vulgar. It came out in Rome in June 1943 and was withdrawn almost immediately under the impact of events.

While Rossellini was making this mediocre contribution to nationalist ideals, films by Genina and Alessandrini in praise of Fascist colonialism were also overtaken by events. Genina had still to complete *Bengasi*, glorifying the conquest of Libya, when the town fell into the hands of the Allies, and the film was never released. Propaganda films had had their day and now had a dangerously false ring about them, as the situation worsened everywhere, on the battlefields abroad and inside Italy, among the dupes of Fascism and among the intellectuals who realized that the end of repression was at hand. In this ambivalent situation of confusion and hope the cinema miraculously survived, but, artistically, only one attitude was possible – wait-and-see, or rather, as Lizzani writes, indifference to external events; and this period of expectancy enabled Italian film-makers to devote all their attention to the cinema. Most of the directors then working followed the example of Blasetti and Camerini. They skated round the problem by producing careful treatments of themes taken from the common fund of great literature or more often from the Italian provincial novel. For the umpteenth time came versions of Manzoni's *I Promessi Sposi*, by Camerini, Oxilia's *Addio Giovinezza!*, revived by Poggioli, and many others. But we can already detect in certain films a feeling for humanity, similar to that found in the otherwise very different films of De Robertis, and an attachment to authenticity which finally weaned the Italian cinema from convention and scenic stylization. In this context we may mention *Piccolo Mondo Antico* (*Old-Fashioned World*), adapted from Fogazzaro by Mario Soldati, a novelist turned film director. Writing in *Cinema*, De Santis has this to say about the film: 'Here, for the first time, is a landscape breathing reality, the antithesis of vulgar picturesqueness, and landscape which is in perfect harmony with the humanity of the characters. . . .'

No doubt the neo-realist revolution has led critics to neglect these films, whose importance is nonetheless great. They are as far from the decadent films of the golden age with their glittering sets and gesticulating *dive* as they are from the first neo-realist films. They form the bridge between these two styles in every respect, be it their use of location shooting or the restraint shown in their sets and acting. For this transitional period was marked by the emergence of a new generation of actresses whose simplicity, youthful charm and loveliness are qualities totally lacking in the 'sacred monsters' of the former age. Assia Noris (of Russian origin), Maria Denis, Elisa Cegani, Alida Valli and Clara Calamaï all made their début at this time. The first truly Italian film comedies also appeared, with the famous Petrolini (in *Nerone*), Angelo Musco, and above all the De Filippo brothers, from Naples, who continued the tradition of the *commedia dell'arte* and played an important role in the rebirth of Italian comedy.

There is a strong flavour of romantic literature about the best films of the directors who were to be labelled 'calligraphers'. Apart from the reasons already mentioned, this was due to the fact that the writers of the day – Emilio Cecchi, the director of Cines, Pirandello, who had turned scriptwriter, Mario Soldati, the novelist, who moved into the cinema in 1931, and turned director in 1937 – were so active in the cinema, and also to the fact that the assumed if undefined superiority of the traditional arts to the comparatively humble art of film-making gave them the right to impose their traditional techniques on the creation of a film. Lizzani, whose comment this is, continues:

The literary origin of Italian formalism was thus to be both its limitation and its saving grace. The 19th and 20th centuries were 'discovered' yet again and pillaged, and our cinema-goers were once more offered plots, characters and settings that were often artistically satisfying and invariably alive, certainly more so than anything else at the time.

Among the rather muddled films of Blasetti and the gently popular productions of Camerini, the hyper-refined style of the 'calligraphers' really got under way with Mario Soldati, who had already been responsible for many of Camerini's scripts. We have already mentioned *Old-Fashioned World*, made by Soldati in collaboration with Alberto Lattuada, who worked on both the script and the sets. Lattuada subsequently worked his way up through the various jobs connected with the making of a film, as many Italian film-makers have done before and since.

At around the same time, the young and impetuous Renato Castellani was working with Camerini and Blasetti, notably on the famous *Iron Crown*, with which he made such a mark for himself that the following year he was entrusted with the direction of his first film, *Un Colpo di Pistola* (*The Pistol Shot*), the inspiration for which came from Pushkin, and which he adapted for the screen with the help of half a dozen colleagues, including Mario Soldati. So the novelist-director was involved in the début of the two directors who were to determine the future development of 'calligraphism', a pejorative term applied to works that were soon to be regarded as brilliant arabesques in the void. The whole body of critics was behind these young directors, but they were opposed by the new school gathering force under the cloak of officialdom, which endeavoured to undermine this formalism.

Giuseppe De Santis, the spokesman of the anti-conformist group, wrote about the work of Castellani and his scriptwriters, work which had given rise to lively controversy when presented at Venice:

The society described by Pushkin was arrogant and melancholy and self-destructive. . . . In place of this we get a pretentious outmoded arabesque, full of sunshades, embroidery and lace trimmings. The public is not fooled by all this: these ivory pillars, these alabaster candlesticks are a gigantically enlarged projection of what were, in the most bourgeois period of our cinema, the famous white telephones that are so decried today. This is the saddest flirtation with fine calligraphy that we have ever witnessed. . . .[5]

It took more than this to discourage the impulsive Castellani, who, the following year, produced *Zaza*, a French comedy of the *belle époque*, in which the young 'calligrapher', like a child with a new toy, indulged in 'a frantic carousel of travelling shots, amid lace, crochet work, white curtains and black stockings, with each movement measured to the millimetre'.[6]

Did Castellani himself have any illusions about his orgies of what Nino

Assia Noris, Massimo Serato in *Un Colpo di Pistola* (Castellani, 1941)

Frank called 'styleless style'? This was his début in a craft that interested him passionately, and first of all he had to learn the tricks of the trade. His excesses drew as much praise as criticism, and he was hailed by some as 'the only Italian director with an international style'. This was flattering at a time when so many other young men – De Santis, Lizzani, Antonioni, Aristarco, Viazzi – were chafing at the bit in the obscure ranks of criticism or adaptation.

Castellani later filmed *La Donna della Montagna* (1943), 'a film without a plot', followed by *Mio Figlio Professore* (1946), another excursion into calligraphy, but showing traces of life as it is lived, and made partly for the great actor of the day, Aldo Fabrizi.

A similar direction was taken by Alberto Lattuada when he made his first film in 1942, *Giacomo, l'Idealista* (*James the Idealist*). From the way he talked about it to me some fifteen years later, I would say that Lattuada was still quite fond of his first film. The subject was taken from a novel by Emilio De Marchi (a Lombard writer who died in 1900), a melodramatic tale of love between a young idealist and a warmhearted chambermaid. There are romantic shots of the misty lakes and leafless forests of the Lombard plain. 'A cold yet compelling work,' says Nino Frank. In this début Lattuada fell into the same trap as Castellani, by giving his frail plot more polish than it could stand, borrowed as it was from a work of literature itself outmoded and unreal. De Santis, as hard to please as ever, did not spare the newcomer: 'We must deplore once again the marriage between the cinema and literature; it is totally arid and sterile, frigid and uninteresting.'[7]

From the outset Lattuada was dismissed as a conservative and a 'calligrapher'. In spite of this, the film interested both the public and the professionals. 'This formal quality,' Lattuada told me in 1958, 'has meant that the film has remained intact to the present day.'

Far from abandoning literature as De Santis required of him, the young director again chose to film a novel, this time by Luciano Zuccoli: *La Freccia nel Fianco*, which he adapted with the collaboration of three well-known writers, Moravia, Zavattini and Flaïano (who later worked with Fellini). Several previous projects had been turned down by the authorities. Following the release of *Giacomo*, Alberto Lattuada had been forced to go into semi-hiding in Rome as a result of the events in Milan. *La Freccia nel Fianco* was accepted and begun in 1943, but work on the film was halted by events and it was not completed until two years later.

To talk about the 'calligraphers' as a school is misleading; though their common concern with form led to their being grouped together under the same label, they were really very different. Along with Soldati the forerunner, Castellani and Lattuada, other directors subscribed, temporarily at least, to this style, notably Luigi Chiarini, the director of the C.S.C., with a number of films possessing refinement but little warmth: *Via delle Cinque Lune* and *La Bella Addormentata* (*The Sleeping Beauty*).

Other productions on the lines of the anodyne little films of the 1930s provided attentive observers with indications that interest in the comic or tragic aspects of daily life was gaining ground in the Italian cinema. Poggioli, who had made his début in 1941 with a new adaptation of *Addio Giovinezza!*, exemplified this new trend in unpretentious films that were far from perfect but by no means contemptible: *Sissignora*, the story of a little chambermaid, and a version of *The Taming of the Shrew* set in Rome. The trend was also apparent in a social study by Palermi, *La Peccatrice*, and above all in three films which already displayed a completely new approach: *Fari nella Nebbia* (1941) by Gianni Franciolini, *Quattro Passi fra le Nuvole* (*Four Steps in the Clouds*, 1942) by Blasetti, and *I Bambini ci Guardano* (*The Children are Watching Us*, 1943) by De Sica.

The first (in which Georges Sadoul rightly detects the influence of Marcel Carné) shows, as Barbaro wrote at the time, 'a section of humanity whose living conditions are determined in the first instance by their work'. And Barbaro gave an accurate forecast of the future when he wrote: 'There can be no doubt that the Italian film will attain the peak of perfection once it has

Gino Cervi, Giuditta Rissone in *Quattro Passi fra le Nuvole (Four Steps in the Clouds*, Blasetti, 1942)

learned to express the anguish and the hopes, the joys and the sorrows of men such as these.'

Though similar in theme, Blasetti's famous *Four Steps in the Clouds* is completely different in its doggedly optimistic approach. Here poverty goes hand in hand with good humour. The banality of a life burdened with care, the petty worries of everyday life, the solidarity of the working people, cheerfulness in the face of hardship, a gift for escaping from drudgery into the world of dreams – the soul of Italy was omnipresent in this bitter-sweet comedy.

The mere existence of this simple film amounted to a denunciation of the meretricious Fascist cinema, with its facility and braggadocio. 'After being obliged for so long to watch himself parading up and down on the screen disguised as a soldier, the man in the street could at last recognize himself in the overworked employee who is the hero of the film.' And referring to the hilarious coach outing Georges Sadoul continues: 'Everything in this charming film was falling into ruin, and this comedy thereby bore witness to the age when the cracks in the regime's grandiloquent façade had begun to foretell the imminent collapse of Fascism.'

Irony and pamphleteering are always the harbingers of political decay. The satirical effect of *Four Steps in the Clouds* may not have been entirely intentional, but in itself the image of Italy that it presented marked the beginning of a new era.

Blasetti's direction was equally free; it contrasted agreeably with the inflated style of the Geninas and Brignones of the Mussolini era. The first part of the film in particular is full of life and humour. *Four Steps in the Clouds* has thus remained the important film that it was hailed as on its first appearance. Yet the time has come to take note also of the scriptwriters – here, as so often, numerous – whose names figure in the credits. We find the names of Piero Tellini (who was to work with Fellini) and above all Cesare Zavattini, who had drawn attention to himself as early as 1935 with his script for Camerini's *Darò un Millione* (*I'd Give a Million*). Zavattini also worked on the adaptation of a novel by Cesare Giulio Viola, *I Bambini ci Guardano* (*The Children are Watching Us*), filmed in 1943 by Vittorio De Sica, the actor, who had been a successful director for several years.

Beneath the psychological plot and the author's moving treatment of childhood, we can detect in this film the image of a bourgeois society whose agreeable elegance covers a multitude of weaknesses and vices. After the vengeful laughter of Blasetti comes the restrained yet all-pervading bitterness of De Sica's film about the suffering of a child exposed to his parents' problems. These films, very different in style yet marked by a common concern with life as it is actually lived, would have been clear indications that something new was afoot in the Italian cinema even if, in 1942, *Ossessione* had not already shown with brilliant clarity the way to neo-realism.

Luciano De Ambrosis in *I Bambini ci Guardano* (De Sica, 1943)

The world outside, France in particular, knew practically nothing of this lengthy and intricate chain of developments. Italy was cut off from its foreign markets, split by its political conflicts, ravaged by poverty and war, despised for its sudden shifts of policy (the reasons for which remained misunderstood), ridiculed and humiliated; in the eyes of the world, whether friend or foe, it simply did not count. It was as if a decade of blunders had cancelled out the history of twenty centuries, and the arrant supremacy of a single political party had made everyone forget that Italy had a soul.

How could anyone have foreseen that within the space of a few years it would come to dominate – artistically, this time – the entire cinema world?

5. The Period of Neo-Realism (1943–50)

Italian neo-realism has indubitably given rise to a greater volume of literature than any other event in the Western cinema. It has been studied as a historical phenomenon in its political and economic context, it has been defined from the point of view of ethics and of aesthetics. Critics have gone beyond stylistic considerations and considered it as a school, with its own artistic creed and codified sets of rules; it even became, at Parma in December 1953, ten years after its inauguration, the theme of a congress attended by film-makers and critics.

A 'cinema of reality' had long been felt as a desideratum by those who wished the cinema to assume its full role in the intellectual and moral life of the nation. Yet some of the assumptions made about neo-realism are open to question. Any codification of any art marks its downfall. Rules are useful only inasmuch as they guide the art towards its maturity; beyond that, their effect is merely stifling. The word 'school', so overworked by contemporary critics in every field, has in any case lost, since the atelier system went out, whatever meaning it may once have had in the fine arts. When art becomes the product of a school, it ceases to be creative; to reduce an original art form to this narrow notion inevitably tends to stifle all invention and sensibility beneath scholasticism.

There is a danger that the original aims and values of the Italian neo-realist cinema will be increasingly distorted by an exaggerated interest in the theoretical aspects of the movement. Essentially, neo-realism was a product of political and social circumstances. And it is this *revolutionary* aspect of neo-realism that I should like to discuss first of all. Before it existed in its own right, with definite aims and sectarian interests, neo-realism – which was still nameless – was *opposed* to a state of affairs which increasingly stifled and oppressed the expression of truth – a state of affairs that existed, as we have seen, long before the Fascist era.

Hence the further error of considering the new Italian cinema as something that came out of the blue. Obscured by the luxuriant growth of costume films, the seeds of realism had, as we have seen, been germinating for many years before the fall of the regime allowed them to burst into full flower. The rejection of artificial sets in favour of location shooting, and the use of non-professional actors, had been practised, in *L'Inferno* and *Cabiria*, even before the realist experiments made in Naples in 1915 gave them a precise and real social context. These features that were soon to become characteristic of the new trend were not, moreover, especially Italian: Feuillade, and after him Renoir, had used outdoor settings, Epstein and the Russians had foreshadowed De Sica and Visconti in their casting of fishermen, peasants and workers, and in Italy itself, in 1933, Ivo Perilli had employed non-professionals, and a veristic and popular manner, in *Ragazzo*. But none of these directors succeeded in making their methods the basis of a style. This was to be the achievement of Italian neo-realism.

The aim underlying the outward characteristics was to make the cinema an extension of the literary realism that had developed at the end of the 19th century, especially in the novels of such verists as Giovanni Verga, Luigi Capuana, Antonio Fogazzaro, Edmundo De Amicis and others, whose works frequently inspired the neo-realists. Neo-realism was thus a revival of the Risorgimento, the 'unfinished revolution' which the young polemicists intended to complete, while at home and abroad the regime was giving increasingly clear signs of its imminent collapse.

The term 'neo-realism' was used for the first time in June 1943, a month before the fall of the regime, by Umberto Barbaro, then teaching at the Centro Sperimentale, in the Rome review *Il Film*. Barbaro used the term with reference to *Quai des Brumes* and the French pre-war cinema: 'If we in Italy wish to abandon once and for all our trashy histories, our rehashes of the 19th century and our trifling comedies, we must try the cinema of realism.' And he later advocated 'a renewal of the former Italian tradition of *Sperduti nel Buio*'.[1]

Barbaro's wholesale condemnation of the golden-age veterans, of the literary 'calligraphers', and of the light-weight comedies in the style of Camerini was based on the revelation of *Ossessione*, which stood head and shoulders above the mass of commercial films continuing to appear at an un-diminished rate even in the heyday of neo-realism.

Luchino Visconti was the first to give concrete form to ideas, or rather criticisms, that had been bandied around for several years; his was the film everyone had been waiting for. But its impetus was immediately transmitted in several very different directions, notably towards the problems posed by the new situations resulting from the fall of Fascism and the new social perspectives resulting from the war. Hence this movement must be seen, above all, as the manifestation of a national awakening – in Lizzani's words as 'echoing the physical and moral revolt of an entire nation'.

What is known, rightly or wrongly, as neo-realism was the product of this revolt. It was not a set of artistic values but an explosion, as it became possible to express the emotions, realities and problems which, since the Risorgimento, first the bourgeoisie and then the Fascists had attempted to camouflage, and which as early as the turn of the century were being highlighted in the writings of Giovanni Verga and the verists.

A story by Verga was precisely the subject with which Visconti had planned to make his début as a director. After working in England and France – as Jean Renoir's assistant – this left-wing aristocrat had returned to Italy. He again worked alongside Renoir on *La Tosca*, which Visconti himself completed with the other assistant, Koch. The films of Renoir that influenced Visconti most were *La Chienne* and *Une Partie de Campagne*. It was his intention to use what he had learned from Renoir in a version of *L'Amante di Gramigna* by Verga, but the project was rejected by the Fascist authorities 'on the pretext that stories about brigands were unacceptable'.[2]

Meanwhile Visconti had joined the editorial team of the review *Cinema*, which at that time was edited by his friend Gianni Puccini and which, as we have seen, published contributions by De Santis, Antonioni, Viazzi, Casiraghi, Pietrangeli, Lizzani and others. Hence Visconti was at the very heart of the revolt that was in progress among the young intellectuals of Rome and Milan. What at that time guided the aims of the young theorists still more than the native tradition of realism (*Sperduti nel Buio* and *Assunta Spina*) was no doubt their knowledge of great films from abroad – the American *film noir*, the Soviet classics, French poetic realism. It is revealing that Visconti turned to an American theme, James Cain's *The Postman Always Rings Twice*, about which he had heard from Renoir, to inaugurate the revolution. In Visconti's own words,

I adapted this story with my colleagues De Santis, Alicata and Puccini. The result was the script of *Ossessione*. The Fascists let it through. But they breathed down my neck all the time I was shooting; they insisted on seeing the rushes as I sent them off to be developed and they came back to me in Ferrara with orders to cut certain passages. According to them I should have cut everything. I turned a deaf ear, edited my film the way I wanted, and organized a showing in Rome. The effect on the audience was explosive: they couldn't believe they were really seeing such a film.[2]

Part of the financial backing had been supplied by Visconti himself. In addition to the names listed in the titles, almost all those connected with *Cinema* had helped with the shooting-script. Even before it was completed, therefore, *Ossessione* looked to be a kind of manifesto opposed to the 'white telephones' and optimistic bourgeois intrigues of the official cinema; as Fabio Carpi says, it substitutes 'tragedy for idyllic bliss, passion for mawkishness, adultery for marriage, real sex for sentimental hypocrisy, and restlessness for staid bourgeois stability'.[3] All that Visconti took from the American novel was its 'sordid love plot'; he transposed the action into the Italy of his day and portrayed it in violently sensual and realistic terms. He chose as his setting the Romagna region which Antonioni was later to use for *Il Grido* (*The Cry*). The actual filming was done almost entirely outside the studio, in the Po valley and delta, in the terraced streets of Ancona, and in Ferrara, inaugurating at the same time as Blasetti in *Four Steps in the Clouds* a 'veristic' style of shooting that was to become characteristic of the new movement in Italy.

For his part, Pietrangeli says: 'With *Ossessione* our cinema was invaded by brutal reality.' Indeed, the important thing about Visconti's film, especially from the historical point of view, is that this foreign theme, rethought and reshaped by people with the same outlook, gave rise to something authentically Italian: banal yet realistic characters in a popular, even sordid, environment. *Ossessione* was the sudden intrusion of social and psychological authenticity into a cinema that had previously thriven on the novelettish and the two-dimensional. It was the revelation of an Italy completely different from that of the romantics and the tourists, an Italy of poverty and suffering, yet still mindful of its past grandeur.

'This artist brought Italy to life for us – the Italy of Ferrara with its empty piazzas and its teeming streets, the Italy of Ancona and its fair, the Italy of the Po with its broad sandy banks; a landscape threaded with dusty roads on which cars and people circulate like streams of black blood.'[4] Neo-realism was to share this preoccupation with authenticity of place. *Ossessione* may truly be said to have marked the starting-point of a movement, liberating the Italian cinema from the artificiality of the costume film and even of the 'calligraphers', who tended to express an artistic distillation of reality rather than the thing itself.

Similar developments occurred in the documentary short film, whose concern with authenticity was of course more direct. Its practitioners included Pasinetti, Paolucci and Cerchio – whose *Comacchio*, a documentary about a small port in Venetia, received some attention when it first appeared. Then social intentions appeared, in *Pianto delle Zittelle* by Giacomo Pozzi Bellini about a local pilgrimage, and especially in the first film directed by Antonioni, *Gente del Po* – delayed, postponed and mutilated, as *Ossessione* had been, for daring to portray the truth behind the Fascist façade.

To return to *Ossessione*. On the film's completion, the Fascist censor refused to pass it. The young critics protested and approached Mussolini, probably via his son, the director of *Cinema*. Mussolini saw the film, found nothing to object to, and passed it with a few cuts. In December 1942 the official organ *Cinedoc* commented in its bulletin: 'The plot of this film is a bold new departure in current production.' But this masterpiece of understatement was not the end of the story.

When the last Mussolini government took refuge in the North, they took my film with them, cut it, and presented it in a new version; and they destroyed the negative. The prints in existence today are copies of a duplicate that I had made.[5]

Ossessione remains a great film, the portrait of a miserable, greedy, sensual, obstinate race at grips with the daily struggle for existence and with instincts that they are unable to master. For, over and above its neo-realism, this film has the ingredient indispensable for its lasting greatness: poetry, the sensual poetry of the spell that binds two creatures together, holding them to 'a dark kind of mystery through which they grope eternally towards one another, obsessed with their warmth, their desire, their physical contact'.[6] The essential feature of the film is that it marks a turning-point in the Italian cinema as an expression of humanity much more than of social authenticity. Its heroes 'are not representative of any given social class, and their voices are in no way the voices of protest'.[7] Yet this is no reason for refusing to see *Ossessione* as the first example of neo-realism; to do so is to interpret the movement in a purely political sense; and this can only limit it, if not distort it.

At the end of the war, none of the films that heralded a new departure in the Italian cinema was known abroad, and *Ossessione* was banned for reasons of copyright. It was with *Roma, Città Aperta (Open City)*, presented at the Cannes Festival in September 1946, *Un Giorno nella Vita* by Blasetti, and *Il Bandito* by Lattuada that the world had the sudden revelation of neo-realism. Political events had had a very great influence on this explosion of realism and given it, at the outset, themes appropriate to that exaltation and lyricism which were decisive in winning for it admirers and emulators all over the world.

In this respect, Rossellini's *Open City*, too, is a starting-point of neo-realism – social and epic in contrast to the individually psychological *Ossessione*. Like Visconti's film, Rossellini's had to undergo the vicissitudes of this

Clara Calamai in *Ossessione* (Visconti, 1942) with (*right*) Massimo Girotti

troubled period; its conception and realization were inspired by immediate circumstances. In hindsight we can say that the film's historical importance is greater than its aesthetic value. To measure that importance, therefore, we need to consider the work in its historical context.

On 10 July 1943 the war had moved onto Italian soil. In Sicily, fighting continued, while pressure from the political parties forced the King to have Mussolini arrested and to nominate Marshal Badoglio in his place. The collapse of Fascism was greeted with almost universal joy, but this domestic liberation met with brutal retaliation from the Germans, who occupied the peninsula and succeeded in freeing Mussolini. The Duce re-established himself at the head of a Republican Fascist government at Salò on Lake Garda. As the Allies closed in,

lorries sped northwards, taking away the last reels of film and the last cameras, to Venice perhaps, leaving Cinecittà deserted, Cinecittà whose studios were to become barracks or silos.

This was the great liberating event that had been lacking hitherto: Cinecittà, the pompous symbol of the Fascist cinema, tarnished and began to rust away.

A cinema is dead. Long live the Italian cinema.[8]

Northwards, then, the equipment and films emigrated. Later, in Venice, Antonioni recovered part, and only part, of the negative of *Gente del Po*. For the moment, like Rossellini and many of their friends, he had to go into hiding. Gianni Puccini, the chief editor of *Cinema*, was arrested, along with Visconti, charged with helping partisans. As De Sica later wrote,

> The war was a decisive experience for us all. Each of us felt the wild urge to sweep away all the worn-out plots of the Italian cinema and to set up our cameras in the midst of real life, in the midst of all that struck us with dismay.[9]

Breaking with Hitler, Italy signed the Armistice on 3 September and on 13 October joined the Allies by declaring war on Germany. Seven months went by before the liberation of Rome in June 1944. Fighting continued until the spring of 1945. The Allies advanced into the north of Italy where the Duce ineffectually presided over his phantom government. The end came in April. The partisans took Mussolini prisoner and on 28 April shot him dead.

It was during these dramatic events that Rossellini embarked upon a film that was at first intended to be merely a modest short film: *Open City*, which was made in the via Tasso in the aftermath of a Gestapo swoop. Rossellini had signed up two music-hall comedians, Aldo Fabrizi and Anna Magnani. Here is how the director himself describes the planning and shooting of his film.

> In 1944, immediately after the war, everything in Italy, including the cinema, had been destroyed. Almost all the producers had disappeared. The few attempts to get things started again were very small affairs. At that time directors had an entirely free hand; the absence of any organized industry favoured the least banal undertakings. The field was wide open for innovation. . . .
>
> These were the conditions in which I began shooting *Roma, Città Aperta*, which I and a few friends had scripted during the German occupation. I shot this film on a tiny budget, scraped together as I went along. There was only just enough to pay for the raw film, and no hope of getting it developed since I didn't have enough to pay the laboratories. So there was no viewing of rushes until shooting was completed. Some time later, having acquired a little money, I edited the film and showed it to a few people in the cinema, critics and friends. It was a great disappointment to most of them. *Roma, Città Aperta* was shown in Italy in September 1945 under the auspices of a minor festival and was booed by part of the audience. It may be said that the critical reception was unanimously and unreservedly unfavourable.[10]

However, the film got a warm reception from the public, becoming the biggest box-office success of the 1945–6 season.

Hailed in New York and Paris, Rossellini's film created a world market for the Italian cinema, and its success ensured the success of the style that it introduced.

Detailed analysis of the film would bring out the hoary truth that scant resources and difficult conditions of work are often beneficial to art. The fact that shooting had to be done in real streets and real houses for lack of a studio, the greyish photography due to the absence of power units, and the brusque cuts due to the fact that the editing was done in bits and pieces and frequently improvised, gave this 'reconstituted actuality' a semblance of documentary authenticity. But these weaknesses become qualities in Rossellini's film because the director himself was the first to feel the shock that he communicates to the spectator. This uncompromisingly direct film is a cry of revolt and suffering. And it is because the cry was heard that *Open City* was hailed as an event. As we have seen, neo-realism had been prefigured in Blasetti, and brought into existence by Visconti. But it was Rossellini who thrust it into the limelight, thereby giving it the magnificent impetus that was to carry it along for several years to come. The film is less a tragic tale of the Italian Resistance than a stripping of the mask, with Italy exposed in her squalor and poverty, and united (the priest and the Communist work side by side) in the quest for her authentic identity. *Open City* (what irony in that title!) is no longer the Rome of the *palazzi* but the Rome of the suburbs, the Rome of misery, of children playing amidst tragedy, of simple-mindedness, of strife, and of death. This world laid bare in *Open City* was soon to become the theme of all Resistance films.

We have followed the chain of cause and effect that could not help resulting, sooner or later, in the explosion of neo-realism. That explosion occurred with Rossellini, who provided neo-realism with a method and a style. The difficulties surrounding its emergence, which were not to be dispelled for some time yet, did not of course create the inspiration, but they forced the director to find solutions, and in doing so to draw on his invention and his genius. Thus, as is the rule in all true aesthetic movements, it was the creative act that determined the theory, and not the other way round. Because Rossellini had no studio, no sets, no lights, no sound trucks, the Italians were to go on shooting in the streets, rejecting fine lighting effects and pretty photography, and shooting without sound, which was post-synchronized. This necessity was to be the surest way for them to free themselves of bourgeois settings, white telephones and period trimmings. Poverty was to be their luxury and their grandeur.

Turning to the cast, we find, alongside the two comics whom the director turned into tragedians and the small-part actors, the nameless crowd whose faces jostle and mingle on the screen. Rossellini throws them all into the action with indiscriminate violence. Analysis has revealed that in scenes such as the death of Anna each frame participates directly and necessarily in the establishment of a truth. Rossellini's style is that of the newsreel cameraman. It is evident from the way the director writes and punctuates his story that one

Anna Magnani in *Roma, Città Aperta* (*Open City*, Rossellini, 1945)

personality is in complete control. Yet, as Lizzani has written: 'Even today, some people wonder whether the process that led Rossellini to create *Open City* was conscious or not.'

It seems certain that, in this film at least, *un*consciousness, or rather intuition, was a potent ingredient of Rossellini's makeup. Lizzani, who worked on the film with him, has described him as being as sensitive as an exposed nerve. Carried away by the force of events, he reacted with the violence for which he has become famous. His sincerity gave force to his testimony and kept his inspiration alive. His second film, moreover, was to heighten the interest of the testimony with the beauty of a mature and perfect style.

I have deliberately dwelt on *Open City* because of its importance – to its director and to the Italian cinema as a whole. There is less to say about *Paisà*, a much more distinguished film but merely the logical outcome of *Open City*. Like its predecessor, it is a poignant document about the events of those terrible years; like its predecessor, it presents (with a marvellously adroit mixture of tragedy, humour, subtlety, cruelty and human kindness) a significant selection of episodes from the reconquest of Italy. It is more than all this: it embodies the damaged beauty of this land of grace and humanity,

Giovanna Galletti, Maria Michi in *Roma, Città Aperta* (Rossellini, 1945)

innocence outraged, love pursued, poverty endured, serenity violated and bravery insulted. It reveals the beauty and poetry of those buildings and landscapes racked by madness and death. Not only events, but also their setting, contribute to the pathos. If *Open City* was a cry, *Paisà* is a hymn. Both films are landmarks in the field of events as well as in that of aesthetics; both mark the flowering of a genre which was to give the Italian cinema a unique position for several years. That position rested on the realism of the themes and on a style of expression which freed the film as a whole from the artifice and convention rife both in Italy and abroad. For, whether Italian, French or American, the pre-war cinema was for the most part theatrical. Everything was manufactured, from the characters (annihilated by the actors interpreting them) to the sets, the lighting and the grouping. Continuing the successive experiments of Epstein, Renoir and Pagnol, the Italian film was to bring to the world as a whole (the influence of neo-realism was all-important in Japan) a new conception of the seventh art. It was to set up its cameras in the streets and in the fields, demolishing the studio walls, and restoring contact with life as it is really lived. This was what made the Italian cinema neo-realist, and not the theories that could only define the phenomenon after the event.

L'Apocalisse (Scotese, 1946)

Before tackling this period of artistic crisis and renewal, we need to emphasize another frequently neglected fact. This is that throughout the political upheaval, the explosion of neo-realism, and the aesthetic revolution, the Italian cinema did not once cease to pursue what was at that time condemned with particular savagery by the critics, namely the big spectacular, mythology, opera, melodrama. In 1944, with the peninsula ravaged by war, Giorgio Ferroni filmed *Senza Famiglia*. As early as 1946, despite all the difficulties, a thirty-year-old director, G. M. Scotese, followed in the steps of his elders with *L'Apocalisse*, a cavalcade, as it were, of nineteen centuries of human history which used more extras and sets than even the famous *Iron Crown*. In the same year, Riccardo Freda directed *Aquila Nera* (*Black Eagle*). The musical film untiringly revived the masterpieces of *bel canto*: *Il Barbiere di Seviglia* by Mario Costa, *Lucia di Lammermoor* by Ballerini, and *Rigoletto* by Gallone, while Mastrocinque filmed a *Donizetti*. The other traditional genres also forged ahead, the romantic film with *Daniele Cortis* and *Eugenia Grandet* by Soldati, followed soon after by a new adaptation, by Lattuada, of a D'Annunzio story, *Il Delitto di Giovanni Episcopo* (*Giovanni Episcopo's Crime*, 1947). In 1947 and 1948, when I was in Rome, Milan and Venice for some articles, I heard much more about gigantic sets and ancient Rome than about neo-realism, and the studios contained such people as Jean Cocteau, Christian-Jaque, Jacques de Baroncelli, Erich von Stroheim, not to mention Victor Stoloff, Sarah Churchill, Gérard Philipe and Maria Casarès, together with such veterans of the Italian golden age as Tullio Carminati, still happily playing elderly patricians.

It would be quite wrong, therefore, to believe that traditional production had been supplanted by neo-realism. With the first co-productions organized by Scalera in Rome and Discina in Paris, two or three years after the war, hopes were raised in some circles that a new golden age was in store for the industry. In 1948, Marcel L'Herbier undertook yet another version of the sempiternal Pompeii theme, while in the festive atmosphere of Rome Marcel Carné was planning *L'Espace d'un Matin* (*In the Space of a Morning*), a project whose sole, unhappy distinction was that of living up to its title. This effervescence was as necessary for the industry as neo-realism was for the art. The producer Scalera told me in 1947:

The only way we can stand up to the Americans is to extend still further the system of co-production, either with France, or even with England. At this moment 500 American films are on the market in Italy – a great danger for the Italian film and even for the French film. The first thing we have to do is to bring in the public with productions that are not too highbrow; we have to give them what they want – action. At the moment Italy can produce sixty films a year. Scalera alone will produce a dozen of them. The high standard of our dubbing enables us to envisage co-production with as much certainty as national production. In the future I intend to enlarge this Latin bloc, which is the only way of ensuring sufficient outlets for our products, to include Spain and even South America.

Universalia, a new company founded by Salvo D'Angelo, professed similar ambitions, but was soon obliged to drop its plans for Carné's film and for a film by Robert Bresson about Ignatius de Loyola. In addition to L'Herbier's remake mentioned above, Universalia produced a new version of *Fabiola* (1948) by Blasetti, of a triteness unredeemed by its realist aims. Before the studios at Cinecittà had even been cleared of refugees, the large firms (Scalera, Universalia, Lux, Minerva) returned headlong to the costume film – a constant in the Italian cinema that cannot simply be shrugged off, even if its achievements have had little to do with art.

In view of this, it is permissible to think that little attention was paid in 1947 or 1948 to a few directors working out in via del Tritone or in the suburbs on stories about bicycles or the black market. Yet today these films are the only ones from that period which count in the history of the Italian cinema. Could one have existed without the other? Are they not rather the twin aspects of a single phenomenon which thrives, like man himself, on contradictions?

We can thus agree with Nino Frank when he writes:

The Italian cinema was born to all intents and purposes in 1945, if by this we mean a cinema comprehensive, catholic and of global importance; a cinema that ... reassembled the scattered pieces of its past into a coherent whole and accepted that past impartially – the contributions of Cines and Caserini along with those of Cinecittà and Camerini; a cinema that . . . acknowledged its specifically Italian nature and dared to resort to improvisation and eloquence.

The great event of 1945 was not so much the definitive disappearance of Mussolini or the . . . restoring of communications between Italy and the more enlightened regions of the world outside. . . . The great event was the solid, tangible, overwhelming fact . . . of a nation's rebirth . . . and its immediate encounter with the struggle for survival in all its forms.

This national re-emergence from the harrowing of Fascism and war brought much soul-searching among those for whom the cinema meant commitment and not merely art or work. In his excellent study of the origins and evolution of neo-realism,[11] François Debreczeni quotes several particularly revealing comments of directors working at that time. 'We sought to redeem our guilt,' writes De Sica; 'we strove to look ourselves in the eyes and tell ourselves the truth, to discover who we really were and to seek salvation.' *The Children are Watching Us* was an early illustration of this line of thought. 'After the war, our subjects were ready-made,' says Fellini. 'They were problems of a very simple kind: survival, war, peace. These problems were preordained, they stood out a mile.' But it was Lattuada, a director who has never won the recognition he deserves, who, in a brave and lucid article published in June 1945, defined what was to be the mission of neo-realism:

So we're in rags? Then let us show our rags to the world. So we're defeated? Then let us contemplate our disasters. So we owe them to the Mafia? To hypocrisy? To conformism? To irresponsibility? To faulty education? Then let us pay all our debts with a fierce love of honesty, and the world will be moved to participate in this great combat with truth. This confession will throw light on our hidden virtues, our faith in life, our immense Christian brotherhood. We will meet at last with comprehension and esteem. The cinema is unequalled for revealing all the basic truths about a nation.

The response to this appeal was to enable Italy to recover the trust of the world. 'The Italian cinema emerged from obscurity and blossomed profusely,' writes Nino Frank, 'like all the other vital and constructive activities of Italy which since 1945 have been a source of wonder throughout the world.'

Within the realist movement there sprang up several sub-genres, led mainly by the younger and more enlightened directors and producers. Closely linked as the movement was with the portrayal of the immediate, it went through several stages and developed several genres in close response to the events that changed the face of the land and to the frequently tragic problems with which it had to cope.

Open City had set things moving. The hitherto latent struggle which now burst into the open was the essential truth that had to be made known to Italy itself and to the outside world. The world had to know that Fascism was not Italy, that the political volte-face *vis-à-vis* Germany was not facile opportunism, and that all the political parties and social classes, from Christians to Communists, had joined together to throw off the yoke that had oppressed the nation. Henceforth the Fascists were the enemy along with their Nazi allies. The war of liberation was also a civil war.

Two documentaries testify to this struggle: *Giorni di Gloria*, directed by Giuseppe De Santis and Mario Serandrei with the collaboration of Visconti and Pagliero; and *La Nostra Guerra*, a 400-metre short by Lattuada about the liberation of northern Italy. But the documentary was not to be the Italian film-makers' preferred form; they chose to reconstitute actuality, in fictional narratives directly inspired, as in Rossellini's work, by revolt, hope or fear. In the years between 1945 and 1948, films were to portray with energy and bitterness the strife and anguish sown by disorder and death in the hearts of the Italian people. The liberation became a tale of many cities: Naples, Milan, Genoa, Leghorn, the coasts of Sicily, the canals of Venetia, the grey plains of the Po – all the provinces that Rossellini had epitomized in his admirable *Paisà*. As early as 1945, commercial directors such as Mario Mattoli or Giacomo Gentilomo – the former with *La Vita Ricomincia*, the latter with *O Sole Mio* – attempted to portray the Resistance in Naples. Young directors such as Pietro Germi were to make their début in this genre. But those mainly responsible for this renaissance, later christened neorealism, were the former pupils of the Centro Sperimentale, the young theorists and critics of the G.U.F., working in every branch of production, which they frequently had to improvise on their own initiative.

Here we need to stress an aspect of the Italian cinema which is peculiar to it and gives it unusual vitality. Whether critics, directors or writers, the men who were to be the masters of the new cinema all worked together in a common cause. Alongside Rossellini in the credits of *Open City* stood the names of Sergio Amidei and Federico Fellini. Before that, the collaborators on *A Pilot Returns* included Michelangelo Antonioni, and those on *Desiderio* included De Santis. More and more critics or scriptwriters were to become directors, writers abandoned their pens for a while in favour of the camera (as Soldati had already done), and directors occasionally became actors. This mobility stands in sharp contrast to the setting up of permanent teams like those formed in France with Carné and Prévert or Cayatte and Spaak; in Italy, collaboration took a much more flexible and independent form, the aim being less the production of individual films than co-operation on a broader ideological front. This is why the interminable credits of so many films contain the same names again and again; although frequently the collaborators have been forgotten, and the acclaim has gone, rather arbitrarily, to the director alone.

Yet the scriptwriters played an important role in the preparation of these films. In the pungent style of his *Cinema dell'arte*, Nino Frank describes their meetings in the closing weeks of the war:

I can see them now, sitting at the marble-topped tables in their cafés like groups in a mannerist painting, talking excitedly, yet keeping a wary eye on the few remaining German soldiers: they were all there, all the princes of the scenario, bald smooth Zavattini, the veteran of *Four Steps in the Clouds* and *The Children are Watching Us*, who, sitting with Suso Cecchi d'Amico, can talk of nothing but *Bicycle Thieves* and *Springtime*; Piero Tellini chips in with his ideas for *To Live in Peace* and outlines the film that he is to direct himself, *Uno tra la Folla*; and then there are the front-liners, Federico Fellini, the specialist of Aldo Fabrizi the comedian (Aldo Fabrizi the co-tragedian of Anna Magnani being the affair of Sergio Amidei, Rossellini's scriptwriter); also a quick-witted little Sicilian, Vitaliano Brancati, novelist and man of the cinema, who is preparing *Difficult Years* and who wins the enthusiasm of Perilli, De Benedetti, Napolitano, Franci, Fabbri, and the rest.[12]

In between films, or while waiting for the chance to shoot the films they had in project, directors turned actors. Mario Soldati, an old-stager already, acted under the direction of his young colleague Renato Castellani in *Mio Figlio Professore*, while the Communist Lizzani played the part of the priest, a Resistance fighter, in the film of his elder, Aldo Vergano. This co-operative effort, and the prevalent atmosphere of enthusiasm and optimism, welded the early productions of neo-realism into a coherent whole.

The first individual efforts by some of the pioneers did not appear until comparatively late – De Santis, for example, in 1947 with *Caccia Tragica* (*Tragic Hunt*), Antonioni in 1950 with *Cronaca di un Amore*, and Lizzani in 1952 with *Achtung! Banditi!* – even when they were in at the start of the movement, and when some of them, such as De Santis, were among its forerunners. However, the latter's name appears in various capacities in the credits of Visconti's *Ossessione*, in films by Rossellini and Pagliero, and in the fine film by Aldo Vergano, *Il Sole Sorge Ancora*, where there are reasons for believing that his contribution was considerable. Thus the films about the Resistance and the liberation, the first subjects treated by neo-realism, were spread out over several years, inevitably losing their early spontaneity as time went on, until the renaissance came, rather late in the day, from 1960 onwards – a consecration of the genre and perhaps in part a response to the resurgence of a neo-fascist spirit.

Hence 1946 saw the emergence of a genre that had nothing in common with the atrocious war films being produced in America at this time. Whether partisans, Fascists or Germans, the characters in Italian films are first and foremost human beings, even in moments of horror, cowardice or anguish. For this war was being waged in the very heart of the nation; it concerned the whole population, and not merely the fighters. Very soon, indeed, first the social problems and then the psychological problems created by the war and its aftermath took the place of the actual struggle, as the cinema revealed the appalling state of a country torn apart by rancour, hardship and degrading poverty. As Lattuada had wished, the Italian film-makers displayed the festering sores of their land to the world at large: the black market, theft, prostitution, the death-march of evils engendered by war.

Yet this cry echoing from film to film down the years was a cry of horror or suffering; it was never a cry of hatred or despair. The noblest and most profound message of Italian neo-realism is its human kindness, its sincerity, and the austere restraint of its style. The basic qualities of Italians – their sensibility, their ebullience – are apparent from such shots in the films of that period as Marcella's farewell to Italy on the beach at Leghorn in *Senza Pietà*; the peasant in *Caccia Tragica* (*Tragic Hunt*) driving away the 'bandits' with thrown handfuls of earth in a gesture that is both a rejection and a pardon; the women in *Riso Amaro* (*Bitter Rice*) covering the corpse of their friend with a shroud of that rice that meant toil and sustenance to them; the childish hand that saves the hero of *Bicycle Thieves* from despair.

The suffering or fallen race of men depicted by neo-realism never finds its justification in violence or cruelty, in bitterness or cynicism. These men are human in their refusal to give in to the misfortune pursuing them, in the tenderness towards life that they somehow preserve, even when life plumbs the depths of misery. Thus it was not long before a smiling humour reappeared in the works of Castellani with *È Primavera* (*Springtime*) and *Due Soldi di Speranza* (*Two Pennyworth of Hope*), and a more truculent variety in Luigi Zampa's *Vivere in Pace* (*To Live in Peace*).

This rapid survey of the early forms of neo-realism cannot absolve us from underlining a few exemplary works, exemplary in the sense that they displayed the mature talents of their creators and influenced subsequent developments in one way or another.

The tenderness of Zavattini and De Sica in *Sciuscià* (*Shoeshine*) contrasts strangely with the direct, virile testimony of Rossellini in *Paisà*, all the more so since the theme of *Sciuscià* is the infinitely tragic clash between childhood innocence and adult injustice. *Sciuscià* shows the backlash of war on those who are alien to it, just as adultery had been portrayed as the cause of the child's suffering in *The Children are Watching Us*. Social tragedy here becomes the tragedy of the individual. *Sciuscià* takes a general problem of the day and portrays its effects in a particular case, that of the two children, two friends,

Andrea Checchi, Vivi Gioi in *Caccia Tragica* (De Santis, 1947)

whose purity is gradually contaminated by the world in which they live, with one assuming the role of torturer, the other of victim. As early as 1946 the authors have transcended the limitations of external circumstances; their film is more than a piece of evidence, it is a universal denunciation of human wrongs.

The two films by Lattuada, *Il Bandito* and *Senza Pietà*, are not concerned with the war either, but with its bitter aftermath. Suddenly abandoning formalism and his usual literary approach, Lattuada shot *Il Bandito* silent with a 120 camera and post-synchronized it, as was the custom. The film deals with the problem of demobilized soldiers, horrified to discover the depths to which their country has sunk during the occupation. In Lizzani's words:

The opening of the film is breathless and anguished, with crowded railway stations, packed trains, people seeking an aim in life, views of Turin by night with its ruined houses, its deserted poverty-stricken streets, where the only sign of life is a jazz tune or an open-air gambling hell for down-and-outs in search of easy money.[13]

The conditions in which the film was shot gave the director considerable freedom of action, and it comes as no surprise to find Paul Eluard calling *Il Bandito* an example of 'expressionist cinema recalling the strangeness of the silent films'. But the Italian propensity to melodrama rears its head in the second part of the film, and frequently dominates the plot of *Senza Pietà*, the tragic love affair between an American Negro and a prostitute in liberated Leghorn. This film was shot while the events he describes were actually happening, in the streets, the bars and the docks, with extras roped in on the spot. (They sometimes took a great deal of convincing that Carla Del Poggio was not a real prostitute.)

Senza Pietà won acclaim for its generous spirit, vigorous style and profound humanity. The humanity of *Senza Pietà*, however, is a far cry from that of *Sciuscià*. Lattuada's impassioned violence, his exaltation of action, whether leading to bed or the grave, stands in marked contrast to the sensibility of De Sica. Lattuada's love story about two generous human beings trying vainly to escape from their sordid environment has the rawness and authenticity of a chronicle. Fast-moving, convincingly played by Carla Del Poggio and the American Negro Kitzmiller, with an incisive, essentially visual style in which sound serves as a counterpoint, this cruel document of a period that brought out both the best and the worst in men is also an affirmation of hope in its portrayal of the love of two human beings in defiance of their circumstances, their different-coloured skins and the hatred around them. With *Senza Pietà*, Lattuada moved beyond realism – while remaining invariably realistic – and attained a kind of lyrical pathos seen at its best in Marcella's leavetaking on the beach. This grief-stricken farewell to Italy is an unforgettable piece of cinema, beautifully played by Giulietta Masina.

Lattuada's collaborators on the script of *Senza Pietà* were Tullio Pinelli and Federico Fellini; it was with Lattuada also that the latter was to make, in 1950, his first film, *Luci del Varietà*.

The new Italian cinema was already moving away from its pristine realism towards lyricism and the epic; it transcended everyday reality, and attempted to describe poetically the essential and eternal aspects of human existence.

The epic character of the Resistance film is particularly apparent in Aldo Vergano's *Il Sole Sorge Ancora*, notably in the admirable sequence portraying the execution of the two Resistance fighters. This famous scene, punctuated by the crowd's responses to the priest's litanies as he walks to his death, is a masterpiece of montage, the dramatic effect of which has rarely been equalled.

At the other end of the scale, this transcendence of reality is present in the tragic farce by Luigi Zampa, *To Live in Peace*, a burlesque demonstration of the absurdity of war. It is also present in the reticence of Blasetti's *Un Giorno nella Vita*, in which lyricism goes hand in hand with a gentle austerity matching the austerity that governs the nuns' relations with the partisans whom war brings to their convent. This film could easily have lapsed into novelettishness or worse; but the emotion is maintained throughout with considerable tact – surprising in Blasetti, whose exuberant nature so often leads him into extravagance. The perfection of the images, down to the final tableau of the dead nuns in their long white robes, keeps this film on the borderline between anecdote and symbol, the point where the mundane acquires a timeless quality. For a moment, two worlds intersect: the gentle abnegation of the nuns and the ferocity of men blinded by their ideals. These are peace films rather than war films.

Other films dealt with the fighting that led to the liberation: Gemmiti's *Montecassino*, Gallone's *Davanti a lui Tremava tutta Roma* (*Before Him All Rome Trembled*), and Pietro Francisci's *Io t'ho Incontrato a Napoli*. Others again portrayed the strange atmosphere of those years: *Gioventù Perduta* (*Lost Youth*) by Pietro Germi, about the corruption of young bourgeois in the postwar period, Zampa's *Anni Difficili* (*Difficult Years*), a disillusioned chronicle of the troubled times, and in a similar vein of bitter irony, Carlo Borghesio's *Come Persi la Guerra*, featuring the comic Macario. Finally there was the astonishing film by Marcello Pagliero, *Roma, Città Libera*, a highly distinctive tale of strange nocturnal happenings in Rome.

In the economic renaissance which occurred in the Italian cinema with the revival of the spectacular alongside the realist movement, the young intellectuals meant to keep their independence and to attempt the experiments that had been impossible under Fascism. A case in point was the critic and scriptwriter Giuseppe De Santis, who turned to directing on a corporate basis. His first film, *Caccia Tragica*, was produced on a co-operative footing with backing from the various political parties, as *Il Sole Sorge Ancora* had been. The script itself was another instance of co-operation, since De Santis enjoyed the collaboration of a great many wartime friends: Carlo Lizzani, Lamberto Rem Picci, Michelangelo Antonioni, Cesare Zavattini, Corrado Alvaro, Umberto Barbaro and Gianni Puccini.

Starting from a news item published in the *Corriere Lombardo*, De Santis's team concocted a tale of intrigue studded with big scenes, violent, untidy, frequently confused, which provoked sharp comment from some critics. 'I am loth to narrate the plot of a vulgar thriller illustrated with "sensational" pictures worthy of the gutter press and overloaded with crude or trite allegories amid scenes of sadistic suspense, whether of the grand-guignol or the instant-thrills variety.'[14] But we should not be too severe; the sincerity of the approach is in the long run more compelling than the novelettish detail.

The actual events had occurred in Romagna, in the month following the armistice. A group of bandits held up an agricultural co-operative; whereupon the peasants organized a round-up, blocked all roads and bridges, and finally recovered their money. In his début as a director, the critic Giuseppe De Santis had much – probably too much – to say. His conception of a new cinema for Italy (though inspired by his long-standing admiration for Eisenstein, Dovzhenko, Renoir, and the lead given by Visconti), his social and political ideals (he has been described as 'a primitive and vaguely Christian Communist, and perhaps more superstitious than Christian'),[15] and lastly his natural generosity were as much against De Santis as for him. The novelettish element, already apparent in *Caccia Tragica*, gradually swamped his films to the detriment of psychological verisimilitude and even of simplicity of approach. In his first film, however, as in so many other Italian films dating from this period, these faults tend to be redeemed by the urgency of the protest and the epic sweep of the narrative.

The participation of Romagna peasants as unpaid extras, and the exclusive use of authentic outdoor and indoor settings, give the film external verisimilitude. But it was clear that De Santis needed to forget his academic notions and to adopt a simpler approach.

He failed to do so. His second film (*Bitter Rice*, 1948) shows the same characteristics, notably an epic manner aiming to point his critique of the social structure. From political conviction De Santis wished to express the practical virtues of 'solidarity'. *Caccia Tragica* had already fulfilled this aim both in its production (with co-operative backing) and in its dramatic theme. The individual, robbed, downtrodden and exploited, can obtain justice only by resorting to strength of superior numbers. For De Santis, then, the social balance will be restored by co-operation in every field. To quote Lizzani:

> The problem for De Santis is that he is unable to base his films on the most flagrant conflicts in our society. Politics apart, there is no denying the dramatic value of certain aspects of modern life – strikes, squats, sit-ins – familiar to us all, regularly reported by the press – but impossible to film.

De Santis had no option but to cloak his intentions in plots which were often extravagantly novelettish. A case in point was *Bitter Rice*, whose original aim was to expose the misery of the *mondine*, exploited by the large rice-growers of northern Italy and the parasitic go-betweens who take a percentage of their wages for signing them on.

In the Vercelli marshes, knee-deep in water, supervised by *caporali*, the *mondine* toil in the heat all day for a derisory wage: 40,000 lire and 40 kilos of rice for four months' work. To make matters worse, the *mondine* are split by the rivalry between the contract workers – often factory girls from all over Italy – and the casual workers hired on the spot.

This political and social theme went hand in hand with a critique of contemporary youth, corrupted by romantic magazines and escapist cinema:

> Against a backdrop of the rice fields, I tried to show how certain sectors of the younger generation in Italy have become Americanized in outlook. These youngsters are incapable of understanding where their own interest lies. Instead of joining forces for the struggle, they drift into a life of facile pleasure which condemns them to extinction.

The need to sugar his pill for general consumption accounts for the uneven quality of almost all De Santis's films. One is tempted to criticize him also for the exuberance of his style and technique. In his search for effect and mass he is forever jostling his script from one theme to another. He makes his cast act at full stretch, occasionally hitting upon the perfectly appropriate tone and attitude and crowning his feverish quest with success.

Bitter Rice is first and foremost a kind of epic poem about the rice fields, sometimes grandiose, sometimes puerile, shot through with a primitive, violent eroticism by the seductive Silvana Mangano and a number of dance sequences. This eroticism made the film a world-wide success. Yet it was inherent in the subject and not a commercial additive. The documentary portrayal of the back-breaking work in the rice fields – the mud, the mosquitoes, the long hours, the songs improvised for purposes of communication (talking being prohibited) – is likewise an integral part of the action; in itself it was sufficient justification for making the film.

As in *Caccia Tragica*, the final scene in *Bitter Rice* is symbolic, and has earned De Santis a great deal of criticism. Silvana has betrayed her fellow *mondine*, but her suicide earns their forgiveness. As they cover her body with

Vittorio Gassman in *Riso Amaro* (*Bitter Rice*, De Santis, 1948); *below*, Raf Vallone, Dante Maggio in *Non c'e Pace tra gli Ulivi* (De Santis, 1949)

rice from the harvest, we realize that she was the victim of her false dreams and hence, indirectly, of the world in which she lived.

De Santis's early films may be seen as a trilogy about Italian peasants in widely differing sets of circumstances: farmers, rice workers, shepherds. Each of the three films carries the message that only through solidarity can the workers defeat their exploiters, who so frequently shelter behind middlemen.

Non c'è Pace tra gli Ulivi (*No Peace among the Olives*) completes the trilogy on that note of melodrama and impassioned violence to which, it must be admitted, De Santis is peculiarly prone.

In this film about sheep-stealing and rivalry in love, we find once again the crimes, the problems, the wretched circumstances of peasants condemned to exploitation by their ignorance and weakness. Once again the unscrupulous usurper is punished – though this time he remains unpardoned and unabsolved.

The story, which has little to recommend it, is never more than a pretext for the author to exalt the solidarity of which he dreams. 'I want to show others what I believe to be just, to give them hope, to show them where progress lies.' This he does by choosing his subjects and characters from real life. For *Caccia Tragica* he had lived among the peasants of Romagna, for *Bitter Rice* with the *mondine* of the Po valley; now he settled in Ciociara south of Cassino to film *No Peace among the Olives*.

I made it in Fondi, the village where I was born. I signed on all my childhood friends, not to mention my nurse. I myself tell the story in the commentary.

Critics have perhaps paid too much attention to the real-life plots in De Santis's films, the living portrait of Italian rural life, so different from life in the towns, less familiar, harsher and frequently tragic. Yet this aspect of the films is much more than mere picturesqueness, even when picturesqueness appears to come to the fore, as in the songs of the *mondine* or the procession in *No Peace among the Olives*. It is also an appeal (over-eloquent at times, hence less effective) for greater social justice. Where De Sica denounces the social evils of city life, De Santis exposes the injustices of the peasant world. Their methods are very different, but their objects are the same. Pietro Germi followed a parallel path with his early films, inspired as they were by the same preoccupations. It is this social and documentary line which justifies the work of Giuseppe De Santis. Even the novelettish excess that mars his films may, in a sense, represent a faithful portrayal of this humble race of men, puerile, archaic, superstitious rather than Christian, passionate and violent by nature.

De Santis had further plans in store. In the spring of 1950, he talked to Jacques Krier of *L'Ecran Français* about his plans for a Franco-Italian film on the notorious problem of land distribution in southern Italy. Its title was to be *Our Daily Bread* and it was to be set in Calabria.

It is a region of appalling poverty. The land belongs to the *baroni latifundisti*, or feudal barons. It is a real Far West: the barons go around wearing revolvers. There are no cemeteries: they bury their dead at sea and on the way home they fish to have something to eat. The soil is very friable and doesn't bind with the bedrock: whole villages are literally sliding down the mountains into the valleys.

The peasants want to occupy the uncultivated land. But the baronial Mafia keeps them off and kills them if necessary. My film will be about a peasant who joins forces with his friends and neighbours, and rises against the exploiters.

This dramatic problem besetting the Italian economy has been tackled in several films, but none of them has managed to tell the whole truth.

The film was, for obvious reasons, never made.

In the three films we have just been discussing, De Santis was assisted by Carlo Lizzani. In his own right Lizzani managed to produce a number of short films on social themes, one of which (*Nel Mezzogiorno Qualcosa e Cambiato*) dealt with the problem referred to by De Santis. This 800-metre documentary dealt with the occupation of some of the *latifundia* by landless peasants. But the young critic's real début came with a war film. The leaders of the Genoese Resistance movement invited Lizzani to make a film about their activities; Lizzani accepted immediately and left for Genoa to gather material and to organize the raising of funds by subscription. The partisans accepted the outline scenario and collected the funds. The national partisan organization subscribed in its turn, but there was still not enough to cover the estimate. The collaborators, technicians and cast thereupon invested part of their salary on a co-operative basis. Gina Lollobrigida, the film's heroine, took a share worth 5 million lire. And in 1952, in and around Genoa, Carlo Lizzani shot *Achtung! Banditi!*, which was banned for export and did not appear in Italy itself until it was too late for it to make any impact.

This was because, during the past few years, Italian neo-realism, concerned as it was with immediate issues, had already gone off on another tack. War films had been superseded by social films depicting modern Italy, always closely defined in terms of time and space, at grips with the difficulties of material existence. The Italian's struggles, thoughts, setbacks and hopes are in fact those of every man: within a tiny particular framework is posed the enormous problem of life in general.

Two films dating from 1948 are magisterial illustrations of this trend and are indeed its masterpieces: *La Terra Trema* by Visconti, and *Bicycle Thieves* by De Sica. These two classics have lost none of their beauty and none of their value as exemplars of neo-realism at its most authentic (with non-

Achtung! Banditi! (Lizzani, 1951)

professional actors, real settings, etc.), yet finding in its social theme material for excursions into lyrical poetry and tragedy respectively. The subject is the same in both films: the misery of the isolated worker, his position of dependence in a society which he serves but which does not serve him. Yet these works are not manifestos, nor are they protests. They state a set of facts, a reality from which the spectator can draw his own conclusions. The films themselves neither propose nor suggest any solution whatsoever. At the end, Ricci and Antonio return to their misery, one to the dole, the other to his exploiters. The conclusion, not stated on the screen, is borne in upon the spectators' awareness by the formal beauty, honesty and truth of what has been revealed.

Needless to say, neither film was easy to make. And the fate of Visconti's film was particularly cruel.

After *Ossessione*, Visconti had worked with Antonioni on two projects that were never completed. His imagination had continued to be haunted by the work of Giovanni Verga, the verist novelist. In 1947, having spent the previous years in the theatre, he went to Aci Trezza, a small fishing-port in Sicily where Verga had set his novel *I Malavoglia*. When this 'Red duke' (as Nino Frank calls him) disembarked on the shores once terrorized by the

Cyclops, his intention was to indulge his interest in Verga with a documentary on the fishermen. But his contact with the Sicilians and the fishermen at Aci Trezza led him gradually to transform the documentary into a much more ambitious narrative. Before long he developed this idea into a vast projected trilogy dealing with the fishermen, the miners and the peasants.

Only the first part was ever made – not without difficulty – but it is worth reproducing part of an interview with Georges Sadoul in 1952 in which Visconti talks about his project as a whole.

As I wandered about the island, my vast scenario was dictated to me by men and objects. For instance, a labourer who told me the story of the mine. A sulphur mine had been abandoned by its owner. Fifteen of his workers had then started it up again. I went with them to the mine: it was a veritable descent into hell. At the end of a 500-yard tunnel was the vein of sulphur with naked miners sweating in the volcanic heat of nearby Etna and the perpetual racket of the pneumatic drills. Then the men, crawling on all fours, dragged their little trucks to the surface. . . .

The peasant episode came to me in the centre of Sicily. This is a region of the *latifundia*, the immense domains left uncultivated by their rich owners. These huge plateaux are like the most spectacular landscapes in Mexico. Suddenly there came the sound of galloping horses. Hundreds of peasants galloped up from over the horizon. The sound came closer, the ground trembled (whence the title of my film) under the feet of these battalions carrying red banners and tricolours. They were coming to occupy the uncultivated lands. A great feast began, with food brought by the women. . . . But at that time such conquests were never peaceful affairs. The notorious bandit Giuliano turned his Mafia against the conquerors. The battle for the land, a battle ending in victory, will be the theme of my final episode.[16]

For the only episode that was undertaken, Visconti shot 12,000 metres of negative. Here, in his own words, is how he went about this film, which would surely meet the strictest requirements laid down by the advocates of *cinéma-vérité*.

The film resulted from my conversations with the fishermen of Aci Trezza. I met my hero at the harbour, where he is a fisherman. His two sisters are the daughters of the little restaurant-owner. Their noble faces framed in their black kerchiefs have the grace of a portrait by Leonardo. I told my 'cast' that we were going to make a little documentary that would be over in a week. The work lasted for seven months. . . .

The first thing we did was to take the entire 'family' which I had just constituted to Catania, where a local photographer took the family portrait that plays an important part in the story. Then the story grew from day to day, following the more or less logical order of a scenario that was more often than not suggested to me by the actors themselves. This method led me away from the temptation to play for effect. It has sometimes been said that *La Terra Trema* is too slow. But this film is a reflection of life at Aci Trezza, where the day is invariably slow-moving and laborious. In my film I deliberately kept this rhythm, which also governed our rate of work. For the episodes that take place at sea, we had to spend more than a month in the fishing-boats, generally at night, lit with difficulty by generators. . . . My photographer, Aldo, had started the film without conviction. It made him famous. He was a theatre photographer and didn't think he could cope with the cinema. But before long he was carried away by the general enthusiasm. . . .

All the dialogue and business in *La Terra Trema* was the result of close collaboration with my cast. They put what I asked them to say into their own words. One of my assistants wrote down their suggestions. The phrases were polished up and then rehearsed and recorded. In this way they provided me with every episode in the film, but without really understanding its overall meaning. When the two 'sisters' finally saw *La Terra Trema* in Venice, they were moved to tears by the fate of their 'brothers'. . . .

These Sicilians hit upon poetic *trouvailles* that no one could ever have discovered by remaining behind a desk. None of them had any 'camera complex'. They behaved exactly as they did in real life.

G. R. Aldo – born Aldo Graziati, under which name he is generally listed in Italian filmographies – was not a theatre photographer, as Visconti claims, but a stills cameraman, very well known in France where he had made his entire career. Antonioni had met him in Paris during the shooting of *Les Visiteurs du Soir*, and introduced him to Visconti.

Thanks to Aldo, I was able to see (clandestinely, from the projection room) the first shots of *La Terra Trema* while Visconti was editing the film in Rome in 1948. Above all, I was struck by the physical beauty of the film, notably the scenes at sea, and by awkwardness in the islanders' acting which reminded me of the Breton films of Jean Epstein. But it was not until seventeen years later, in 1965, that the film became available in its entirety. The 'commercial' version released in France in 1952 was only half the length of the original; this deprived the film of all its breadth and grandeur. A version shown in Rome in 1958 was still more savagely slashed, to a mere forty minutes' showing time; it was also in a deplorable condition. Only the unexpurgated version affords a true basis for judgement. On this basis, there can be no doubt that *La Terra Trema* is the masterpiece of neo-realism.

The plot serves to illustrate the social problem and is continually transcended by the true theme. The experience of the young fisherman is the central pivot around which Visconti elaborates the dramas of the individual, the family, and the society in which they live. The social drama is concerned less with class than with a way of life. When everything has gone against him, Toni finds the entire village is against him too. Having lost everything, all he can do to pay his debts is to go back to sea in the boats owned by his exploiters. The scene in which he signs on, mocked by the onlookers, is heart-rending, and the single glance with which Toni answers his adversaries is one of the most pathetic moments in the neo-realist cinema. But the calm determination of this glance suggests that Toni does not intend to leave things at that. His

La Terra Trema (Visconti, 1948)

defeat implies future victories, despite the hostility or indifference of those among whom he lives.

Some critics have taken Visconti to task for his studied composition. It is evident that, despite its total adherence to the tenets of *verismo*, the film was conceived and directed in conformity with certain aesthetic requirements. It may be that a few hauntingly beautiful shots are impressive to the detriment of pure emotion: the women waiting on the shore, for example. But more often than not these shots are an integral part of the narrative, they *are* the narrative. . . . The lighted fishing-boats leaving harbour, the shots of the sea and the village, the angry fishermen throwing the scales into the sea – every scene, by dint of its harsh and tragic style, is part of a narrative that surges forward with a curiously powerful rhythm, in which violence alternates with quiet interludes such as the nocturnal outing to the sound of a harmonica.

Accompanying the images, or rather bound up with them, are the voices calling to each other, the songs sung at sea, and the Sicilian dialect, as harsh and uncompromising as the faces themselves, which together create an ambience of sound that takes the spectator (one ought to say the witness) to the very heart of this regional tragedy. The cry that emanates from *La Terra Trema* is the cry already heard in the works of Eisenstein and Pudovkin;

it is the cry of *Two Acres of Land*; it is the cry of human suffering.

Let us bear in mind, then, that beneath the appearance of spontaneous brutality found in this neo-realist film there is a highly disciplined creative intent matched by equally striking stylistic qualities. *La Terra Trema*, as Willy Acher puts it, 'inaugurates Visconti's grand manner, pungently poetic, penetrating and dramatic, in that style which deserves to be known by the proud name of humanism'.[17]

If De Sica's *Bicycle Thieves* enjoyed a happier fortune than *La Terra Trema*, it was not made without its share of difficulties. Failing to interest the producers in so trifling a subject as the theft of a bicycle, De Sica was finally obliged to raise the money himself. The script, based on a novel by Luigi Bartolini, was the work of Cesare Zavattini. Zavattini was already an important figure in the Italian cinema. As the scriptwriter of *Four Steps in the Clouds* and *The Children are Watching Us,* he had been in at the start of neo-realism and had been connected with most of the pioneering works in the new style. He had collaborated with Blasetti, Camerini, Germi, De Santis, Zampa and Castellani, and continued to work in close co-operation with his friend De Sica. Mario Verdone regards Zavattini as having had a decisive influence on the Italian cinema. His warm sympathy for his fellow men was largely responsible for steering neo-realism towards the humanitarian outlook that can frequently be detected even in its most sordid and violent works. Yet it would be going too far to credit him with the authorship of De Sica's films; these were governed as much by the director's outlook as by that of the scriptwriter, whose fluency was not always as disciplined as it might have been.

The controversial success of *Bicycle Thieves* justified the enthusiasm of the critics and demonstrated the film's importance. *Bicycle Thieves* defined the aims and aesthetics of neo-realism to a degree denied the mutilated version of *La Terra Trema* available at that time. Though now held in some suspicion by certain critics, the film seems as cogent and moving as ever. Once again, as with Visconti's Sicilian fisherman, an amateur performance, this time the acting of a steelworker, attains an authenticity more convincing than the art of the greatest professionals. And, though planned down to the smallest detail even for the scenes shot in the streets of Rome, De Sica's direction seems as authentic as the acting.

There is little point in repeating here what has already been said at length in so many excellent critical studies. However, it is perhaps worth stressing once again that the greatness of this film goes beyond the scope of neo-realism. Henri Agel has drawn attention to the dream-like behaviour of the hero. In the light of this observation, the film should be seen above all as a tragedy of solitude, expressed through a social theme, but constantly

Ladri di Biciclette (*Bicycle Thieves*, De Sica, 1948)

transcending reality and moving into the domain of the spirit. What is more, despite the apparently negative nature of their dénouements, these two masterpieces of neo-realism, *Bicycle Thieves* and *La Terra Trema*, both end on a note of hope. When the hero of *La Terra Trema* throws himself at his oars in the admirable closing shot, he is not beaten, but convinced of the rightness of his actions. Similarly, it is with renewed confidence that Ricci plunges into the crowd at the close of his day of anguish. . . . In stylistic and spiritual terms alike, such images belong to the supreme achievements of the cinema.

Visconti, De Sica – and Rossellini: these were the three giants of the Italian cinema at this period. After *Open City* and *Paisà*, Rossellini's reputation stood high on both sides of the Atlantic. Already his own intention was to go beyond the frontiers of Italy, to see and to portray the consequences of similar events in other countries and to evaluate the problems confronting other nations. Like Zavattini, Rossellini could have said, 'First and foremost I want to be a contemporary.' Even though his passion for Anna Magnani had led him to shoot Cocteau's *La Voix Humaine – Una Voce Umana* – in Paris, Rossellini intended to abide by his original manner and direct the third and final part of what was to be a trilogy about war. Germany, defeated and in ruins, provided him with a rich vein of experience. After his first trip there in 1947, he decided to shoot in Berlin *Germania, Anno Zero* (*Germany, Year Zero*), having, as he says, 'a very clear idea of the film in my mind'.

In June, Carlo Lizzani, who was to be his assistant, left for Berlin in his turn, a month before shooting was due to commence, and from his talks with journalists gathered material for discussion with his director when the latter arrived.

The Germans were human beings like the rest; whatever had brought this disaster upon them? False values (the very essence of Nazism), the usurpation of humility by the cult of heroism, the exaltation of force rather than that of weakness, pride versus simplicity?

That is why I chose to relate the story of a child, an innocent creature whose distorted, utopian upbringing leads him to perpetrate a crime in the belief that he is performing a heroic act. But the tiny flame of morality is not extinct in him: he commits suicide to escape from his malaise and his internal contradictions.

In the end, I was able to shoot *Germania, Anno Zero* exactly as I wished. When I see the film again today, I am overwhelmed; it seems to me that my judgement of Germany was a fair one, not complete, but fair.[18]

In fact, many difficulties – with Rossellini, often the consequence of his private life – had cropped up. Very much *persona grata* in occupation-army circles, he ran the entire social gamut in the company of Anna Magnani who, unconnected with the film, probably did much to distract him from it. His

Edmund Moeschke in *Germania, Anno Zero* (Rossellini, 1947)

work and his love no longer coincided; and in such circumstances Rossellini is too fond of the good life to deny it the major share of his attentions. The script had still to get beyond the draft stage. Shooting went ahead for around twenty days in the tragic setting of ruined Berlin, improvising at the rate of one scene a day. In September, unable to stand the cold, Rossellini decided to return to Rome and shoot the indoor scenes in the studio. The thread was broken, and it was doubtless this paucity of authentic background which earned the film, in Rossellini's own words, 'a very poor reception'.

Rossellini's pride prevented him from admitting the weaknesses in the conception and execution of his film, and (despite a few remarkable sequences such as the child's flight and death) all the consequent shortcomings of un-inspired improvisation.

In the meantime, *Una Voce Umana* remained unknown. 'I found myself with a forty-minute film that was practically unsaleable since we are the slaves of the standard cinema programme. I had to find another story of the same length. Then Federico Fellini, who usually worked with me, told me the story that I filmed under the title of *Il Miracolo*.'

Even with a theme such as this, lyrical and symbolic at the same time, Rossellini remains a realist. His two characters live in a primitive landscape

Anna Magnani in *Il Miracolo* (episode in *L'Amore*, Rossellini, 1948)

of hills, paths and stones, all deprived of life and colour by the oppressive white glare from the sun, with its shrill message of heat and solitude. The film also shows a characteristic Fellini theme – the accession of an unthinking brute to the true human condition, that is to say to spirituality: her faith in her illusion makes of the goatherd, certainly not a saint, but at least a woman, a mother. It is also the drama of suffering in solitude. But, from whatever viewpoint it is considered, *Il Miracolo* demands from the spectator the most direct kind of faith. And Catholic circles themselves were frequently hostile to it.

It is clear from this last film how far the Italian cinema had moved away from the social themes of neo-realism. Yet these were the themes that engaged the young director Pietro Germi in *In Nome della Legge* and *Il Cammino della Speranza* (*The Road to Hope*), two fictionalized treatments of the problems of the day: the fight against the Mafia in Sicily, and illegal emigration, which had already been the theme of a film by Soldati, *Fuga in Francia*. *In Nome della Legge* is the story of a young judge who, in his attempts to enforce law and order, clashes with the local Mafia, owned by the powerful baron and his main tenant.

Turi Vasile, now a director, wrote at the time in the *Revue Internationale du Cinéma*: 'This is the first Italian film that has had the courage to propose a solution to the problem – something clearly contrary to the principles of neo-realism, which is expected to limit itself to the *exposition* of a problem.'

For his part, the Italian critic Ugo Casiraghi claims that in this film Pietro Germi's style came close to that of Rossellini's two years before and De Santis's in the future.

The young director's social outlook is evident. It is difficult to decide whether or not to believe in the film's optimistic ending; what matters is its message. Pietro Germi offers us the image of a Sicily unknown to the tourists, a Sicily of stone seared by the sun, a land where mankind has remained primitive and brutal.

And here is how the film's hand-out described this aspect of Sicily:

In this land, human sentiments seem to take on dimensions different from those found elsewhere; the cult of individuality becomes indistinguishable from idolatry. The overriding preoccupation is with being 'a man'. You have to be a man and prove that you are a man, that you can take care of yourself, that you do not need to run to the police to defend your honour and your property, and that you rely on nothing but your own wits, your strength, your cunning, your friends. This attitude is reinforced by the inefficiency of the authorities and by the fact that the principles upon which the authorities act are unacceptable to the very people who are expected to submit to the law.

The problem of banditry in Sicily has been the subject of many films, not all of which were able to deal with it as frankly as might be wished. This film stresses the feudal origin of the Mafia, which is concerned more with the interests of the big landowners than with tradition. According to Casiraghi, Pietro Germi was obliged to submit his script to a Mafia leader and to accept a compromise: 'The film virtually idealizes the Mafia. The *mafiosi*, their leader in particular, are portrayed as knights of honour.'[19] The judge triumphs because his cause is acknowledged to be just, but his victory brings no recognition of the power of law and order as such.

For non-Italians, the main attraction of this film is the gripping beauty of the photography. With *In Nome della Legge* Pietro Germi reveals considerable gifts for composition enhanced by austere, direct editing with no fading in or out, a sequence of shots captured by a fixed, objective camera. Like De Santis, Germi seems to have taken as his model the films of the Russian school – there is clear evidence of this in the sequence where the peasants, answering the summons of the alarm bell, gather on the village square, in the close-ups of tense faces, and in the social-documentary aspect so frequently found in *In Nome della Legge*.

The Road to Hope has a similarly forceful opening, a rapid succession of frozen images, with the peasants motionless in front of the sulphur mine which has just closed down, depriving them of their livelihood.

Germi and his producer, Luigi Rovere, had got the idea for the new film during the shooting of *In Nome della Legge*. One morning in March 1948 they were waiting for the boat for Sicily at Villa San Giovanni, in Calabria, when they noticed a group of emigrants – women, children, old men – going in the opposite direction. This incident was to provide the theme of *The Road to Hope*, though it was only later that Germi and Rovere, then shooting at Sciacca in central Sicily (with the sometimes wary assistance of the local population), learned the explanation for it: the closure of the sulphur mines in the Agrigento region, which had caused a considerable stir among the workers. One of them then related an adventure that had previously befallen a group from the region, cheated by a swindler who was supposed to be arranging for them to be smuggled into France.

Two faults, detectable also in *In Nome della Legge*, detract from the quality of *The Road to Hope*: the excessively romantic character of certain episodes which mars the epic character of the main theme, and a heavily moral tone designed to satisfy the producer and the censor. The result is an artificial ending which provides an over-simple solution to a problem that is far from simple. But here, too, as long as the plot – or rather the problem – absorbs our attention, Germi's work remains forceful, honest, humane. . . . Yet the conclusions of these two works are diametrically opposed. In the earlier film, truth emerges because the law is respected; in *The Road to Hope*, by contrast, the heroes are saved by the frontier guards' disregard for their duty, that is to say for the law. The authors' intention was surely to demonstrate that legality is no substitute for humanity.

Lattuada, too, turned to romanticism – the literary romanticism of which he was so fond – with *Il Mulino del Po* (*The Mill on the River*), adapted from a novel by Riccardo Bachelli about the 19th-century agrarian struggles and the birth of socialism in northern Italy. This film, like Blasetti's *1860* before it, thus seems to perform a neo-realist synthesis of a historical theme and a modern social problem. Nervous montage sequences in the Soviet style alternate with panoramic, slow-moving shots reminiscent of the majestic river, and the finale attains a breadth of lyricism which was to become characteristic of the second phase of neo-realism.

For the rest, improvements in technique had brought a renovation of style and a new access of quality to every genre; even that most unlikely genre, the hagiographic film, acquired an accent of truth. With a young and unknown cast, Augusto Genina filmed the story of Maria Goretti, *Cielo sulla Palude* (*Heaven over the Marshes*). Here, too, we find a sober authenticity of approach that makes this tragic story extremely moving.

But it was Renato Castellani, the young 'calligrapher' of *Zaza*, who set the fashion for humour and gaiety, his example being quickly followed by Luciano Emmer with *Domenica d'Agosto* (*Sunday in August*). Castellani, however, also initiated a less laudable trend for facile picturesqueness.

Spurned by the neo-realists, Castellani was inactive for three years, until *Mio Figlio Professore* enabled him to make a cautious comeback. Realizing that the days of 'calligraphy' were over, and tempted by the vogue for truth that had overtaken the Italian film, Castellani sought a way of getting back into the swim. He was to do so successfully, his gift for observation allowing him to turn everyday problems into films full of life and gaiety. As his assistant he engaged one of his former actors, Fausto Tozzi, a voluble *afficionado* of the cinema and a fund of anecdotes about himself. Listening to Tozzi and combing the old quarters of Rome, Castellani hit upon the idea that was to make him famous overnight.

Over a period of a year Castellani, Tozzi and their collaborators collected material for their plot. They had to live on a shoestring while waiting for a producer, then turn their mass of observations, reminiscences and anecdotes into an artistic whole, and finally find a cast of unknowns capable of giving life to this chronicle of demotic life in hard times.

Despite numerous artistic flaws, the work beguiled audiences with its movement, gusto and spirited acting. But once the plot emerges – fortunately quite late on – the film lapses into banal melodrama. Presented at the Venice Festival in 1948, *Sotto il Sole di Roma* was awarded the Presidency of the Council Prize – which suggests that officialdom was not displeased by this excursion of neo-realism into comforting optimism. Castellani's merit was to have adapted his style to, and blended it with, the movement of his narrative. He is not content with merely *photographing* his characters; his camera follows their gestures, seizing upon an eloquent detail, and assumes, as it were, their volubility. The incident of the belt being passed from hand to hand during the match is an example of this highly original style, enhanced by extremely swift and skilful intercutting.

But Castellani's vigour sometimes lapsed into farce. He was portraying an essential feature of the Italian race, its insouciance in adversity, the occasionally naïve optimism that had helped it to recover so quickly; and it is because his subject was young people coping with the problems of the postwar period in their own way – not always the orthodox way – that Castellani was led to use comedy as one of the ingredients of his realism. But is it really comedy? It is more like an irresistible vitality whose prime wish is to assert itself. It has been said in this connection that Castellani was 'the director of youth'. All his later films were in fact concerned with very young heroes still imbued with all the ingenuousness and sincerity – sometimes the selfishness and cruelty – of childhood. In this, Castellani looks forward to a new kind of realism. He

Sotto il Sole di Roma (Castellani, 1948)

helped the realist movement to avoid the pitfall of becoming, to its impoverishment, too faithful a reflection of a given period. With *Sotto il Sole di Roma*, *Springtime* and *Two Pennyworth of Hope* he has given us a brilliant triptych on the life of an eternally youthful race.

For *Springtime* Castellani used the same technique as for its predecessor.

The story is not my own. Since the hero was to be a soldier, I did the rounds of the barracks. There I came across a Campanian, Antonio, whom I was unable to use as an actor, but who was extremely good at telling a tale. We became acquainted, and I got him to talk.

In going to the people for his inspiration, in choosing a cast unconnected with the cinema, and in relying entirely on real outdoor or indoor settings, Castellani was not taking the easy way out. Work on the successive stages of the script often took more than a year. There was also the important language question, on which Guido Aristarco has this to say:

The dialogue of *Two Pennyworth of Hope* is one of the finest and richest in the Italian cinema. It probably owes a great deal to Titina De Filippo or rather the school of Eduardo De Filippo. *Two Pennyworth of Hope* attacks the problem of language in the Italian cinema and helps to explain why all the best postwar Italian films are spoken in dialect. Italian is more of a literary language than a spoken language, a language for scholars rather than for an entire nation. In Italy most people speak, not Italian, but one of the several dialects. Now that the Italian cinema has become realistic, it cannot do otherwise, precisely because it is popular, than resort to the different dialects to express rebellion, suffering, hope, and to win the sympathy, understanding and support of the public.

But the need for being understood throughout the country gave the script-writers a delicate task of transposition.

The language of Castellani (and of Titina De Filippo) is a kind of translation from Neapolitan which preserves many of its words, dialect expressions, constructions, contractions, repetitions, errors, and its frequent use of adverbs, proverbs and popular sayings. In Castellani's film, the dialect expressions bear within themselves the real strength and lifeblood of the popular language, with no literary constraint.[20]

Springtime is a farce, about the amours of a randy young Florentine. While stationed in Sicily, he gets married; posted to Milan, he repeats the performance from pure kindness of heart. *Two Pennyworth of Hope* owes less to fiction and more to observation, for this hilarious yet profound film is first and foremost a study in *mores*. The story is told in a brisk, sparkling manner that forms a perfect foil to the richly eccentric characters.

Beneath this façade of gaiety, however, both films portray the problems then confronting the younger generation in Castellani's country – above all, the problem of unemployment. But Castellani is concerned with *stating*, not with protesting or criticizing. Social circumstances, though crucial to the heroes of *Two Pennyworth of Hope*, never succeed in quenching their tremendous appetite for life or the enjoyment they expect to get out of it. Confronted again and again with routine, tradition and convention, the young fight them, flout them, and finally, since they cannot defeat them, despise them. When Antonio strips his fiancée before the bewildered villagers, and covers her with his own shirt so as to owe nothing to her miserly parents, his gesture recalls that of Saint Francis of Assisi in stripping off the clothes he owed to his father so as to enter the service of the Lord a free man.

Spontaneous yet disciplined, charged with pathos but rich in comedy, Castellani's work is, when all is said and done, a valid testimony – to the poverty and suffering, but even more to the heroic qualities of a race whose 'two pennyworth of hope' is more permanent than the greatest good fortune.

Castellani, then, subscribed, in his approach as well as in his themes, to the methods of neo-realism. However, his choice of visual material leaves nothing to chance, even when his film appears spontaneous to the point of disorder. In addition, Castellani helped to free neo-realism from the cult of misery (*miserabilismo*) in which it sometimes wallowed on the pretext of remaining faithful to the mission of protest assigned to it by Marxist criticism.

Mario Angelotti, Irene Genna in *E Primavera* (Castellani, 1949)

What is so admirable about this film is that it is, at one and the dame time, the most pitilessly precise of documentaries on the state of Italian rural society in 1951, and a wonderful love story, one of the finest that the cinema has ever produced, poetic in a perfect, timeless way. In this context it is not presumptuous to invoke the names of Marivaux and Shakespeare: *Two Pennyworth of Hope* is *Romeo and Juliet* on the dole. The apparent contradiction between realism and poetry is thus resolved and transcended. Castellani's work has the documentary discipline of a social report, but it is full of humour, tenderness, and the poetry of character and events that make for greatness in literature or the theatre.[21]

In this last remark, André Bazin puts his finger on the fact that neo-realism could not survive unless it went a stage further than the problems of the moment – if, that is, it forgot the perennial requisites of the work of art.

For having opened the way to optimism, that is to say to a more facile realist cinema based on national temperament rather than on ethical or metaphysical problems, Castellani has been repudiated by some critics. Granted that his role in the first phase of neo-realism was relatively unimportant, his contribution nevertheless accounts for the explosion that occurred around 1950 and opened up immense possibilities for the younger generation of Italian directors.

6. The Masters of a Difficult Decade (1951–9)

From *Open City* to *Two Pennyworth of Hope*, the new cinema reflected the evolution of the Italian nation itself. After anguish and death came frenzied enjoyment; after destruction, rebirth. This dynamism, quite as much as American aid, allowed Italy to make a fantastically rapid recovery. By 1951, the average individual income was already above the pre-war level. During the years that followed, it continued to climb; industry and agriculture progressed at an equal rate. Despite political clashes and strikes, the boom continued unchecked. These political confrontations, indeed, appear actually to have stimulated the economy. True, not every problem was solved: there remained unemployment, the Southern question (despite highly publicized investment) and, above all, social inequality. The Italy of 1950 is epitomized by a scene in De Sica's *Miracolo a Milano* (*Miracle in Milan*): a luxurious express train crosses the misty Barboni region, two alien worlds pass each other by, separated by a pane of glass like a wall and soon parting, the denizens of the first heading for some *dolce vita*, those of the second trudging along in their misery yet clinging to their 'two pennyworth of hope'.

Though the postwar period failed to bring universal well-being, or to cast off the old chains of a bourgeois morality dating from before Fascism, it freed Italy and its inhabitants from fear, oppression and the psychological stresses caused by tyranny. Understandably, this liberation sufficed in itself to divert from anxiety to hope, from reticence to flamboyance, an art form so closely bound up with social realities. Since, however, the struggle waged by the neo-realist cinema was not yet over, and because many problems had still to be solved and much suffering relieved, the men who had conferred on the cinema its new social role were unwilling to see it abandon this role and yield to the attractions of psychology or spectacle – returning, in short, to the diversity that is equally one of its privileges.

This split led to much talk of a crisis, when in fact it was a sign of progress. 'The crisis of neo-realism,' De Sica wrote at the time, 'is due precisely to the fact that we have exhausted the particular reality which characterized the German occupation and the postwar period, which had to be filmed in a restrained, almost documentary style that is totally inadequate to represent the new reality, that is to say the raw material available to film-makers.'[1] But the left-wing critics saw other reasons for the crisis: 'The general falling-off of neo-realism is bound up in great part with the political evolution of Italy. The clerical offensive, the increasingly stringent censorship, the growing hold of the Christian Democrats have played a capital role.'[2] They did recognize, however, that 'the main cause was financial, for the social film did not make money.'

In this respect, the success of *Open City* had been a momentary exception, because it had touched a nation-wide chord. But as neo-realism moved on from the Resistance film to the social film its audience dwindled. In Italy it was equally unpopular with the upper classes, whose peace of mind it disturbed, and with the lower and middle classes, who had little desire to see their problems and sufferings displayed on the screen. Hence neo-realism in its original form was doomed and had to evolve or perish.

At the start of 1949, Italian production was going downhill. The cessation of the aid programme, together with uncertainty about the future, led to paralysis in the production companies. Protest meetings held in February called for a new programme of aid and for protective measures against the invasion of Italy by American films.

A new aid law was passed on 29 December 1949; it was based on proposals tabled by Andreotti providing for subventions and quotas, but gave the government discretionary powers over the economics of production and the choice of subjects. The subventions granted are revealing: *Don Camillo* got 216 million lire as against the 6 million allotted to *La Terra Trema*. And the form of pre-censorship implied by the allocation of subventions gradually discouraged the kind of outspoken comment on social topics that had given neo-realism its strength.

In the eyes of left-wing critics, social comment was the essence of neo-realism. The convention held in Parma in 1953 brought together critics and directors. But, in the words of Borde and Bouissy,

there was a lot of talk about 'human' cinema and not enough about the real enemies of neo-realism. There was no real dialogue, nor were there any concrete proposals: it sounded like the talk at a wake. In 1953, the Italian social cinema was already in the throes of a crisis. Its content was getting poorer every day and the Parma convention was incapable of halting this process of decline.[2]

It was thus the intention of the Marxist critics to limit neo-realism to a purely social role. What this amounted to, surely, was interference with the cinema's freedom (its power to reflect immediate events) by imposing criteria as questionable as those of the Fascist era. If this view had prevailed, neo-realism would have become a pretext for special pleading and propaganda rather than a testimony to the truth. The extraordinary single-mindedness of the period of hardship had given the Italian cinema the semblance of a school; now that the danger was past this unity came to an end as logically and ineluctably as that of the political parties.

Having broken with the past and found a style of its own, which could be applied in many different fields, the new cinema, enriched by its experience, now needed to explore new paths. The much-heralded demise of neo-realism was in fact a rebirth. The important point is that it never abjured its humanity, never ceased witnessing to a reality whose scope extended beyond daily life and social considerations to embrace fantasy and the hidden reaches of the mind – a *universal* reality created in the mind of the onlooker. By refusing to submit to the codification that would have stifled it, neo-realism spelled freedom for the creator and for the form: fantasy, imagination and mysticism are as much the domain of realism and reality as are welfare, labour and equity.

Nonetheless, the implementation of the Andreotti plan and the political vicissitudes of the era were to play a vital role, and not always a beneficial one, in the evolution of the Italian cinema of the 1950s. Whereas production rose considerably, in particular international co-production, which moved from ten films in 1949 to twenty-five in 1953, the proportion of quality productions decreased continually; and there was growing trouble with the censor.

As early as 1953, this last fact is stressed in Zavattini's journal. In the same year, Carlo Ponti, the producer, speaking to the Association for Cultural Freedom, stated:

Today, anyone intending to produce a film has to cross a minefield of compromise, intimidation and all kinds of pressure. . . . If a producer is brave enough, he can take a risk, but only once. The second time, he prefers to invest his money in films of pure entertainment, from which he is sure to get a return and which invariably bring him a subvention 'for exceptional quality'.[3]

The directors were obviously affected in the same way, as De Sica confirmed with a reference to 'self-censorship':

When preparing, writing or shooting a film, our hands are tied. Out of consideration for our producers, we cannot make a film which might become hard to sell as the result of a verdict from the government or the church. So, without always realizing it, we start making concessions.[4]

Many films, indeed, never got beyond the planning stage or were totally deformed by cuts later on. Nevertheless, despite its artistic and professional crisis, the Italian cinema miraculously produced an impressive array of outstanding films in the course of the 1950s. There could be no better proof of the impetus given by the earlier renaissance, or of the potential energy that neo-realism possessed in its content and form. The socialistic trend was to be joined, moreover, by a more spiritual trend concerned with problems of a different order which were nevertheless just as relevant to the human condition.

True, the unity of purpose that De Santis was demanding as late as 1957 had become a pure delusion. Such unity is possible only at times of crisis. The break-up of neo-realism was to result in the emergence of a few figures producing works of exceptional diversity and quality. When output had already reached enormous proportions, encumbered as it was by the products of international trade, the personalities of these men set the tone for the cinema of their day and gave it its value. It therefore seems logical to discuss this period in terms of these great figures who did not merely mark it but created it.

After *Bicycle Thieves*, De Sica and Zavattini felt the need to go a step further, to do something else, to say more. While remaining faithful to what might be called their mission, that is to say their desire to demonstrate the need for human solidarity, they were to consider the problem from the other side of the fence, by turning from a hero overwhelmed by society's indifference to a hero who is not only radiantly happy himself but possesses a strange capacity for making all those around him happy. From the tragedy of solitude they turned to the fable of togetherness; but their purpose was the same and their conclusion may seem just as bitter. If the only way out for Ricci in *Bicycle Thieves* was to carry on the fight with renewed courage and confidence, the *barboni* of Milan have no solution but to escape from a society in which money always has the last word into 'a kingdom which is not of this world'. But the miracle of this escape is mainly symbolic. It suggests, as Ricci's drama had already done, that the solution for man's eternal quest for happiness lies first and foremost in himself.

However, this kinship of inspiration, this attachment to a metaphysical –

Brunella Bovo, Francesco Golisano in *Miracolo a Milano* (De Sica, 1951)

almost a transcendental – view of social problems, is expressed in two completely different modes – a fact which amply proves the creativity of the authors. The discreet understatement and restrained melancholy of *Bicycle Thieves* is followed in *Miracle in Milan* by an exuberant *joie de vivre* full of lively, inventive, bitter-sweet humour. This is indeed a fable, but a fable rooted in reality of the most authentic and vivid kind. None of the tenets of neo-realism is distorted or betrayed in this film; the intention is merely to show that there can be no question of imposing on neo-realism restrictions that would ultimately lead to the appearance of new conventions as deplorable in their way as the old ones had been. The diversity of life should be reflected in an absolute freedom of expression.

Zavattini's idea for the story went back a good many years, to the time when he was beginning to collaborate with De Sica; circumstances alone had prevented it from being made sooner. In 1950, it was possible to think that the time was ripe for innovation. Things were looking up, and the prospects that inspired the optimism of Castellani also opened the way for the fantasy of Zavattini. Hence *Miracle in Milan* brought the cinema back to its true aesthetic standpoint while remaining faithful to the moral values with which it had been enriched by neo-realism. This development did not fail to cause concern among those who were afraid that the cinema would return to its tricks and entertainments, its 'calligraphy'. The political discussions that separated the Christian and Communist groups into two distinct camps found much fodder in this film. The ambiguous protestations of the authors, declaring that their film was merely a fable, were hardly calculated to convince their adversaries. Every fable has a moral; it was on what the moral *was* that the two camps could not agree. By virtue of this very disagreement, *Miracle in Milan* proclaimed its allegiance to a cinema with firm roots in the social and human fields.

It is the fable form, a 'free' form with no commitment to the here-and-now, that has enabled the cinema to retain its youth and poetry. The form itself is eternally young, and in this film it went hand in hand with stylistic qualities which, while never indulging in effect and avoiding clever trick shots, creates a totally convincing world of fantasy.

This work, then, was a turning-point. Not only did it give neo-realism a new tone, as Castellani's films had done, it freed it from a tendency to become fixed in one style. It proved that there was more to be gained from the personal approach – the imaginatively free approach of the poets – than from following lines of conduct dictated from outside.

That this enlargement of the creative function of the cinema was no betrayal became clear immediately afterwards with *Umberto D*, a scrupulously orthodox extension of the most absolute tenets of neo-realism. In this new work, which many have regarded as their masterpiece, Zavattini and De Sica returned to an extremely austere depiction of reality, a dramatic statement of a distressing social problem of our time: old age in a society which has no place for it.

Exemplary in its humanity, *Umberto D* is exemplary also in its neo-realist approach. It comes closer than any other film to Zavattini's ideal: the portrayal of life as it is lived from day to day, with no concessions made to abstract composition or conventional effects.

Like the earlier films from the same hands, *Umberto D* has been the object of much discussion and much excellent analysis. I need mention here only the famous successive sequences of Umberto's bedtime and the maid's morning in her kitchen. With the passage of time, we can now appreciate the full and novel significance of these scenes, with their 'dedramatization' and their depiction of reactions occurring in the innermost recesses of the mind.

Umberto D already foreshadowed the cinema of 1960, the cinema of the mind – its inner workings and outward manifestations. Hence the historical importance, so seldom mentioned today, of these films by De Sica. In addition, they reveal, in the close collaboration between the scriptwriter and the director, an affection that is all their own, a warmth of the spirit that somehow infuses the most burning issues with compassion and hope without detracting from their truth and impact. Their very restraint, the measured tones of their accusations, are, it seems, even more disturbing than any amount of vehement protest. These films incommode too many consciences to have escaped the direst reproaches: of wilful pessimism, revolutionary tendencies, calumny. Such was the opposition that Andreotti himself, as the junior minister responsible for the cinema, invited De Sica and his disciples not to be content with 'describing the injustice and suffering of one system and one generation'.

For De Sica the problem of finance was always acute. His success as an actor during the same period helped him to make good the deficit. He turned down offers from Hollywood because he had no feeling for the subjects; but he eventually compromised with *Stazione Termini* (*Terminal Station; Indiscretion of an American Wife*), filmed in Rome with an American cast and American backing. The theme was watered down until the film became just another star performance in which the neo-realism of the setting was merely a superficial embellishment. The indulgent reception given to this film is almost as incomprehensible as the attacks mounted against its successor *L'Oro di Napoli*, in which Zavattini and De Sica recovered their independence and gave free expression to their warmth, their humanity and the lively style that is all their own. *L'Oro di Napoli* is a series of episodes, with none of the faults usually associated with the genre. Those who have criticized it for being larger than life know nothing of Naples with its teeming streets, its magnificence, its misery, its fanatical exuberance in everything concerning religion and death.

To deny this film is to deny the *commedia dell'arte* and the harlequinade, not to mention the theatrical mentality of the Neapolitans, to whom De Sica belonged by birth and upbringing.

L'Oro di Napoli is a key work which reveals the other side of De Sica's personality, the comic actor and creator of *Buongiorno Elefante!* and *Roma, Città Libera.* Mutilated (two of the six episodes were cut, one of them being the best of all according to Bazin), misunderstood, judged by the irrelevant criteria of traditional neo-realism, *L'Oro di Napoli* was nonetheless extremely original and personal, and most of the major scenes were highly effective in their complex theatricality. Like so many others, this film deserves to be revived and rehabilitated.

Its merits should soon have become plain, for *Il Tetto* was to reveal the weakness of conformist neo-realism, not really coming to grips with a grave but psychologically uncompelling problem. In *Il Tetto* we find, in lieu of tragedy and austerity, a spiritless and witless cautionary tale. Faced with the choice between a free approach (condemned in the name of neo-realism) and faithful adherence to a henceforth banal stereotype, Zavattini and De Sica seem to have lost their nerve. More than five years went by before they worked together again, and their significant work was all done in this earlier period. But their contribution to the Italian cinema was important both for the quality of the works they have left us and for the features in these works that departed from the beaten tracks of neo-realism.

It is impossible to talk about Rossellini's work without at the same time discussing his ideas and his life. He himself has stressed this:

Each of my films is more than a film. My professional life has always been closely associated with my private life. The two go hand in hand. Every film I make expresses my problems, worries or enthusiasms of the moment.[5]

The circumstances of his life, his love-life in particular, were to govern his career and give his films a physical and moral likeness to their leading actresses. It would be interesting to study the relationships obtaining in the life and work of great artists and their interpreters: Chaplin and Paulette Goddard, Rossellini and Ingrid Bergman, Fellini and Giulietta Masina, Antonioni and Monica Vitti – not to mention Molière and Armande Béjart, Racine and La Champmeslé. . . . The situation is not new; but the form that it takes in the cinema *is* new, more intense and withdrawn. What we have here is something quite different from the wife's collaboration in the life and work of a scholar. For the man whose mission is to express passion and human sentiments, the woman in his life becomes, quite literally, his interpreter. It is her look, her voice, her gestures, her appeal that allow him to express himself. It is as if he marries her a second time, by imparting to her his dreams, thoughts and aspirations, since she, receiving them, makes them her own and communicates them to others. There is every reason to think that Ingrid Bergman made, as Rossellini's interpreter, a great contribution to his work, not only by her acting, but by her presence, by her aura. It is this presence and this aura that were to give *Europa 51*, *Viaggio in Italia* (*Voyage to Italy*), and *La Paura* (*Fear*) a psychological quality that they might not otherwise have attained.

On 8 May 1948, I received a letter from Ingrid Bergman: she had seen *Open City* and *Paisà* and she would have liked to make a film with me. . . . I wrote back to Ingrid immediately and on 17 January 1949, five years to the day after the first shots of *Open City* were taken, I arrived in Hollywood to discuss the idea of *Stromboli*.

Ingrid Bergman was then at the peak of her fame. The biggest producers in Hollywood vied for her services. She had eclipsed all her rivals in America and Europe; she was the new Garbo. And this woman who had everything, this glitteringly successful actress, begged as a favour to be the interpreter of a director who a few years earlier had been completely unknown. To begin with, Rossellini was flattered; then he realized with satisfaction how useful the backing of a star could be for a director. Not so very long since, he had been obliged to sell his furniture to finish *Roma, Città Aperta*. And no doubt he also admired Bergman as much as she admired him.

Rossellini wanted to lose no time in making this film. For he is impulsive, he believes in his luck, he knows that every success in his life has been due to his boldness and tenacity. Ingrid expected him to reply with a flattering telegram, or a synopsis, or a script. . . . Rossellini himself considered these possible lines of approach and rejected them. He wanted to transform Ingrid's vague proposition into a concrete reality. He had no doubt but that he would succeed, provided he was on the spot to speak for himself. He was counting on his powers of persuasion, his eloquence, his irresistible warmth and enthusiasm.[5]

He was right to do so. All who know him grant him these qualities that have enabled him to extricate himself from the most difficult situations.

The same year, 1948, Rossellini undertook a new film for which, as usual, he was also co-producer, *La Macchina Ammazzacattivi*, but which he left unfinished. It was shown commercially only in a few *avant-garde* cinemas and film clubs.

In Hollywood, Rossellini carried all before him. He had no need to convince Ingrid, but he got her to come to Italy; he convinced Dr Lindström, her husband and agent; he persuaded the American producers to let him shoot the film his own way – without a shooting-script or production schedule. This, more eloquently than anything else, proves the persuasiveness of this formidable man. For all that, rumours and gossip followed Rossellini from

Rome to Hollywood. Ingrid heard about his love affairs, his extravagant spending, his financial problems.

At the beginning of March, having finally settled the production of *Stromboli*, I returned to Italy, where Ingrid joined me on 19 March [1949].[6]

To reach the chosen location, the Aeolian island surmounted by its volcano, Rossellini embarked with Ingrid on a sailing ship, the *San Lorenzo*, which cruised through the Tyrrhenian Sea in the wake of Ulysses. Here he undertook on a personal basis, before turning the experience into another film, *Viaggio in Italia* (*Voyage to Italy*, 1953), the journey of discovery that introduced the nordic Ingrid to Italy. This was also a way of winning her heart.

The *San Lorenzo* reached Stromboli on Easter Sunday. Rossellini himself says:

At the beginning of April, we began shooting at Stromboli; and at the same time the scandal about our private life broke out.

What was behind it all? Why did such a colossal scandal arise from mere rumours of divorce and remarriage, when the film world – the American film world in particular – had long since institutionalized divorce and made it seem part of daily life?

Rossellini has given his own detailed account of this scandal, which does not concern us here. Anna Magnani, the rejected wife, riposted by starring in a *Vulcano* directed by an American, William Dieterle; but victory in this 'war of the volcanoes' went to Ingrid.

For Rossellini, however, *Stromboli* was a commercial and (for the most part) critical failure. His method of working carries great risks as well as advantages. In this instance, the weak script, the feeling of improvisation, and the excessive prominence of the actress, hence of the heroine, spoil the ambitious theme, whose pretensions necessitated great care in its working out.

The story is that of a 'displaced person' who, to escape from the horror of the camps, agrees to marry a former prisoner, an Italian fisherman who takes her home to his island. The tragedy lies in the utter incomprehension that soon divides these two people of different language, race and character. The only contact between Karin and her husband (and his compatriots) occurs at times of danger. Once again Rossellini's chief preoccupation is moral solitude – a solitude damningly endemic to an age that uproots human beings from their own environment and climate, leaving them stranded wherever wars and other catastrophes choose to wash them. This incomprehension is also, however, a quest – but a hopeless quest, because the heroine has never been sincere. A total failure faced with death, she prays. 'Her prayer may be a reflex, or it may be the expression of a sublime truth. Either way, it is the expression of a deep mortification which may also be the first glimmer of conversion.'[6]

In their book on Italian neo-realism, Raymond Borde and André Bouissy stress the misogynous aspect of this first film of Rossellini's to have Ingrid Bergman as its star. It is a fact that in this film, as in Rossellini's other films with Bergman, the woman is endowed with a kind of fatal flaw which cries for redemption. This sense of guilt is responsible for the particular thematic slant of *Stromboli*, *Europa 51*, and *La Paura*.

But the director's intentions, whatever their emotional source, are frequently spoiled by an over-assured faith in his own genius, a lack of critical judgement and objectivity, which stems ultimately from a lack of humility. The intentions are not always fulfilled; these films are distinguished by a number of large, inspired fragments (in *Stromboli*, the fishing for tunny that becomes a symbol of the drama); elsewhere, bad workmanship and confusion baffle the spectator, who goes from the work to the man, and not, as his more obsequious apologists do, from the man to the work.

It is remarkable how often in the *Cahiers du Cinéma* interview Rossellini harps on the incomprehension he claims to encounter – incomprehension amounting to a conspiracy to destroy him. His sincerity, here as elsewhere, leaves no room for doubt.

When guided by his imagination, Rossellini can be brilliantly inspired; when his imagination comes up against historical facts the risks are proportionately greater. For proof we have *Francesco, Giullare di Dio* (*Saint Francis of Assisi*), a film which many people hold in high esteem for its austerity, its cinematographic asceticism. Now a work of this kind can be studied from many points of view, but first and foremost it must be studied in relation to its subject. And, if the work throws light on the personality of Rossellini, it distorts that of Saint Francis, both in the choice of the eleven *Fioretti* ('little flowers') and in the way they are illustrated.

The first thing to be regretted is that Friar Juniper receives more attention than Francis himself, and this detracts from the profound significance of the *Fioretti* and from their charm. Some critics have been shocked by Rossellini's portraying these monks as childishly playful imbeciles. That was indeed their reputation in their own day. But the film's failure to explain this naïveté, this infantilism, in terms of the joy and gaiety which were its cause, or even to present Francis as the poet that he was – all this destroys the aura which transfigured the extraordinary adventure of the Friars Minor. An attempt has been made to defend Rossellini's film in the name of realism. In my view, however, its most obvious fault is precisely its lack of realism, despite its setting and despite (or rather because of) the authentic Franciscans who form its cast. These 20th-century monks, fat and contented, comfortably clothed in grey homespun, the disciples of an order which is now part of the religious establishment, have nothing to suggest the original Franciscans, vagabonds in every way – half-starved, ragged, and so sickly-looking that they frequently scared women and children. Nor is there anything in the chosen setting to suggest the Umbria of the Franciscans, with its forests, its ravines and fast-flowing streams, its remote caves, where winter is harsh but summer magnificent. A certain imprecision of time and place would have been justifiable if the hero himself and his deeds had been depicted outside their times and their setting. But in Francis, besides his loftiness of purpose and purity of life, there was the spirit of a troubadour, the quintessential spirit of his age which is so conspicuously absent from Rossellini's film, and a total commitment to reality which became the very essence of Franciscanism.

True, *Saint Francis of Assisi* can be seen as an image of sainthood, but in a rather abstract, impersonal manner that is the direct opposite of Francis's personality. This so-called asceticism seems merely an intellectual artifice that is particularly alien to the subject and its hero, who strenuously avoided dialectics.

Financially, *Saint Francis of Assisi* was another failure in Rossellini's career. Ever since *Paisà*, there had been a growing gap between his work and his public, between himself and his supporters – directors, producers, critics. The solitude that he expressed in the child in *Germania, Anno Zero*, in the exile in *Stromboli*, and in the madwoman of *Il Miracolo* was a solitude that he himself felt; hence his astonishment and anger at the incomprehension with which his work was met. The entry of Ingrid Bergman into his life and work is no more responsible than that of Magnani for these repeated failures, failures which often occurred with films in which neither was present. Rossellini has never sought success the easy way – and that fact alone should earn respect for everything he undertakes. His work expresses an ethic, and by that ethic it stands or falls. He has never seen himself as working *for* the public, or trying to satisfy it, but as speaking *to* it and, often, warning it against itself and the abuses of its period. His work is nothing if not courageous.

And he was finally to achieve his ambitions in three successive films, the high quality of which marks an epoch in his career. It is perhaps not unduly hazardous to attribute their quality of firmness to the new equilibrium in Rossellini's life, to the presence of Ingrid Bergman, who is the interpreter of all three films. The harmony thus established between his personal life and the requirements of his art imparted to his work the stability that it had previously lacked. These three films, *Europa 51*, *Voyage to Italy* and *La Paura*, so different in tone and theme, express a common thirst for sublimity, a thirst which made the presence of an actress of Bergman's class imperative. After the chaotic *Stromboli*, the art of the director and that of the actress were in every way wedded to each other.

The first of these films, *Europa 51*, marks a kind of turning-point in Rossellini's career. The title – like that of *Germania, Anno Zero* – suggests that the author set out to give his testimony on a specific place and period. The actual film, however, makes its title appear ambiguous. The story is merely a particular example of something universal and eternal – it could as well take place in the Middle Ages as in 1951, in Mexico or Egypt as in Europe.

The story revolves round a society woman whose life is devoted to the frivolous pursuit of pleasure. The death of her child, for which she is indirectly responsible, plunges her into a state of distress through which she gradually becomes aware of a new compassion for the poor and unprovided. Without going to the extent of experiencing poverty herself, she comes into contact with the suffering of a world unknown to her previously and dreams of devoting herself to sharing and relieving that suffering. This impossible scheme meets with opposition from all around her: her husband, her mother, her friends, the police, the doctors. Her 'revelation' is interpreted by modern society as madness, and she ends up in the hands of the psychiatrists. Even the priest does not 'recognize' her. Only the poor exclaim: 'She's a saint.'

The subject is unusual and ambitious. Its value lies mainly in the fact that Rossellini does not treat it exhaustively, but deliberately leaves a number of loose ends: this is the story of an aspiration rather than an action. The heroine, who for this very reason is no saint, does not take her madness to its ultimate consequences; she gives in, and by so doing passes judgement on a society in which noble actions are no longer possible.

If no other nation has as many saints as Italy, it is because no other nation has felt so strongly, for two thousand years, the fraternity – or Franciscanism – which attracts men to their fellows, and inclines them towards indulgence and mutual forgiveness. In *Europa 51* we have the same theme as in *Miracle in Milan*, expressed differently. The later film, even more than the earlier one, is very precisely in the vein of the *Fioretti*.

Alongside this spiritual aspect, however, the film comprises a testimony in the neo-realist vein – the portrait of a period and a culture, whose economic and social structures are exposed in all their precariousness and unreality by the tragic action of the heroine. But what counts in the film is not the testimony itself but the heroine's 'revelation' to which it gives rise. In Rossellini's career, this film confirms the new departure which began with *Stromboli* and culminates in the masterly *Voyage to Italy*.

In this film, nominally about a domestic crisis, Rossellini deals with the very meaning of life and happiness. It is a kind of second courtship between his hero and heroine, as they slowly discover in the beauty of a strange land and the simplicity of its people the sheer absurdity of their married life, the stability of which is as futile and unreal as that of the society in *Europa 51*.

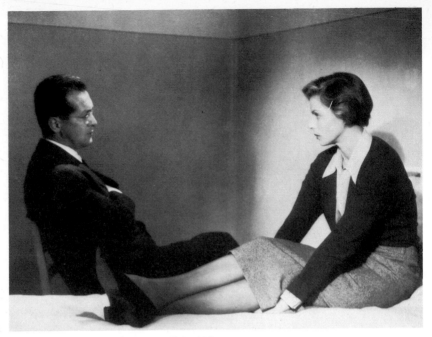

Ingrid Bergman in *Europa 51* (Rossellini, 1952)

Voyage to Italy contains all Rossellini's love for mankind and for his country.

It is easy to see where a theme like this, which is essentially a conflict of character, could lead. Rossellini departs from traditional psychological analysis and facile dramatic motifs. He follows his characters with total empathy, observing their most banal actions and their least expressed thoughts. He takes us into a universe in which everything is seen through their eyes. In this way we discover their mutual solitude, their need to communicate, and the joy that finally saves them in the fine procession sequence.

Few directors have shown such disregard for the so-called laws of dramatic construction. *Voyage to Italy* has virtually no action, no Aristotelian peripeteia. Nothing happens; everything comes from within, and there is only the slenderest link between the characters and the spectator. In his criticism of the film, Maurice Schérer[7] makes a remark which holds for many other films of the same type. While watching the film, he suddenly realized that his thoughts were sometimes wandering 'a thousand leagues from the action itself', yet without destroying the tenuous link between the characters and himself. This kind of distraction is really an extension of our receptivity to beauty; in the cinema, it occurs only with works of the highest order, not

Ingrid Bergman in *La Paura* (*Fear*, Rossellini, 1954)

those which rivet us to our seats with suspense or the more elementary emotions. 'Spectator involvement' is really a shoddy aim, and for its victim a second-rate satisfaction. The greatest literature sets up a resonance extending far beyond the immediate illusion that it creates; and the best films are those that have us *accompany* the characters as their friends rather than step into their shoes.

In terms of its importance for our understanding of the cinema of the 1960s, *Voyage to Italy* ranks with De Sica's *Umberto D*. But, whereas De Sica's achievement is in the field of the emotions, Rossellini's is in that of the spirit. All his characters are in search of their souls. This brings him to depict aspirations rather than actions, because his Christian outlook leads him to see life in terms of what he calls 'the sense of eternal life'.

La Paura, the third film in this quasi-trilogy was an adaptation of Stefan Zweig's novella *Angst*. 'I want to show the importance of confession,' Rossellini said. 'The woman has done wrong and can free herself only by admitting her guilt.' He deliberately rules out any kind of external event in this third film, which portrays only the evolution and clash of feelings and thoughts. All the action takes place in the minds of the characters, involved in a drama for which they are entirely responsible. The domestic crisis expressed in *Voyage to Italy* is given a new twist of extreme cruelty and suffering.

The French journalist Georges Beaume, who drove with Rossellini in his Ferrari at 140 m.p.h., recorded this confession:

Yes, speed means a great deal to me. When I drive at this speed, or faster, I get such a feeling of living more intensely, such a feeling of power, that I feel capable of knocking any obstacle out of my path. All my personal and professional problems resolve themselves when I'm at the wheel, particularly at night.[8]

How can this 'will to power' bring such a man to sing the praises of Franciscan humility and self-abnegation? How can this playboy be a Christian? These contradictions are also part of Rossellini's nature. 'Being a director means nothing to me,' he told Georges Beaume. 'I simply do the best I can to set out objectively the problems with which I am concerned.'

Thus, his 'will to power' expresses itself in the field of ideas, just as in others it takes the form of political or financial domination. In his favour Rossellini has his charm, which is another essential feature of his make-up and one of the factors governing his success. He has many enemies, particularly in Italy. In Rome, everyone is agreed that it is impossible to resist his charm or his will-power.

Ingrid Bergman is one of many people, men and women, who have reaped the rewards and paid the price of his domineering character. She tried in vain to make him see reason; the struggle lasted for years, before the end finally came in yet another glare of hateful publicity.

Once again a film project was to upset his life and disorient his career. It dated from 1955; and it was intended as the first film to do justice to India. The sub-continent had fascinated Rossellini for some time, and he had gathered material of every kind. Philosophy, ethics, history, fiction, travel, journalism, news snippets – he read them all, and took advantage of his stay in Paris to write a script which, like *Paisà*, was intended to convey, through a series of variegated episodes, both the face of modern India and its eternal underlying truths.

The enormous amount of work done subsequently in India was accompanied by numerous love affairs, and the net result was, not surprisingly, disappointing. Jean Herman, who was Rossellini's assistant, has given us, in *Cahiers du Cinéma*[9] and *Cinéma*,[10] an account of the expedition:

On his return home, he [Rossellini] organized the film into nine episodes preceded by a general introduction designed to remove the prejudices and misconceptions that people in Europe and elsewhere have about India.

Following a trip to Delhi, the Indian government, whose guest Rossellini was, decided to co-produce the film with Rossellini's own company, Aniene. The Film Division – a government body (sponsored by the Ministry of Information) which produces the majority of short films in India – provided the greater part of the team of technicians and some of the equipment.

Shooting began in earnest at Cawnpore.

The rest of the team, with the generators and arcs, had come there to rejoin us. The nearest telephone was fifty miles away. We had no water apart from the river, and no piped electricity.

After working for several months that summer and travelling 12,000 miles by all manner of transport, Rossellini was left with an enormous mass of material: 48,000 feet of film and 4,000 stills, enough for several short films and for seven of the nine episodes planned.

In the midst of all this there is Rossellini.

He moves around, searching, observing, driving his car, demolishing the ideas he had the day before.

What many of those around him take for a fundamental instability is merely his strange capacity for being so close to things, events and situations that he moves at the same speed as they do.

Fellini's place in the history of the Italian cinema is rather special. His career dates effectively from his collaboration with Rossellini in 1943, though it was not until seven years later, in 1950, that he was to direct, or rather co-direct, his first film. Thus, though he served his apprenticeship in the period of neo-realism, by the time he made his real début as a maker of films the neo-realist style had been considerably modified. Fellini himself took the process a stage further by at once revealing a highly personal and poetic style.

His activities during the six years which he spent as scriptwriter or assistant, or in both capacities, undoubtedly impinged on the work of several of his colleagues. His influence was not, of course, decisive, since his scripts or adaptations were almost always written in collaboration; but alongside the harsh, left-wing neo-realism of Visconti, Antonioni, De Santis, Lizzani and the rest he introduced a tone of tenderness, even lyricism. His friend Lattuada finally gave him the chance to co-direct with him *Luci del Varietà*.

Taking full advantage of his opportunity, Fellini achieved at once a true director's film; the subject, like those that followed, was essentially auto-biographical, and he was completely free (the co-directors were also co-producers) to handle it as he thought fit. Fellini is so obviously a poet that one cannot begin to understand him without first recognizing this fact, which emerges clearly from his characters, so dominated by their dreams. Whether pathetic like Gelsomina, gauche like the Fool in *La Strada*, or ferocious like the *bidoni*, they are all dreamers, carried away for better or worse by their imaginations. The characters in *Luci del Varietà* were undoubtedly chosen to meet the wishes of Fellini. These touring music-hall artists, with their gilded

Luci del Varietà (Lattuada and Fellini, 1950)

poverty, their delusions of grandeur and their nostalgia for the open road, are typically Fellinian characters – a blend of the chimerical and the real, always ready to exchange the disappointments of actual life for the consolations of a mirage. The irony here is biting and sometimes cruel; we encounter also what has been the major theme of the Italian cinema for the past twenty years, the sense of human solitude. But with Fellini this solitude was to become almost a tragic condition of life, highlighted by the way in which the outer world (composed of individuals vainly hoping to forget *their* solitude) is shown always in the frenzied pursuit of pleasure or noise. The alternation of scenes expressing this contradiction was to constitute one of Fellini's most important dramatic devices. There is a similar alternation of reality and fantasy, of enthusiasm and disappointment, of strange wanderings through the night with cruel awakenings on deserted squares at dawn. With the exception of *La Strada*, which is concerned with the interplay of three characters, all Fellini's films present a small group of people isolated within the larger group to which they belong: the young *vitelloni*, the girls in *Cabiria*. United and alone, dependent and misunderstood, they are engaged in a quest, not for happiness or love, but for the truth of their dreams, the meaning of their destiny.

Fellini's films are among the most controversial in the contemporary cinema. Their complexity and richness of invention, and the personality they reflect, never fail to attract commentary and discussion; and no director who receives so much critical attention, favourable or otherwise, can be regarded as unimportant.

Each of his films has been examined in detail: their ideas, their form, their rhythms and imagery. But the really striking element which, from the very beginning, stamps them unmistakably as the work of an authentic artist is their creation of a peculiarly Fellinian universe. His work is all of a piece: the same themes recur or overlap from one film to another, their characters and sometimes even their scenes are repeated, with an effect of enhanced depth and illumination, like some obsessional leitmotiv.

The unity of his work stems less from the style or the construction or the choice of a genre than from the ideas and personality of Fellini himself. It is first and foremost his own life which inspires his work and confers on it an internal unity while allowing it a considerable margin of external diversity.

What is called Fellini's *universe* is as tangible as that of Chaplin or Utrillo. Other directors, admittedly, have succeeded in creating a world in the image of their own minds. But very few have been more intensely dominated by their characters. Chaplin created types, René Clair created puppets, others have created monsters. Fellini creates characters at once particular and authentic – people so credible and three-dimensional that they entirely dominate the work in which they appear.

This calls for qualification, which will also explain part of Fellini's secret: Fellini loves the characters he creates. His sympathy for his characters is obvious and illumines his whole work with an endearing warmth. Whether they are brutes like Zampano, seedy old-stagers like those in *Luci del Varietà*, *bidoni* or prostitutes, Fellini is unmistakably compassionate towards his heroes – witness the way he shows us Fausto, unaware of the harm he is doing to those around him, or Alberto the drunkard sobbing after his sister has left him, or the long-drawn-out death of the *bidone* at the roadside.

Only one of his films, the first he directed alone, *Lo Sceicco Bianco* (*The White Sheik*), differs from the rest on this score. Here all the characters seem to be deliberately conceived as hateful and despicable.

At the end of Chaplin's career came *Monsieur Verdoux* to smash the myth. Conversely, *The White Sheik* seems to have been a kind of liquidation of the past in preparation for the emergence of the Fellinian universe, a chance for the author to work off his hatreds and rancours. If he never actually wrote for romantic magazines himself, he had close connections with those who did. He had been a journalist, a cartoonist, and had worked on comic strips. This was the life he rejected before recalling those wanderings on holiday beaches and in cities by night that were to provide him with his real characters. *The*

Giulietta Masina in *Lo Sceicco Bianco* (*The White Sheik*, Fellini, 1952)

White Sheik is a line drawn at the foot of a page – and who can tell how many family ghosts it laid?

By comparison with the depth of other Fellini characters, those in *The White Sheik* present only the sham veneer conferred on them by pulp fiction (Wanda), bogus grandeur (the 'Sheik'), or ready-made ideas (the husband). They are futile, without depth, non-existent. They are mere shadows.

At a more personal level, it seems equally significant that Fellini did not give the part of Wanda to his actress wife. He chose not to do so because he despised Wanda; and to have shown Giulietta Masina, his 'inspiring muse', as someone he despised would have lowered her in his own estimation and in that of the public. Instead, he gave her the only scene in *The White Sheik* that foreshadows the world of his later films: on the deserted nocturnal square where the husband has finally collapsed there suddenly appears the enigmatic dancing figure of a prostitute. Masina's astonishing performance, the atmosphere of the scene, and the sudden appearance of the fire-eater exude all at once the climate of strangeness that was to be the hallmark of Fellini's films. In the midst of this story of puppets, these silhouettes in the night suddenly point the way to truth and life. They alone are alive, because they are free, unattached, human. Then the parenthesis is closed, but its aura remains as a symbolic foretaste of the future. We realize why Fellini brought in Giulietta Masina at this point: with her, it is Gelsomina, Cabiria, Anita and Giulietta who enter this first film like a premonitory dream. To return to our comparison, she is to the Fellinian myths what the scene in *Monsieur Verdoux* with Marilyn Nash was to the myth of Charlie Chaplin: the resurgence of truth in the midst of the absurd.

The works that followed from 1953 to 1956, from *I Vitelloni* to *Le Notti di Cabiria*, were to develop further certain aspects of this strange episode: its esoteric appeal to the unconscious, and its peculiar style that was to lead Fellini towards a baroque form of expression all his own. Both these aspects of his art have been praised and denigrated in equal measure, mostly from preconceived standpoints. Fellini makes no mystery of his Christian conception of human destiny. This is the yardstick by which he measures the metaphysical potentialities of the problems that attract him. That is to say, social considerations attract him only insofar as they impinge on human conduct, illuminating or hampering the progress of the soul. His problems are not unemployment or the distribution of land, but charity and love. What he seeks, beyond the human condition, is the spark of the divine. What he denounces is poverty of the spirit, the void in the soul.

This outlook gave rise to a succession of three admirable films – *I Vitelloni* (1953), *La Strada* (1954) and *Il Bidone* (1955) – about which much ink has flowed. They well merit discussion, and if the innumerable articles and books about them have not succeeded in exhausting interpretation it is because these three films touch upon the most essential features of human existence. They develop a single theme: man in search of his soul. The *vitelloni* wander like lost souls through their void of pleasure and inchoate anguish. 'I was portraying, not, as people have claimed, the death throes of a decadent social class, but a certain torpor of the soul,' Fellini has said about his film.[11] Yet we do not need to look very far to discover among the causes of this torpor the consequences of a bad upbringing, the moral bankruptcy of a certain section of the middle class. Fellini was himself a *vitellone* and to some extent his memories form the subject matter of the film. If we accept that this moral anguish is in fact social guilt, Fellini's satire has a double edge, even if he chose to represent only one aspect of his theme. He does so with such truthfulness, force and nostalgic sincerity as to create a mood that is unforgettable. Of all Fellini's films this is perhaps the most bitterly convincing, even if others have a deeper message and more complex implications.

La Strada, as its title suggests, is the obscure progress of a soul from ignorance to awareness. Zampano, the central figure in this triangular drama, is an ignorant and incorrigible brute: neither a man's death nor a woman's love is capable of revealing him to himself. It takes the slow welling-up of

Anthony Quinn, Giulietta Masina in *La Strada* (Fellini, 1954)

bitterness and regret to bring him one day to the deserted beach where he finally receives, in a kind of revelation, the gift of tears. *La Strada*'s symbols of the victim and redemption, its aura of mysticism and its thematic implications, make it a profoundly Christian work; similarly, *Il Bidone*, though a much harsher film, contains obvious reminders of damnation and redemption as the *bidone* pays for his transgressions in his moments of agony. Even if we refuse to accept this Christian interpretation of Fellini's films, we are bound to acknowledge the presence of the human problem in all its complexity and implications, once we admit that man does not live by bread alone. This is the central issue. Never does this great Christian director lapse into mere edification; and it is surely wrong to criticize him for remaining true to himself, or to regret that *La Strada* was not 'a survey of life on the road'.

In any case, whether we accept or refuse its theme and conclusions, each of Fellini's films brings the proof of a technical mastery and, still more, an originality even his detractors cannot deny. One must admire his talent, his wonderful sense of mood and authentic detail, his dazzling lyricism, his pictorial sensuality.

A year later, in 1956, *Le Notti di Cabiria* was to confirm, though doubtless applied to a more lightweight theme, the same qualities of style and the same undefined aspiration of mankind for something greater than itself, 'the expression of an irresistible and providential force, innate in us; an incoherent, intermittent force that cannot be gainsaid – the anguished longing for goodness'.[12]

Visconti's eclecticism is at first sight disconcerting. He left the fishermen of Aci Trezza in order to stage Shakespeare in settings by Salvador Dali. For several years he was to be active in the cinema and the theatre simultaneously, with the latter taking up more and more of his time. In six years he made only one film – *Bellissima* (1951), a story of a mother's vain hopes of social betterment for her daughter – though he did contribute two episodes to collective films, one of which, *Siamo Donne* (*We, the Women*, 1953), also had the collaboration of Rossellini.

But these two aspects of Visconti's activities were not so much parallel as convergent. The theatre, the opera and the cinema were to unite in *Senso* (1954), a masterly work bringing together all the author's familiar themes. *Senso* may well be Visconti's masterpiece.

In the course of a discussion published in *Cahiers du Cinéma*, Visconti talked about the inception of his film:

My original idea was concerned with the historical aspect. I even wanted to call it *Custozza*, after the scene of a great Italian defeat. There was an outcry from Lux, the ministry, the censor. . . . So the battle originally had much more importance. But the idea was to use history as a backdrop for the personal story of Countess Serpieri, who was ultimately no more than the representative of a certain social class. What I was interested in was the story of a bungled war, a war waged by a single class and ending in fiasco.[14]

Whatever the work *might* have been, as it stands it is overwhelming, despite last-minute cuts and alterations. At the press conference he gave in Paris on 26 January 1956 for the opening of his film, Visconti made a punning reference to the relationship between his first, theatrical conception and the idea of the film: 'I've blasted *Il Trovatore* across the footlights, into a story of war and rebellion.'

The plot of *Senso* mainly concerns two characters who, *a priori*, have nothing in common, but who are united by passion – a romantic passion which is merely augmented by the obstacles in its path: the young woman betrays, one after the other, her husband, her country, her brother and her own dignity. But the passion is unreciprocated and undeserved.

Visconti's heroes are not merely characters, they are also the symbols of the decomposition of two social classes: the Italian (here, Venetian) aristocracy, manœuvring for survival between collaboration with the enemy and the incipient Resistance groups, and the Austrian military caste, the fag-end of a society whose charm has already a taste of ash. This decomposition is revealed gradually, mainly in the person of the Austrian lieutenant – charming, elegant, cultured, quoting Heine pertinently and with apparent feeling, but gradually lapsing into falsehood and cowardice in order to make the best of his tedious war. What the countess denounces in him is his cynicism and indifference. But the great achievement of *Senso* is not so much its characters or its social comment as its dramatic construction and its visual beauty.

Stated at the outset with the production of *Il Trovatore* at the Fenice Theatre in Venice, the link to which we have referred develops both in the film's content – from the characters on stage to those in the box – and in its style. Visconti exploits to the full all the possibilities of the stage and the screen, all the wealth of a spectacle that sometimes assumes the grand manner of opera. Throughout the film Visconti frequently adopts the viewing angle of the opening sequence, that of a spectator in a theatre: the oblique high-angle shot. The screen becomes a stage and is treated as such visually. This is apparent, above all, in the closing sequence, as brief and austere as the opening sequence is ornate and complex. The execution is seen from a distance, from above, reduced to a scenic epilogue. While the off-screen singing continues, the groups dispersed at the four corners of the screen disappear, and the stage empties on a note of derision, with the drama suddenly depersonalized and rendered insignificant.

Its use of colour made *Senso* a landmark as important in its day as Renoir's

Senso (Visconti, 1954)

Carrosse d'Or (*The Golden Coach*). Besides Aldo, Visconti had the services of the admirable Robert Krasker. Between them, they gave *Senso* a colour to match the film, sumptuous and warm: composite colours in the tones of the great Venetian painters, with the dominant golds and greys (as in the dresses of Alida Valli) splashed with garnet-red. Finally, with music borrowed from the symphonies of Bruckner and used with perfect understanding, Visconti achieved the total spectacle that is the aim of opera. The style of *Senso* is undeniably operatic – in the best sense of the term – and we can agree with Doniol-Valcroze when he says that 'grandeur, though never directly striven for or proclaimed, bursts out of this film, masterfully and overwhelmingly.'[13] This exceptional film, thanks to this multiform quality, can be counted among the few masterpieces of the last twenty years.

The operatic form, the colours of Titian and Tintoretto, the music of Bruckner, blend into a harmonious whole recalling Renoir's achievement in pressing Mérimée and Vivaldi into the service of his *Carrosse d'Or*. This harmonization of apparently discordant elements is also practised on the stage by Visconti, when he links together ballet and comedy, epic poetry and Shakespeare, Beethoven and baroque.

Senso has been well described as the first Stendhalian film, because of its composite nature and the acting of Alida Valli, who would have made an ideal Sanseverina. Visconti would have liked to film *La Chartreuse de Parme*:

If my film had not been cut, and if it had been edited the way I wanted, it would really have been Fabrice at the Battle of Waterloo, Fabrice *behind* the battlefront. And Countess Serpieri was modelled on Sanseverina.[14]

Years went by before a new film by Visconti appeared on the screen. It was at Venice, in September 1957, that *Le Notti Bianche* was presented to the elegant festival audience and the critics.

The fact that the film was a co-production was a formidable handicap at the outset. It was no doubt for this reason that Visconti adopted an extreme approach and rethought entirely the theme and circumstances of the action. Was it possible for an Italian to reproduce the atmosphere of Dostoyevsky in an Italian setting, with a Latin language, and French, German and Italian actors? A faithful adaptation in such conditions would have resulted in the kind of hybrid turned out so successfully by Carmine Gallone and Riccardo Freda.

Visconti chose otherwise. He eliminated every precise reference to time or place. The action of *Le Notti Bianche* takes place in a world as strange and imprecise as that of *Il Cappotto* (*The Overcoat*) by Lattuada – another adaptation from the Russian in which the director adopted an equally intelligent approach.

But Visconti's transposition went far beyond outer appearances. He transposed the subject itself into something quite different.

In *Le Notti Bianche*, indeed, we can say that scenic conventions govern the whole *mise en scène*, even the characters. We know nothing about them apart from their appearance, their gestures, their comings and goings in a narrowly defined universe. All the action takes place on an imaginary stage that is never seen in its entirety, though its presence is felt from beginning to end – a dramatic *locus* in which the characters are as it were enclosed. Other figures cross their paths without entering their lives – the unknown inmates of this claustrophobic universe which resembles less a prison or a camp than a mental hospital. Around the two central figures, even in the most intimate scenes, there are always witnesses, motionless in the background or passing and repassing. They belong, not to the setting – which Visconti wished to be theatrical, stylized, unreal – but to the mood. These figures seen merely in outline are perhaps the actors in another tragedy. Some of them, the prostitute for example, intersect with the drama being enacted for us.

As with a symphony, the interest of this slow build-up of mood can only be appreciated retrospectively. The interminable comings and goings around the bridge, the characters rushing in search of each other, in pursuit of each other, in flight from each other, and the mood of endless night create a tension that only breaks when the heroine topples, as it were, from dream into reality during the astonishing dance-hall sequence. This is also the moment, the only one, when the main figures mingle with the others, approach the latter's state of intoxication, first lose and then find one another again. This is the moment when the hero talks about himself to Nathalie, who does not hear him, because she is breaking out of her 'circle' as she watches the dancing couples. After this dramatic and aesthetic climax, the film resumes its progress towards a state of dream.

Understandably, a dramatic approach as strange as this puzzled the critics and the public. *Le Notti Bianche* was a commercial failure, but it is a film to see again – intellectual rather than sensuous, an interesting attempt at abstraction rather than austerity. It represents a further step in Visconti's quest for a film form that would merge rather than interact with that of the theatre. This quest is not without its dangers. But the aesthetic experiment was worth trying for its own sake and is completely in line with the searching mind and art of Visconti.

Michelangelo Antonioni belonged to the spearhead of neo-realism: as early as 1940 he worked on the editorial staff of *Cinema*, the importance of which has already been stressed. Before long he was helping to adapt or script a number of films. Yet it was not until ten years later, rather like Fellini, that he presented his first full-length film, *Cronaca di un Amore*, at a time (1950)

Lucia Bosè, Ferdinando Sarmi in *Cronaca di un Amore* (Antonioni, 1950)

when, as we have seen, neo-realism was entering its second stage. In the interim, Antonioni had not been idle; but his début was difficult, hampered and delayed by political events and his own demanding nature. Yet his first short film, *Gente del Po*, is important, stylistically and thematically, in the early history of neo-realism, even if its importance has been somewhat clouded by its belated appearance and the cutting to which it was subjected. The peculiar nature of his art, the psychological overtones with which he was subsequently to endow the most realistic settings, is already apparent in another short film, *Nettezza Urbana*, in which empty streets and the dingy light of dawn prefigure the achievements of *The Eclipse* or *The Red Desert*.

It is already clear that in these essays – in the original meaning of the word – Antonioni is seeking a way to apprehend another side of reality, the most profound of all. He goes far beyond the social neo-realism implied in the subjects chosen – the poverty of the inhabitants of the Po regions, the work of the street-cleaners in Rome. Similarly, the convolutions of the police investigations in his first feature film, *Cronaca di un Amore*, are of no more than superficial interest. This film at once earned him a niche alongside his elders and contemporaries. At the same time he differed from his fellow directors in that he deliberately chose to depict a middle-class environment; but he chose to do so in order to stress its instability in the face of a primordial emotion. For Antonioni, social problems are subordinate to the basic human problems of love and hate; and the devouring, exclusive passion which demolishes the social barriers between his lovers affirms that we are human beings first, and members of a class or society only second.

It is also interesting to notice that the author makes his story revolve round the girl. It is the heroine who has the decisive role. Antonioni's later work was to take this approach further still: 'The female mind is the best filter of reality I know.'[15]

Despite its importance as a signpost to Antonioni's later work, *Cronaca di un Amore* did not meet with the success that it deserved, both for its choice of theme and for its carefully studied treatment. After this tardy début, the author had to endure for a long time to come, not so much adverse criticism, which would at least have drawn attention to his work, as incomprehension, indifference, a curious myopia, at a time when his persistence and integrity ought to have won him instant recognition.

Added to this were considerable material difficulties of production and distribution, particularly as regards *I Vinti*, which contained three episodes about juvenile delinquency in the immediate postwar period. The suicide episode in *L'Amore in Città* (*Love in the City*) aroused hostility by its ambivalence. As for *La Signora senza Camelie* which followed, its deliberate demystification of the film world was hardly calculated to win the sympathy of the public or to shake the critics out of their apathy. Just as he had stripped

Eleonora Rossi Drago, Valentina Cortese, Yvonne Furneaux in *Le Amiche* (Antonioni, 1955)

the failed suicides of their aura of romanticism, Antonioni stripped the star of her false glory and sham happiness. Each film ends on the same note of emptiness, poverty of spirit, lack of incentive to live.

La Signora senza Camelie, admittedly, was not without weaknesses. In 1953, then, Antonioni was forty-five, far from famous, and only just beginning to attract discreet attention from a handful of critics. Even that pair of masterpieces, *Le Amiche* (1955) and *Il Grido* (1957) failed to establish him fully, though they exhibited a mastery of ideas and form and an originality about which there could no longer be a grain of doubt. With this achievement, Antonioni opens the door to a new cinema which emerged in the 1960s. He does away with plot and 'character', replacing them with what has been well called 'a cinema of behaviour and interiority', with which the seventh art entered a new phase in its development.

Elsewhere I have attempted detailed studies of these two films. All I can do here is put them in their context and ask what features they contain that foreshadow the later, better-known works. For it may be thought that *Le Amiche* and *Il Grido* will come increasingly to occupy a key position that will ultimately necessitate a revaluation. Even if Antonioni subsequently achieved subtler things, we may surely ask if he ever achieved greater ones. Coming at

155

the close of the second period of neo-realism – or rather, its explosion, in 1957 – *Il Grido* seems to contain all the elements that gave neo-realism its peculiar character and beauty: its sympathy for the workers, its poetic revelation of little-known regions of Italy (a feature introduced fifteen years earlier by *Ossessione* and subscribed to by his own *Gente del Po*), and its air of total truth as regards the setting and the behaviour of the characters. But Antonioni compounded these ingredients of neo-realism into a mixture of his own, thanks to the intensity of the psychological drama and (even more) its sublimation into the problem of man at grips with the emotions that bind him, dominate him, and hinder or prevent his self-fulfilment. In this way neo-realism moved from the social to the deepest and most complex human plane, in which a man's destiny is no longer governed merely by external circumstances, but by his inner freedom or emotional dependence – by the lack of ties or the existence of them.

This, from now on, was to be the field of inquiry and discovery in the cinema. Standing on the threshold of this new departure, *Il Grido* continues to exemplify the preceding half-century of film history, an end-stage in the process of technical discovery culminating in the dominant and pervasive role of the image. The ideas which this haunting work embodies are Antonioni's; but it embodies also the photography of Gianni di Venanzo, the music of Giovanni Fusco, the human faces and landscapes of the Po valley, the winter mists shrouding the banks of the river. *Il Grido* is an admirable poem in which intellectual profundity and formal perfection go hand in hand.

Enthusiasm for the first period of neo-realism – the enthusiasm of sudden revelation – has led to an undervaluing of its second period, which, even if it adopted a new approach, or perhaps for that very reason, resulted in a still richer vein of quality works. True, the proportion of quality films in relation to the total output dropped considerably. But are we to deplore the prosperity of the industry in the belief that prosperity necessarily occurs to the detriment of works of art? No film industry, whatever its country, can thrive on master-pieces alone. Run-of-the-mill production has great importance in every country; it is the basic framework of any healthy cinema; it popularizes the basic motifs that a handful of artists manage to create, and establishes links between the public and what is new. The important point here is that between 1950 and 1960, in spite of occasionally excessive output and difficulties with the censor and the government, many excellent films saw the light of day; and it is of secondary importance if those films no longer complied closely with the political and social dictates of neo-realism. These dictates had been a stimulus; if they had been allowed to ossify, neo-realism would sooner or later have run into an impasse of the Fascist or Stalinist type.

Roma, Ore 11 (De Santis, 1952)

From this fate it was saved by the genius of a handful of men, whose achievement left a deeper mark on the period than did the alleged decline, no trace of which became apparent until the close of the decade. What is more, the innovators were not the only directors producing works of quality. Almost all those who had come to the fore at the fall of Fascism continued turning out gifted, conscientious work. The partisans of social cinema lacked neither subjects nor arguments to continue their struggle. In 1952, Giuseppe De Santis shot *Roma, Ore 11*, a moving account of a news item connected with the unemployment problem in Rome; but the following year he brought in psychology as well, with *Un Marito per Anna Zaccheo* (*A Husband for Anna Zaccheo*) before lapsing into the novelettish with *Giorni d'Amore* (*Days of Love*) and *Uomini e Lupi*.

Carlo Lizzani was destined, by his combination of idealism and a some-what theoretical approach, to a distinctly erratic career. Like De Santis, with whom he often worked, and for the same reasons (cultural rather than political), Lizzani never managed to make up the retardation, thematic and stylistic, which he displayed as early as *Achtung! Banditi!* This is clear from the manner in which, in *Ai Margini della Metropoli* (1952) – structurally attractive but technically outmoded – he grafts on to the resolutely popular and romantic detective story the profound theme dear to his heart, the struggle of the classes. Two worlds stand confronted, symbolized by the two women whom the lawyer visits in turn to prepare for the lawsuit, gradually discovering his prejudices, his blindness, and, ultimately, his injustice. The hero, accused of a crime he did not commit, is the victim of his social environment. After giving the details of his life, the lawyer says of him that he is 'tragically alone in a hostile world'. We may say, then, that the plot and the characters are a pretext for the director to generalize about social justice; there is no need to insist on how dangerous this approach can be, especially when the author is moved by such evident conviction. But the prime quality of this film is its intelligence – the intelligent way Lizzani develops his story and his ideas, steering round the points of possible disaster and saying what he has to say with discreet elegance. There is a slight tendency towards mawkishness; but for most of the film, particularly the opening, Lizzani passes quickly over the dramatic scenes and lingers more on the psychological moments.

The author's communism is reflected in the friendship he bears towards his working-class characters and in their solidarity – one recalls De Santis – when misfortune strikes one of their number. (They save the accused man by defying the law.)

The same qualities and defects are found in Lizzani's adaptation of Pratolini's novel *Cronache di Poveri Amanti*, set in Rome in the early days of Fascism. Here again, Lizzani preserves his human touch and his affection for the individual despite his social theme. An attempt at burlesque, *Lo Svitato*, and a large-scale exotic documentary, *La Muraglia Cinese* (*Behind the Great Wall*), sent him off in other directions before, in the 1960s, he returned to his original themes.

Another of the younger directors who did not quite fulfil his early promise, Pietro Germi, changed his manner after making the films discussed in the last chapter. The social questions with which he had been concerned gave way to family problems and problems of the psychological and sentimental type. His interest henceforth was in the individual – but in the individual as a member of society: *Il Ferroviere* (*Man of Iron*) is the story of a railwayman; *L'Uomo di Paglia* (*Man of Straw*) that of a general worker. Both films were presented at Cannes, but met mainly with sarcasm and indifference. This was rather unfair. If his films are melodramatic it is because they are faithful reflections of reality, a reality closely defined in terms of race and class. Germi puts the whole of himself into these two films, even acting the parts of his own heroes. Outspoken, unquestionably sincere, Germi at least merits respect for his honesty. He never resorts to tricks of style or doublethink. He is simple and direct, taking us straight to the heart of his milieu, those 'average' families continental critics and public detest, though for different

L'Uomo di Paglia (*Man of Straw*, Germi, 1957)

reasons. Perhaps Germi has no intention of getting us involved in his 'little people'; but he has chosen to depict them for us at the risk of boring us with their laughter, their anger, their tears, their disputes and their feuds. Neo-realism, as we have seen, is rarely the same thing as reality. Like all true art, it transposes. Germi has the fault of over-scrupulous fidelity.

Melodrama is not merely a form of theatre, it is also a way of life, specifically meridional. The first part of *Man of Iron*, and even more that of *Man of Straw*, are quite remarkable in their way: the characters, the setting and the movement are absolutely authentic – an authenticity which is not confined, as in naturalism, to the outer appearance of objects and people, but which delves to the very heart of the individual and gradually, through his eyes and his reactions, reveals to us the little universe in which he lives. The affair between Zaccardi and his young neighbour is portrayed with quite exceptional tact and humanity. The myth of love at first sight (this being virtually the only form of love recognized by the cinema) is for once left agreeably far behind. Germi's hero is indeed a 'man of straw', tossed hither and thither by his desires, his dreams and his chosen reality, a grey and uneventful life. If Germi could limit himself to this, he would probably be rated higher than he is. But in *Man of Iron*, as in *Man of Straw*, he goes too far: his plots drag on long after they have made their point; hence the forced endings, the calamities which suddenly rain down on his heroes and cause the human adventure to founder on the rocks of the romantic-jejune.

This error of judgement on Germi's part is to be regretted, because the tone of his films, their authentic portrait of a section of humanity, and his own acting reveal an attractive personality.

His sure craftsmanship brought him success with films in which he was less faithful to himself: *Divorzio all'Italiana* (*Divorce, Italian Style*) and *Sedotta e Abbandonata*.

At this period, neo-realist devices were tacked on to a genre that had proliferated while steadily degenerating: the episode film, which prospered from around 1951–2 onwards.

Amore in Città (*Love in the City*, 1953), to which we have already referred, comprised six stories directed by Antonioni, Fellini, Lattuada, Lizzani, Maselli and Risi. It was to form the first issue of a monthly celluloid magazine entitled *Lo Spettatore*. Devised by Zavattini, Riccardo Ghione and Marco Ferreri, *Lo Spettatore* was to treat several aspects of a given theme, taking the realism – as in the episodes filmed by Antonioni and Maselli – to the point of re-enacting events with the actual people concerned. The dangers and limitations of this audacious and questionable experiment, a kind of fore-runner of *cinéma-vérité*, are only too apparent in the two episodes mentioned above.

Lo Spettatore never got beyond its first issue, but the idea cropped up again later on. *Documento Mensile*, consisting of filmed reports, stories and news items, was the fruit of collaboration between writers and directors: Moravia, Visconti, De Sica and others. It, too, had a short life.

The episode-film recipe attracted directors of the calibre of Rossellini and Visconti in such films as *Siamo Donne* (*We, the Women*) and *Amori di Mezzo Secolo*; while Blasetti, as prolific as ever, set himself up as its champion in *Altri Tempi* and *Tempi Nostri*. Latterly, despite the collaboration of excellent directors, old and young, this genre, exposed as it was to all the temptations of facility, lapsed considerably. At all events, *Love in the City* is the only neo-realist specimen of the genre, the characteristics of which tended to be fixed by the least demanding of its disciples, Castellani and Zampa. The latter directed *Anni Facili* (*Easy Years*), a satire that provoked much ire in neo-fascist circles. Castellani's 'optimistic realism' had a descendant in the prototype for a series of similar films, *Pane, Amore e Fantasia* (*Bread, Love and Fantasy*) by Comencini. The sharpness and flavour which marked this and other films in the same vein were found less and less as time went on, until, in certain purportedly neo-realist films by Dino Risi and Bolognini, we find the stale conventions of a latter-day novelette.

Geronimo Meynier, Andrea Scire in *Amici per la Pelle* (Rossi, 1955)

The neo-realist legacy, or rather its possibilities, were better understood by a young director, Franco Rossi, in *Amici per la Pelle*, a minor work but a sensitive one, and full of a promise that has never really been fulfilled.

Other films of this period belong to a different line of derivation from neo-realism: *Cristo Proibito*, directed by the writer Curzio Malaparte, concerns the return of a prisoner of war – an outmoded subject, but here extended to include the messianic theme of the salvation of mankind by the sacrifice of the innocent. This is a remarkable film, marred to some extent by its excessive concern with dramatic build-ups and visual effects – though the result is gripping in scenes such as the procession during the mock crucifixion, with its masked bearers and obsessive drumming. Malaparte did not repeat this incursion into the cinema.

There is, of course, less intellectual rigour in Ettore Giannini's pleasant divertimento *Carosello Napolitano*; but there is the same tenderness and human kindness, as in the face of a girl crying over her first love or in the closing shot of these half-starved people continuing to follow their poor yet joyful destiny in the pale light of early morning.

In the historical genre of *Nozze d'Oro* and *1860*, a realist tradition is apparent in the virtually unique work by Piero Nelli, *La Pattuglia Sperduta* (*Vecchio Regno*), an episode in the 1849 campaign portrayed with non-professional actors and treated in the verist manner – an admirable conjunction of sincerity and austerity.

Alongside these outstanding successes, once the neo-realist phase was over, two former 'calligraphers', Alberto Lattuada and Renato Castellani, confirmed the extent of their gifts. Lattuada in particular has not received all the attention he deserves, owing no doubt to the very diversity of his approach, an ingenuity which occasionally lapses into facility, a mercurial temperament and, paradoxically, a scrupulous concern with the details of his craft. His contribution to the first phase of neo-realism was important, but Lattuada was not a man to remain faithful for long to a single idea or approach; he continually turned from one genre to another, and was equally at home in almost all of them.

Il Cappotto (*The Overcoat*), which Lattuada adapted from the short story by Gogol, is a work of the first importance, quite unlike any of his other films, a fable set in an imaginary world verging on the unreal. Kafka's name has been invoked. The central character (played by the comic actor Renato Rascel), a petty official, is rather like the heroes of *The Castle* and *The Trial* – like Kafka himself, but more naïve, more human, a Kafka revised by Charlie Chaplin. He is the eternal underdog, painfully aware of the fact and yet haunted by great aspirations. This rather abstract literary invention is a compound of several partial truths, the conjunction of which elevates him beyond realism into a symbolic archetype. When things are at their worst, the hero of *The Overcoat*, like Chaplin, adopts a kind of relieved nonchalance admirably expressed by Rascel in the brilliant police-station and ballroom scenes. This is high comedy, and it is astonishing that critics have generally neglected this all-important aspect of the work and seen only the satire or the drama. *The Overcoat* is a great film, complex, moving, satiric.

Its satire is bitter but without the illusions on which, paradoxically, satire so often feeds. If Carmine had belonged to this world of sycophancy and corruption, would he have been any better than the rest? His suffering does not make him altruistic; his hankering after an overcoat owes as much to ambition as to necessity. He is cold because he is alone, rejected, even more than because the wind is cutting through his rags. Carmine would not lend his overcoat to his brothers; he sees no further than his self-centred ambition. Indeed the harshest moral in this fable is that the hero, however pitiful and touching he is (when, for example, he gazes at his coveted overcoat in the crowded streets), it is his plight, not his personality, that wins our compassion.

When finally he gets his overcoat, the poor fellow becomes merely ridiculous, distinguishable from those around him only by his lacking their sly hypocrisy, and contemptuous of those who naïvely believe in his influence. It is the thief who restores him to an authentic state of grandeur by stripping him of the emblem of his pride, thereby leading him to his death and to the silent homage of the officials and the whole town. The funeral sequence, by restoring Carmine in our affection, forms an admirable conclusion to the fable. Like *Miracle in Milan*, *The Overcoat* is a homage to humility and a criticism of all material success, even among the poor.

Castellani also, after his trilogy (*Sotto il Sole di Roma, Springtime, Two Pennyworth of Hope*), set out to extend his field of action: he said at this time that he had no wish to limit himself to 'pseudo-realist formulas'. Like Visconti with *Senso*, he turned to the theatre and colour photography with an adaptation of Shakespeare's *Romeo and Juliet* (*Giulietta e Romeo*). Despite his declared intention of depicting on the screen, with the most absolute realism, the people, the settings, the feelings, the very soul of the *trecento*, Castellani's outstandingly beautiful film is in every way a transposition, for he attempts to discover and reveal 'actuality' in his images of the past. To do so, he uses devices much the same as those he employed in his trilogy: within the real framework of *trecento* Italy he places young actors with little experience, almost the same age as the characters that they play, and as yet unwarped by any stage tradition. But then, paradoxically – and because, after all, Shakespeare is Shakespeare – he has these Italian characters speak English. This extraordinary conjunction of reality and convention, history and poetry, authenticity and artifice, somehow gives unity – purely intellectual no doubt, but singularly effective and convincing – to a work whose quality and tone recall the theatrical productions given in Graeco-Roman

Laurence Harvey, Susan Shentall in *Romeo and Juliet* (Castellani, 1954)

amphitheatres or Gothic palaces: in both cases, the effect is ultimately one of timelessness.

On this occasion also, Castellani was the 'director of youth'. Looks, gestures, movements – the impetuosity (and also the hesitations) of the action as a whole cry the youth of its theme, cast and characters much better than any ardent expression of passion could have done. For all her being a woman in love, Juliet is first and foremost a girl, almost a child; and it is love for her youth which sends Romeo galloping wildly towards their fatal rendezvous.

Castellani devoted three years' planning and seven months' shooting to his difficult undertaking. The technical perfection of the angles and framing, the sumptuosity of the settings and costumes, were further demonstrations of what the trilogy had already made clear, that Castellani's 'calligraphic' period had not been wasted. Neither in the trilogy nor in *Romeo and Juliet*

164

is there any of his former preciosity; instead we find a visual beauty in accord with the subject. Castellani was less fortunate with *I Sogni nel Cassetto* (1957), a return to social problems in a rather melodramatic mode, and with *Nella Città l'Inferno* (1959), set in the women's prison in Rome.

After these major works, the Italian cinema seemed suddenly to undergo the artistic crisis that set in virtually everywhere. In addition, the dictates of the censor and the more or less open opposition of the government and the Vatican discouraged initiative and innovation. This situation led to the manifesto, signed by most of the Italian film-makers, in defence of neo-realism and their freedom of expression.

During the same period, we can observe an increase in the frequently deplorable system of co-production and the start of a series of Graeco-Roman films inspiring belief in something called 'neo-mythologism'. In fact, every branch of production flourished: melodramas, more or less bucolic comedies, pseudo-historical adventure films, and biblical epics.

Around 1955, indeed, a genre new to Italy made its appearance and prospered for a few years: the full-length documentary, which might have given a new lease of life to the exotic film if it had learned a few things from neo-realism. But on the contrary, with the successful films of Enrico Gras and Mario Craveri, it swiftly lapsed, not merely into glossiness and quaintness, but into artificiality and untruthfulness. *Continente Perduto* and *L'Impero del Sole* are merely exotic fictions wrongly labelled as documentaries, and betray the interests of a genre that even then tempted directors of the quality of Rossellini, whose *India 57* has already been described, and Lizzani, with *Behind the Great Wall*. Apart from this, the exotic film joined up with the costume film, which came to the fore once again in this artistic crisis of 1958–9. But there was nothing new or significant in that.

Yet a twofold renewal was imperceptibly in progress. It was to come both from the established directors of the day and from the younger generation.

Anouk Aimée, Ferdinando Brofferio in *La Dolce Vita* (Fellini, 1960)

7. New and Young Cinema (1960–9)

The movement that was to revolutionize the cinema around 1960 was an international phenomenon. In most of the producing countries, the old formulas were becoming worn out, and new styles were emerging. A new generation of directors bore witness to a general need for breaking out of what had become an archaic mould.

In Britain, the birth of Free Cinema raised hopes of a renaissance. In France, the *nouvelle vague* rushed in where the older generation feared to tread. In Italy, by contrast, after the brief slump at the close of the 1950s, the innovating impetus came from the establishment: from Antonioni, Fellini, Visconti and Rossellini. The first two, in particular, did more than restore the strength and vitality of the Italian cinema: they radically altered the traditional forms of construction and expression and came to grips with the dramatic and moral taboos, thereby accomplishing a revolution both aesthetic and thematic. The year 1960 will always be remembered as that of *L'Avventura* and *La Dolce Vita*, two films presented at Cannes, where they caused a stir which marked a definitive break with the dramatic legacy of 19th-century theatre, rocked to its foundations as this had already been by the neo-realism of the 1940s. For this reason, the 'new cinema' can be regarded as a long-term consequence of neo-realism. It is itself a form of realism, even when it indulges in introspection or baroque exuberance.

In the two films mentioned above, plot is ousted by story – a kind of dramatic eye-witness account which unfolds independently of all considerations but its own crises and their evolution. Scenes are no longer included in order to lead an action towards its conclusion, but to set forth an actual state of affairs, a datum, a succession of 'now-situations'. It is significant that the central character of *La Dolce Vita* is merely a *witness* of a world to which at the outset he does not belong; and that the first heroine of *L'Avventura* disappears without trace a quarter of the way through the film.

On the social level, both films are set in the same world, the present-day Roman aristocracy. Both portray this world in a state of decomposition: it is sentimentally degenerate in one film, morally degenerate in the other. And the same hollow characters surround Claudia in Antonioni's film and Marcello in Fellini's. Despite their different styles and aims, both directors share a new-found concern with the social environment, which makes their films first and foremost testimonies on their period. *L'Avventura* is about a sexual crisis, but the crisis is determined – this is the point – by particular social circumstances. Fellini is more comprehensively, indeed uncompromisingly, satirical, and even his bitterest enemies are bound to recognize the sheer force of his satire.

After the hostile reception given to his film at Cannes, Fellini himself gave the following explanation of his intentions in making this 'chaotic fresco'.

La Dolce Vita is intended to be both a testimony and a confession. The film attempts to dedramatize (and not merely demystify) certain aspects of the world we live in, and to accustom us to facing up to our monsters, one after the other. . . .

I have tried to portray a society which no longer has any passions, any guts. What *has* it got? Conventions, clothes, attitudes, smiles, horn-rimmed spectacles, feathers, chairs, tapestries. . . . This was to some extent what governed my style. In my ignorance, I had an intuition that style was the same as substance; in other words, that form mutated into substance. That is what happened. . . .

Finally, *La Dolce Vita* was only a substitute title. I set out with the intention of stressing the permanent aspect (outside time, and above all outside our own times) of the story that I was going to tell. My original title was *Babylon, 2000 A.D.* Then everything fell into place, and *La Dolce Vita* tied up with all my previous films. I have always been passionately interested in human anguish. I am fascinated by modern man and his contradictions: a frenzied, anguished, exciting life – and a terrible, hidebound, motionless void. Yet we rush around, we throw ourselves about. . . . The men go from affair to affair, from woman to woman. . . . And all they do, ultimately, is chase their own tails. In this apparent excitement, which is really inertia, there is no room for faith.

In *La Dolce Vita* everyone can see his own reflection, provided he is sincere enough first to look for it and then to recognize it. Unfortunately, man does not have either enough self-confidence or enough self-distrust. *La Dolce Vita* was intended to be a cry of anguish capable of shaking him from his lethargy.

Intentions and works such as these have always caused a scandal. Fellini's film was no exception. Françoise Duez summarizes its reception in Rome as follows:

A campaign, led by the editor of the *Osservatore Romano*, was mounted against the film; the political and religious authorities were stirred to indignation. The Vatican stated that the film was 'morally unacceptable'; the Christian Democrats described it as 'a singular slur on the dignity of Rome'; the Pope viewed the film and was struck with horror. There was much talk of excommunicating Fellini; his film was put on the Index. The deputy mayor of Rome labelled it 'crypto-porn', and many voices were raised in favour of abolishing subsidies for 'film producers who infringe morality'. . . . The National Heraldic Council issued an official reprimand to those members of patrician families who had taken part in the film. Parliament split into two camps. . . .

In spite of the brouhaha in the press and the pronouncements of prominent per-sonalities, the Minister for Arts and Entertainment refused to ban the film: 'We cannot allow the serious art of the Italian cinema to be stifled and mortified by censorship.'

The *Osservatore Romano* and the Christian Democrat organ, *Il Popolo*, were, indeed, far from having it all their own way. Even in Catholic circles the film had its defenders: Cardinal Siri, archbishop of Genoa, gave it as his opinion that the work could only discourage evil – an opinion shared by Under-Secretary Magri when authorizing the film to be shown to all but minors.

Fellini professed astonishment at the scandal; in fact, it proved that his aim had been achieved. One has to be blind or disingenuous to be unaware of the gulf that separates this terrifying and brilliant genre painting from so many dismally pornographic productions. What is more, the artist has managed to suffuse the background and even the foreground of his painting with a mysterious aura all its own.

I should like to make objects and people 'transparent', in the way that every object, every face, every figure, every landscape is palpably transparent. This is what I was trying to express by unfolding my film against a panorama of funerals and ruins. But these ruins are swathed in a light so splendid, so joyous and so golden that life acquires a peculiar and enduring sweetness, even if the ruins collapse and block our paths.

We may say, then, that the satirical violence of Fellini's film seemed to reinforce the psychological avant-gardism of *L'Avventura*. Both these qualities brought back into the Italian cinema of 1960 a profound originality that for the public smacked of scandal. Despite the forebodings of the critics, who imagined that they were the sole supporters of this revolution, *L'Avventura* was a great popular success and *La Dolce Vita* was the top box-office draw of the season, earning more than 2,000 million lire.

However, still more important than this avant-gardism and its commercial consummation is the fact that these two films shocked people out of their preconceptions about what a film was or ought to be. Indeed, the impact of the themes was due largely to this fundamental departure from convention and its effect on audiences. The film seemed to acquire a new dimension; for us today this new dimension is all the more interesting because it made its appearance in two styles that were so vastly different, indeed almost diametrically opposed. The unwonted length of the works – surprise number one – is ascribable, not so much to the convolutions of the story as to an extensive development of each motif, a slower approach, a novel way of circling round each event before closing in on it. The long, modulating shots of *L'Avventura* are matched by the dramatic luxuriance of *La Dolce Vita*. Differently, but just as radically, the latter film replaces the traditional narrative with a succession of quite independent sequences which are juxtaposed without any preconceived link or progression, like the different scenes in a series of frescoes, the meaning of which emerges from the sum rather than from the parts. The characters are not tied to a plot; they flutter around Marcello like the figures and contradictions of the modern world, but always with extraordinary intensity. If Antonioni and Fellini still cling to a semblance of objective realism, they reject entirely any kind of arbitrary dramatic construction, preferring to be guided by the autonomous dictates of the crisis in question. (Both directors had already, in their earlier works, begun this break with the classical tradition.)

This, then, is the real turning-point of 1960. The aim is no longer to construct a plot, but to show people living with their problems. The cinema of drama becomes the cinema of social, psychological or even metaphysical questions, and the style of expression changes accordingly. There is no longer any progression towards a dénouement, because the dénouement has been abolished, or is regarded as irrelevant. The film lingers over nuances, examples, incidentals. It is addressed to the intellect rather than to the emotions.

Just as the neo-realist approach overlaid a fundamental concern with society, the stylistic development which occurred in 1960 was determined by a simultaneous realization of the existence of new social factors, a new mode of existence and a new state of mind. The two films which mark the advent of this renewal are given a resolutely 'actual' setting: they depict a present and immediate world open to the big questions of the future. What will our feelings be? asks Antonioni. What will our morals be? asks Fellini. And Visconti poses the question: What will society be? But with *Rocco e i suoi Fratelli* (*Rocco and his Brothers*), another monument of 1960, we find ourselves with a work which, both in form and theme, is much less original, concerned less with man in his eternal aspects than with the problems of a society set firmly in the dimensions of space and time.

Visconti is as frank as Fellini – though for different reasons – about his preoccupations and aims:

The keystone to states of mind, to psychology, and to conflicts is in my view essentially social, even if the conclusions that I reach are merely human and are concretely concerned with individuals as such.

In telling the story of Rocco and his brothers, he returns to the Southern question always latent in Italy, but transposes it into the problem of the South's relation with the North.

By means of the purely imaginary peculiarities of my characters and story, I think I have posed a moral and intellectual problem that is typical of the historical moment we are passing through and of the mentality of the men of the South: on the one hand, hope, determination, and belief in a future renaissance; on the other, a constant tendency (in the face of inadequate measures) to sink into despondency or to adopt hopelessly makeshift solutions such as the individual integration of each Southerner into a mode of life imposed upon him from outside.

This is the setting for my story; as you know, it extends to murder, aiming to portray an aspect of the Southern character that strikes me as extremely important: the passions, laws and taboos of honour. The theme of the obstacles and derision with which society greets the most generous individual impulses is a modern theme if ever there was one. However, there are at least two ways of portraying it. There is the complacent, dilettante manner that I unhesitatingly qualify as asocial or even antisocial. The other manner examines the conditions of the failure in the framework of the difficulties experienced by the establishment; it is all the more an incentive to hope and energy since it reveals, via the artistic illusion, the true aspect of the obstacle and the bright alternative. Verga restricted his creation and his analysis to the first phase of this method. Starting with Verga's method, I tried to lay bare the original causes of the problem; I portrayed, at an acute moment of stress (in *La Terra Trema* the economic collapse of the Valastro family; in *Rocco* the moral collapse that occurred at the peak of the economic recovery), a character who, clearly, almost didactically (I am not afraid to use the word), exemplifies these original causes. In *Rocco*, it is not by chance that this character is Ciro, the brother who signs on as a worker: the ability that he shows for adjusting to life is not romantic or temporary; he has gained awareness of the social obligations implied by his rights.

With this intentionally dramatic and extravagant plot, Visconti continues the work already begun with *La Terra Trema*. Here, too, the impact is frequently considerable, but the form of expression is more realistic and indeed more traditional than in the films of Fellini and Antonioni. The characters are uncompromisingly real and human; in Rocco the humanity verges on self-sacrifice, as he seeks to inspire in people an awareness of their spirituality. Hence the social problem is overlaid with a many-sided psycho-

Suzy Delair in *Rocco e i suoi Fratelli* (Visconti, 1960)

logical conflict – dense, captivating, verging on melodrama – which has been well likened to the work of Dostoyevsky. Visconti, however, rejects both the maladjustment of Simone, the brother who kills, and the generosity of Rocco. 'In man-made society there is no room for saints like him. Their compassion causes disasters.'

In the same year two other great directors tried to renew their claims, but the themes and forms they chose belonged to the past: *Era Notte a Roma* by Rossellini and *La Ciociara* (*Two Women*) by De Sica were marred by a certain romanticism far removed from the innovations of Antonioni and Fellini. These films were probably responsible, however, for the revival of the Resistance film, one of many genres which was to mark the years to come.

We need, in fact, to stress right from the start that there was an enormous difference between the renaissance of 1960 and a movement such as neo-realism. The former was not nearly so committed or exclusive, and it operated in the economic field as well as in the artistic sphere. The prosperity of the Italian film industry at that time is all the more surprising since all the producing countries were going through a general crisis: 168 Italian films (including co-productions) were made in 1960, 213 in 1961, 241 in 1962, 239 in 1963, with a total attendance figure hovering around 730 to 750 million, only slightly less than the record figure of 819 million attained in 1955.

In such conditions, exceptional works cannot help being in the minority. Yet it is possible that the publicity and scandal referred to above helped to keep the Italian public cinema-conscious at a time when commercial success was encouraging the producers to try something new. As with the French *nouvelle vague* (and perhaps following its example), the main beneficiaries of the public's interest in the unusual were the young directors, who jumped at the chance to make their mark with new and daring films. New names cropped up right and left: Gian Vittorio Baldi, Bernardo Bertolucci, Giuseppe Fina, Ugo Gregoretti, Nanni Loy, Ermanno Olmi, Pier Paolo Pasolini, Elio Petri, Vittorio De Seta, Florestano Vancini, Valerio Zurlini. It was not a school with fervent aims, but a spurt of growth in which arrivism and sincerity came in through the same door together.

Yet this 'young Italian cinema' did not share the characteristics of the soon-exhausted *nouvelle vague*. Before trying to list its achievements, however, we must take a look at other developments occurring at the same time. This will also enable us to evaluate the importance of this *significant* cinema which is part of the much larger, and necessarily unequal, total output.

Like the American cinema, with which even then it had links, Italian production hit back smartly at competition from television. In 1955, there were barely 150,000 TV sets in Italy; three years later, the figure had risen to a million, by 1960 to two million and by 1963 to over four and a quarter million.

Colour and the panoramic screen were first-rate weapons in the cinema's favour; and, like their Hollywood counterparts, the Italian producers strove to retain their audiences by resorting to big spectacular films. They met with a fair amount of success, as we have seen, mainly because colour and the large screen encouraged and enriched the revival of a genre that had always had a considerable following in Italy.

The recovery had become apparent as early as 1952 with large-scale productions in a very conventional style: *Spartaco* (*Spartacus*, 1952) and *Teodora* (1953) by Freda; *Ulisse* (1954) by Camerini; *Attila* (1954) by Francisci. For all that, in 1957 there were still a mere ten or so costume films out of a total output of 119 films. But in the years that followed the proportion rose continuously: 13 in 1958, 20 in 1959, 37 in 1960, and over 40 in 1961 and 1963 as against a total output that had not even doubled over the same six-year period.

After the famous golden age of the silent cinema and the ambitious experiments of the Fascist era, this third spate of costume films cannot be explained away by commercial considerations alone; nor was it confined to the peninsula, since it was as well-received abroad as in Italy itself. The talk about 'neo-mythologism' (a term coined by Cottafavi) in this connection ignores the fact that this kind of film is a perennial feature of the Italian cinema; but the confusion may have arisen owing to a new approach to the genre inaugurated by Blasetti's *Iron Crown* – an approach in which the younger French critics saw unfathomable virtues.

By the end of the 1950s, several broad trends had emerged within the genre. Pseudo-historical adventure films – about knights errant, pirates, bandits or princes – listed in their titles the names of such old-stagers as Bragaglia, Gallone and Campogalliani (who had now chalked up fifty years' devoted service), and established directors such as Lattuada, Gentilomo and Leonviola. As before, literary adaptation played an important role in these adventure films, whose success was due to the reasons referred to at the beginning of the present book. It is in no way surprising to find in Bragaglia's *La Gerusalemme Liberata* a retelling of Ariosto's story, or in Gentilomo's *Sigfrido* a free adaptation of the Nibelungen legend.

Though fewer in number, ancient history also had its *afficionados*, who once again trotted out the same old war horses: *The Last Days of Pompeii*, *Fabiola*, etc. Biblical themes were virtually excluded from this genre, however, either because the Italian directors shrank from competing with the successors of Cecil B. DeMille, or because the subject appeared too delicate with regard to the Vatican, and unsuitable for the kind of humour and irreverence that were to characterize this revival of the costume film.

This last-named branch of the 'antique film' included such hardy perennials or newcomers as Hercules, whose main biographers were Francisci and

Ercole e la Regina di Lidia (*Hercules Unchained*, Francisci, 1958)

Cottafavi, and Maciste, the famous and perduring hero of *Cabiria* (1914). It was in 1957 that Pietro Francisci hit on the idea of introducing the super-man figure of Hercules, in *Le Fatiche di Ercole* (*The Labours of Hercules*). Sold to the United States for 100,000 dollars, the film made a fortune for its distributors. The character's survival was thereby ensured, and the specialists set briskly and interminably to work. Maciste made his comeback in 1960, with *Maciste nella Valle dei Re* by Campogalliani. The following year brought no fewer than five Maciste films (by Freda, Gentilomo, Cerchio and Leonviola) as against three Herculean adventures (by Cottafavi, Caïano and Bava). The same year saw the highly successful début of the character Ursus, and the years that followed produced strange encounters in the course of which Greek mythology joined forces with cinema mythology and finally the Bible itself: Hercules, Samson and Ulysses united to do battle with the Philistines.

The history of the cinema cannot be written in terms of 'intellectual' works alone. That is why this digression was necessary, even if one does not share certain critics' oneiric ravings at the erotic burlesque of *La Regina delle Amazzoni* (1960) or the scarcely concealed sadism of *Il Colosso di Rodi*. The great popular currents are of prime importance in the evolution of the art;

175

witness the Mack Sennett shorts and the Western. There is little likelihood that 'neo-mythologism' will have quite so much influence, because it arrived rather late in the day; but it may help to counterbalance the rather excessive inclination of the Italian cinema towards realism and introspection.

In fact, this third great period in the history of the costume film was less a revival than a transformation of the traditional genre. If the subjects are the same as before, the style of expression is radically different – so much so that the great virtue of the genre in its early days, its 'bigness', which paved the way for the Americans, is almost entirely lost. There is a general tendency to limit the *mise en scène* to clever effects in order to avoid employing too many extras; and if a few sets remain fairly handsome many others make little attempt to conceal the true size of the budget.

The fact is that even the aims are no longer the same: directors do not set out, these days, to astonish or to move their audiences to tears; they set out to amuse, and they resort to those devices, tried and tested in other genres, which correspond to current tastes. The old-fashioned recipes of melodrama – invincible heroes, *femmes fatales*, ingenuous heroines – are laced with contemporary eroticism and violence. Most of these films, be they Cerchio's *Nefertite, Regina del Nilo*, Bragaglia's *Le Vergini di Roma* or the many Hercules adventures, display a fondness for *risqué* scenes frequently accompanied by torture and massacre – sadistic rather than dramatic. And everything is wrapped in a brand of humour that disarms the censors and sometimes – as with the Bragaglia film mentioned above and (especially) Vittorio Sala's *La Regina delle Amazzoni* – develops into burlesque and parody.

It will be seen, then, that both the tone and the style are far removed from what they were in the golden age. Theatrical grandiloquence has given way to good humour, the knowing wink at the audience. Anachronisms and other errors become gags; and historical truth – if such a thing is even possible – becomes the least of the concerns of directors for whom character and plot are merely pretexts for unbridled fantasy.

This difference of approach is probably due to the fact that we are now able to view the old-fashioned historical dramas in their true perspective. This may also account for the evident desire to debunk the hero as, in collusion with his audience, the author transforms his 'reconstitution of history' into a kind of game.

What will the role of this game be in the future? Its fascination for certain young critics in France amuses their colleagues in Italy, and it has doubtless surprised the directors concerned, who mostly have no pretensions beyond the professionalism often displayed in equally commercial but neglected genres such as melodrama and light comedy. But the nonchalance of approach and the freedom of expression found in these films, as in the archetypal *Iron*

Alice Sapritch, Sophie Darès in *I Due Orfanelli* (Freda, 1965)

Crown, occasionally enable even the feeblest directors to achieve a kind of frenzied extravagance which delights a generation bred on surrealism.

Success in this field is often due less to deliberate intention than to chance. Specialists soon emerged: Francisci, the inventor of the Hercules saga, Bragaglia, earlier a successful director of 'white telephone' films, Grieco, Mario Bava and Vittorio Sala, formerly a director of documentaries. But the two names most frequently acclaimed are those of Riccardo Freda and Vittorio Cottafavi; unlike their fellow 'mythologists', these two directors use the genre as a pretext for a deployment of decorative qualities which amounts to a distinct style.

Both are cultured men of over fifty. Though they both attended the Centro Sperimentale at around the same time, they spent their formative years rather differently, Freda as a sculptor and Cottafavi as an author turned script-writer. They already had a wealth of experience in the cinema before they took up 'neo-mythologism' – mainly for commercial reasons, though the genre doubtless appealed also to their sense of the spectacular. Commercial or not, the genre enabled them to prove themselves as directors. 'I am not in the least interested in banal humanity, everyday humanity,' says Riccardo Freda, and it is therefore not surprising that he has always been an opponent of neo-realism.

What I am interested in is, roughly speaking, the hero: mankind in times of greatness, in times of war. History is full of possibilities for enthralling scenarios. The main thing is to hit upon the decisive moments.[1]

I Giganti della Tessaglia (1961), one of his best films, was a very free adaptation of Jason's quest for the golden fleece, which enabled Freda to deploy a kind of baroque lyricism, including a famous storm filmed in the studio and romantic shots reminiscent of Gustave Moreau and Géricault.

Hailed even more enthusiastically than Freda by the amateurs of the genre, Vittorio Cottafavi displays a peculiar brand of eclecticism, directing both for the cinema and for television (for which he stages the great international classics of Sophocles, Molière, Dostoyevsky and so on). In the cinema, after melodramas verging on the study of manners (*Traviata 53, Una Donna Libera*), he directed several spectacular films – *La Rivolta dei Gladiatori* (*Revolt of the Gladiators*), *Le Legioni di Cleopatra, Messalina, Venere Imperatrice* – in which he attempted to treat in a tragic manner the erotic fortunes of the protagonist. Finally, he took over from Francisci the myth of Hercules: *La Vendetta di Ercole, Ercole alla Conquista di Atlantide* (*Hercules Conquers Atlantis*). The humour with which he spices the adventures of his hero is ample proof that he does not take him very seriously, and there is reason to believe that the whimsical adventures of those virgins of Rome owe more to

Cottafavi, who worked on the film, than to Bragaglia, who directed it. It is obvious from the very way he treats his subjects, as from his knowledge of staging and his use of colour, that Vittorio Cottafavi is a complete professional and probably more besides. However, as Raymond Borde and André Bouissy put it, this comic-strip aesthetic has little value except 'as a seven-day wonder in rural zones, *Cahiers du Cinéma*, the Near East and Latin America'. And not even that audience is likely to rise to the soporific *I Cento Cavalieri* by the same Cottafavi!

Yet Borde and Bouissy's sally is only too true. Apropos the Maciste saga, Unitalia was able to state recently: 'The genre has become a kind of standard recipe, not merely for those who set out to create fantasy, but also for a massive invasion of American, Asian, African and even European markets.'

Is the Italian cinema of today aiming to regain the position that it held in the earlier part of the decade 1910–20? The ambition would be far from unrealistic, considering that the American film has lost its hegemony and will probably decline still further as a result of internal and external pressures. The very collaboration between the two production systems may contribute to the triumph of Italy. Well before the neo-mythological film or the hero series began to show signs of flagging, the Italian producers envisaged competing with America on her home ground by entering the field of the Western. A link-up with Spain seemed likely to provide the European Western with the essential desert landscapes and cheap labour. The venture was taken seriously and by the middle of the 1960s the genre had produced its first fruits: *Per un Pugno di Dollari* (*A Fistful of Dollars*) by 'Bob Robertson' (Sergio Leone), *Minnesota Clay* by Sergio Corbucci, and others. The pseudonym chosen by Leone was typical of the genre at this time: Riccardo Freda signed himself Robert Hampton, Sergio Grieco became Terence Hathaway, and even the actors took to adopting American-sounding soubriquets. Yet it seemed unlikely that the masquerade would last for long, despite the massive investment that the venture represented.

Further American-style ventures included science fiction and the horror films of Mario Bava: *I Tre Volti della Paura* (*Black Sabbath*, 1963), and *Sei Donne per l'Assassino* (*Blood and Black Lace*, 1964).

A further phenomenon became familiar during the early 1960s. Inaugurated much earlier, and stimulated by the contingencies of co-production, the episode film became a typically Italian-French product. To ignore it would be to ignore works by some of the best directors of both countries. The genre takes two forms: either one director takes responsibility for the different episodes (with or without a connecting theme), or the episodes are farmed out to several directors and scriptwriters. Blasetti was one of the innovators in the first form of episode film, to which De Sica also contributed, with *Ieri,*

Messalina (Cottafavi, 1960)

I Tre Volti della Paura (Black Sabbath, Bava, 1963)

Oggi, Domani (Yesterday, Today and Tomorrow), a trio of stories, each star-ring Sophia Loren and Mastroianni. The second type of episode film brought together contributions from De Sica, Fellini, Monicelli and Visconti in *Boccaccio '70*, a feeble effort which seems to have been intended as a kind of prototype. It did in fact give rise to a series of imitations culminating in the films that launched what *L'Espresso* called 'the war of the nude': *Controsesso (Countersex*, 1964) and *Le Bambole (Four Kinds of Love*, 1965). The latter led to Gina Lollobrigida and Virna Lisi appearing in court in Viterbo, along with their directors, Dino Risi and Bolognini, for infringing article 528 of the civil code, which forbids the diffusion of pornographic material. *Countersex* earned Castellani and the producer, together with the distributor and eight cinema-owners, suspended sentences of two months' prison on the same charge.

Eroticism is a dominant feature of the modern cinema. But in the episode film it ceases to be an ornament or consequence of the plot and becomes the sole purpose of the film, and that is doubtless where the problem lies. Antonioni and Fellini, and many others, have included in their works scenes of greater eroticism than the laborious exhibitionism and smut with which some directors waste their time and talents. But what in one case is justifiable as being part of a general theme, in another is merely a way of making money. This was in fact the criterion applied by the government when it condemned 'all films that exploit sex in a vulgar manner and to commercial ends'. Nonetheless, the definition is ambiguous and the condemnation virtually unenforceable, as can be deduced from the following details reported by Pierre Billard:

For many months the Italian cinema has been in the grip of debauchery. Out of 212 films produced last year [1964], 47 were banned to under-fourteens and 61 to under-eighteens. A scrupulous statistician has contrived to establish that 163 of these films portrayed a woman wearing a black négligée (the favourite uniform of the envoys of Satan). Panties, bras, suspenders, and transparent déshabillés are the essential items in the wardrobes of the actresses of Cinecittà.[2]

This branch of the episode film is linked with another genre in favour in Italy, the problem film, to which Zavattini, in particular, has continued to subscribe. *L'Amore in Città* was still imbued with the ambitions and methods of neo-realism. More recent problem films, however, have tended to go in for the fashionable style of *Le Italiane e l'Amore* (*Latin Lovers*), the idea for which was again due to Zavattini, *I Nuovi Angeli* (*The New Angels*) by Gregoretti, *I Fuorilegge del Matrimonio* by the Taviani brothers and Orsini, and *Comizi d'Amore* by Pasolini. Starting with a problem of the moment (women in society, divorce, the younger generation), these films frequently hover skilfully around a point midway between fact and fiction. With *I Misteri di Roma* (1963) Zavattini exploited a rather different vein that discarded fiction in favour of the 'secret document' type of film (frequently of doubtful authenticity), made popular some years before by Jacopetti's *Mondo Cane*. Here the aim was to collect oddities; *curiosa* might be a better word, to judge by the connection between this genre and another invented by the prolific Blasetti, the 'report' on night life in various cities, as in *Europa di Notte* or *Mondo di Notte*. These 'sexy documentaries', as they are known in Italy, more or less pornographic in spirit, are extremely good business for the producers: *Sexy al Neon* made 400 million lire at the box-office – a very gratifying return for a minimum outlay. In point of fact, insofar as the camera is an eye-witness and striptease has become a modern ritual, the Italian name for the genre is not misplaced, and the sexy documentary, for better or for worse, is a commentary on our times.

These various aspects of Italian production could not legitimately be ignored here any more than could neo-mythologism. They are the other side of the medal, with art, unfortunately, conspicuous through its absence.

Art is conspicuously present, by contrast, in the neglected field of the short film. It must be noted here, however, that from the founding of L.U.C.E. in

1926 the documentary represented a large proportion of the annual output.

Both before and during the war, the short film had already furnished the younger generation with a chance to experiment which was to contribute to the revolution connected with neo-realism. *Comacchio* by Fernando Cerchio (later an exponent of the commercial full-length film) came as a revelation in wartime France. And the short film played its part in neo-realism with items such as *Bambini in Città* by Comencini and the admirable experimental films of Antonioni, *Gente del Po* and *Nettezza Urbana*.

Around this time, there appeared a genre that had a natural appeal to Italian film-makers, considering the wealth of their past and their culture: the art film. For a long time, even with encouragement from L.U.C.E., this genre merely took the form of a series of more or less banal travelogues. However, Pietro Francisci's unfortunate attempts to 'animate' famous paintings suggested a device that was shortly to find its justification.

Luciano Emmer's encounter with Enrico Gras around 1939 resulted in the earliest examples of what were called 'art films'. In fact, the film-makers used paintings by Giotto, Carpaccio, Uccello, Simone Martini and Piero Della Francesca to compose *Il Dramma di Cristo* and *La Legenda di Sant'Orsola*. But of course the spectator's interest is directed, not at the 'story' that the authors set out to tell, but at the paintings in which the narrative is conveyed.

Emmer and Gras had no intention of setting themselves up as art critics. 'We had no pretensions of making cultural documents or disseminating propaganda in favour of art,' says Emmer. 'We were interested solely in the possibilities of the camera and we attempted to use it to translate the dramatic elements of fine old paintings into the language of the cinema.'[3]

In so doing, the authors exposed themselves to criticism on another count: the 'dramatization' of paintings. Even though this 'dramatization' was often performed in the spirit of the painter, it shocked the sensibility of the purists – rightly so, in many cases, for drama in a painting is merely a pretext. To limit a painting to its theme seemed to many critics like an ignorant betrayal of everything that art stands for. And to use a painting to compose a work of a different order seemed even worse – a downright destruction of art.

Taken as a whole, however, the authors' intention implied from the start a profound knowledge of painting. 'The aim was no longer to make a short film with a series of photographs of paintings. . . . There was a human content, a linear drama that would come to life in the film. . . .' It was to express this 'content', this 'drama', that the directors were to explore and reveal the painting without any argument but the painting itself.

Hence it is indeed the transposition of the painting into film terms that constitutes the twofold interest – cinematographic and pictorial – of the film. The problem was to transpose a plastic rhythm into a dynamic rhythm, to translate space into temporal terms.

Having understood the painting, Emmer and Gras had to convey their understanding in terms of the other medium, film. To get the drama across, the camera uses travelling shots, pans, intercut shots, blow-ups, studio sets or natural settings, just as it would have done with human actors. Emmer's and Gras's use of cinema does not betray the paintings in question, it reveals them.

Such was the general impression at the congress in Basle in 1945 at which their first films were presented. Photography has completely renewed our knowledge of painting and architecture by its ability to change its viewpoint and viewing distance at will. Nor are we capable of moving around a statue with the same ease as a camera. But it is in the case of the Italian fresco, almost always half invisible high on a wall or in a dark vault, that the contribution of the cinema has been most invaluable. In addition to their frequent inaccessibility, the frescoes are constantly threatened by damp, by damage done to their supporting material, even by graffiti. Giotto's frescoes in the church of San Francesco at Assisi and in Santa Croce, Florence, Leonardo's *Last Supper*, and the anonymous seventh-century frescoes in the monastery of Sacro Speco near Subiaco have all suffered in this way. While ensuring preservation of these fragile works of art, the cinema can, as Emmer's work proves, awaken our eyes to the internal 'movement' that exists within these great paintings and reveal, through close-ups, dramatic expressions and attitudes.

The interest aroused even in the general public by these productions was responsible for a brisk output of art films in Italy. Pasinetti and Blasetti shot a series of shorts on the architecture of Venice, Rome and Milan. The current fondness for realism inevitably encouraged the emergence of a lively documentary style in short films of every kind, from Lizzani's *Nel Mezzogiorno Qualcosa è Cambiato* to Rossellini's *Prélude à l'Après-midi d'un Faune*, Antonioni's shorts, and Antonio Petrucci's stylish 'elegies' (*Autunno sui Laghi, Elegie Romane*, etc.). The travelogues of Pasinetti, Dano, Ugo De Rossi (Venice), Avanzo (the Aeolian islands), and above all Giovanni Paolucci (*Portofino* and *La Montagna di Cenere*) were works of art with a quality and style of their own.

Hence in the ten years 1955–64 the short film became a testing-ground for young directors, many of whom subsequently worked in the full-length commercial film while continuing to make short documentaries; several of them, such as Vittorio Sala and Fernando Cerchio, produced their best work in this latter field.

In quantitative terms, this branch of the Italian cinema was important. Favoured with considerable subventions under the terms of legislation passed in 1955, the production of short films was in excess of 500 films per year – though this total obviously comprises few original works, most being commissions on prescribed topics. This output is little known at home and totally unknown abroad. The international festivals are our only chance to see a few of these films and discover their authors' talents.

Yet most of the directors whose names we shall be encountering served their apprenticeship in the short film: Maselli, Risi, Petri, Zurlini, Vancini, Olmi, Damiani, Loy and so on. Applied to the full-length feature film, the discoveries that some of them made in the field of shorts enabled them to add something new to the tradition of realism. This was the case with Vittorio De Seta and Gian Vittorio Baldi, who achieved some fame before they made a full-length film, and with the young director Giuseppe Fina, who, after shorts on Milan and Sardinia, undertook the social survey that formed the plot of his first feature film. Television, of course, cannot fail to provide opportunities for the short film, whose cultural and artistic value no longer needs to be stressed.

A genre which remains fairly embryonic is the Italian animated cartoon film, probably because it has little contact with the human reality that is the characteristic feature of all Italian film production. Apart from a few prior experiments by young painters and technicians – including Enrico Gras – the first cartoon films appeared towards the end of the war. Two full-length films date from this period: *I Fratelli Dinamite* by the Pagot brothers in Milan, and Gino Domeneghini's *La Rosa di Bagdad* (*The Rose of Baghdad*), begun in 1943 and completed six years later. *The Rose of Baghdad* had an enthusiastic reception in Italy; but there, as elsewhere, the animated film has virtually only one outlet, cinema or television advertising. This has been the path taken by Domeneghini and the Pagot brothers; the results can be quite artistic, as will be seen from the latters' publicity shorts like *La Ruota*.

New firms were founded about this time. One of them was Gamma, a modern-minded team which included Zavattini. Corona, headed by Ezio Gagliardo, produced two full-length films for young people, using a combination of animation and live shooting; the team that made them was composed of Elio Gagliardo (Ezio's brother), Zanorelli and a few others. Emmanuelle Luzzati, painter and potter, also worked for children with *Castello di Carte* and *La Gazza Ladra*, which won the jury prize at Annecy in 1965. Finally, mention must be made of Bruno Bozzetto's films: *Tapum* (1958), *The History of Inventions* (1959), *Alfa Omega* (1961), *I Due Castelli* (1962), his Signor Rossi films, and the eighty-minute *West and Soda*, a parody of the western.

In the mid-1960s, the 'significant' Italian cinema – significant in an ethical as well as an aesthetic sense – appeared to be determined partly by the problem of the generations. Yet if the majority of the younger generation of directors dealt with the psychological, moral and social conflicts resulting from the evolution of manners and the situations which this evolution created, others, especially the men of the preceding generation – those who were thirty at the time of the political upheaval that shook the country – portrayed the tragic years that determined that evolution. The fall of Fascism and the destruction of its myths marked all Italians, not only those who were adults at the time, but also those who were adolescents or children. All these directors look back at those years – no doubt from a wish to understand what really happened – in a detached manner, without any of the partisan passion or lyrical enthusiasm which characterized much of neo-realism. In their book *Le nouveau cinéma italien*, Raymond Borde and André Bouissy put forward the following accurate if incomplete explanation of this phenomenon:

In our view, the Left discovered in the war a kind of anti-Fascist golden age in which the choice was a simple one. . . . The villains of the piece, dressed in black or grey-green, were immured in their uniforms, and could be hated on sight. All hopes were pinned on the future brotherhood of the liberation, the rising sun of Socialism, expected around 1945.

Yet more often than not the revival of the Resistance film tended to demythologize the war and this facile simplification of the problem. As early as 1959–60 several films set the tone: Rossellini's *Il Generale Della Rovere*, De Sica's *Two Women*, Zurlini's *Estate Violenta*. Rossellini's film, if not his best, is one of his most accomplished; and the admirable acting of De Sica makes a truly creative contribution to the work. The topic was a remarkable one and enabled author and actor to express a form of heroism which happily owes nothing to the occasionally facile lyricism of postwar days; here the heroism of action is superseded by moral heroism. The close attention to detail which validates such a work is precisely what is missing from De Sica's *Two Women*. But the film's faults have been allowed to mask its good qualities. Here, Borde and Bouissy's image rings untrue: in the confusion of 1943, the 'liberators' themselves could become the villains of the piece – witness the appalling scene of the rape in the church. This demythologizing of general heroism also occurs in the mundane preoccupations of the countrymen whose lives are unaffected by the war. Similarly, in Zurlini's film, *Estate Violenta*, the lovers live in a universe of their own, remote from the contingencies of the war.

The black-out curtains are drawn. Roberta and Carlo slowly dance, their faces lit with the magic of love. The windows are open. In the distance, the sky is a sheet of flame: an Allied bombing raid is in progress. But the night is sweet and the jazz continues softly in the background like chamber music.[4]

These three films exemplify the new climate in which the revival of the war film was to take place. As against the conventions or the exaltation of neo-realism, the new approach stressed a different kind of reality, less sublime, no doubt, but more human. Thus the Italian cinema remains faithful to its major virtue, which is that it continually returns to humanity and truth

La Lunga Notte del '43 (Vancini, 1960)

despite the digressions and excesses to which it is led by its particular character and its natural lyricism.

More conspicuously successful than in 1945, the genre grew and gave rise to works of value that confirmed or revealed the talents of both the older and the younger generations. Three such works appeared in 1960: Rossellini's *Era Notte a Roma*, uneven, too long, but interesting nonetheless; *Tutti a Casa* by Comencini, in which buffoonery goes side by side with tragedy; and *Il Gobbo* (*The Hunchback of Rome*), in which Lizzani returns to his favourite themes of social action and revolt. Lizzani has said that *Il Gobbo* was the story of one particular character; *L'Oro di Roma* was the story of one particular event, a sell-out at the expense of the Roman Jewish community. The same director's *Il Processo di Verona*, relating the trial of Ciano and the members of the Fascist government, is genuine history, reconstituted with an authenticity and an understanding of his craft which confirms the talents of this somewhat underestimated director.

In addition to Zurlini, who was seventeen in 1943, other young directors entered the lists with films about the war: Gillo Pontecorvo (born in 1919) with *Kapò*, a picture of the women's camps, admirable in its first section but completely unbalanced in the second, which lapses into the worst kind of convention and artifice; and Florestano Vancini (born in 1926), with *La Lunga Notte del '43*, another uneven film, adapted from Giorgio Bassani's novella. Further names and titles could be cited, more or less deserving of attention (though this is another genre which is prone to lapse into the facile). Old hands looked back on the 'black years': De Santis with *Italiani, Brava Gente*, about the Italian contingent on the eastern front, a film whose highminded intentions are spoiled by the far-fetched and heavy-handed treatment; Luigi Zampa with *Anni Ruggenti*, a rather laboured parody of Fascism – an outworn form also used, to no better effect, by Dino Risi in *La Marcia su Roma*.

If we except Comencini's *La Ragazza di Bube*, which is more concerned with characters than with events, two works stand out from this revival of the Resistance film: *Quattro Giornate di Napoli* by Nanni Loy, and above all *Il Terrorista* by Gianfranco De Bosio, a man of the theatre whose treatment of the need for unity in the Resistance over and above party creeds is authentic and stimulating. Nanni Loy's film fails to avoid high-minded clichés in certain secondary episodes, but it does display a quite remarkable feeling for period and authenticity. *Il Terrorista* is set in Venice; like the Naples of *Quattro Giornate*, the city is not merely decorative, but plays an active role in the drama by creating a specific mood.

From around 1960 onwards, there was also a move towards the montage or compilation film. The genre was initiated by the Socialist Party, which financed *All'Armi, Siamo Fascisti* by Lino Del Fra, Cecilia Mangini and Lino Micciche, with a commentary by Franco Fortini. This history of the movement since the North African campaign ends with the anti-Fascist demonstrations of 1960 in Genoa and Reggio, thereby giving the film a polemical twist. Pasquale Prunas and Roberto Rossellini, with *Benito Mussolini*, and Mina Loy, with *Anatomio di un Dittatore*, use archive material to retrace the history of Fascism through a close scrutiny of an individual.

Other films followed, similarly centred on political topics: *Giorni di Furore*, a montage film on the Resistance by a group of young people in Turin; *Il Piave Mormorò* by Guido Guerassio and Vico D'Incerti; *Rivoluzione a Cuba* by Luciano Malaspina; *Il Delitto Matteotti* by Nelo Risi; *Mathausen Mahnt!* by Piero Nelli; and *Il Fiume della Rivolta* (a history of the great social upheavals of the first half of our century) by a then promising young director, Tinto Brass.

Once again, it has not been possible to give more than a rapid survey of this trend, which is virtually unknown outside Italy and will probably remain so.

Peasant banditry, always a topic of burning actuality in Italy, cropped up as the subject of two important films which coincided with the overthrow of the traditional cinema in 1960–1.

Rosanna Schiaffino in *La Sfida* (Rosi, 1957)

Francesco Rosi, a former assistant of Visconti, had made his name in 1957 with *La Sfida*, a film dealing with restrictive practices in the Naples fruit and vegetable market; this was followed in 1959 by *I Magliari*, about more or less dishonest retailers living in Germany. With *Salvatore Giuliano* he undertook a kind of historical inquiry into the life of the famous outlaw who, after the liberation of Sicily, held the police and army at bay for several years. Giuliano was assassinated in 1950; the controversial subject of his life is treated by Rosi with striking originality and force, with recourse to historical reconstruction, documentary evidence, interviews, and an invariably direct vision of reality conferred by a camera that scrutinizes faces as well as rural hovels and sun-scorched landscapes. Rosi's aim is not to explain, to defend or to accuse: he gives evidence, merely, in a dynamic and effective style which is all of a piece. It has been asserted that his account of this complex affair only goes half way, in that it is based on a rigged trial which shielded those really responsible, the Sicilian barons. But a film director is neither a judge nor a lawyer. The indecisive way in which Rosi leaves the drama is the very stuff of reality.

Vittorio De Seta's *Banditi a Orgosolo* is set in Sardinia, and its method, akin to *cinéma-vérité* (De Seta shot it virtually without outside help), argues from cause to effect, whereas Rosi had argued from effect to cause. The story is that of a shepherd who, as the victim of a theft, is forced to turn sheep-stealer himself in order to stay alive – the story of *Bicycle Thieves* in a rural, individual mode, but with the same mood of tragic fatality. De Seta had already made several remarkable shorts on Sardinia. For him, authenticity is never allowed to become a pretext for abjuring beauty in the image – a beauty which is all the more impressive when we consider the crude technical resources at his disposal; like Visconti before him, in *La Terra Trema*, De Seta is an artist first, a social critic second. *Banditi a Orgosolo*, like *Salvatore Giuliano*, revives the epic aspect of neo-realism found, for instance, in *Il Sole Sorge Ancora*, in the films of De Santis, and in some of Lattuada's. The same tone is to be found in a film by Castellani, *Il Brigante* (1961), a slightly over-ambitious tale about a Calabrian forced into banditry by circumstances and injustice.

The assassination of Salvatore Carnevale by the Mafia in 1955 is the subject of a more recent film, *Un Uomo da Bruciare*, directed by Paolo and Vittorio Taviani and Valentino Orsini. The theme is land distribution in Sicily and the dramatic consequences when the interests of the Mafia are at stake. And there is Lattuada's *Mafioso*, in which Alberto Sordi plays the unwitting executant of an organized murder.

Obviously, banditry is merely a *pretext* for these films – a thematic and dramatic device. And the still unsolved problem of the Mafia is probably quite beyond the scope of the cinema; it would appear, indeed, that the Mafia exercises control over the subjects which concern it.

The emergence of these distinct genres extending from pure entertainment to social inquiry has not, however, been the main event in Italian production since 1960. The most representative area of Italian film-making at present is that discovered by Antonioni and Fellini: the study of contemporary *mores*. The questions treated in this way are all the more controversial since Italian society has changed very fast since the Risorgimento. A few of these questions are: the ever-increasing discrepancy between the social classes; the decline of religious feeling; bourgeois corruption; the freedom of the young; the threat of families breaking up; the contemporary sense of alienation.

The concept of alienation has taken on a special meaning in Italy. It is not the Hegelian notion of a frustration of the being in general, nor even the Marxist notion of proletarian frustration. It is the aggregate of affective problems that stem from contact with the modern technocratic world. The economic miracle has strewn the roads with vehicles and the waste lots with office blocks. Without any transition, the mass media have imposed their lowbrow sub-culture on provinces choked with provincialism and dramatically lacking in any kind of national culture. Peaceful villages have been invaded by motor-scooters. Things have moved very fast in the sixties: an implacable and

Salvatore Giuliano (Rosi, 1962)

quasi-traumatic evolution of manners. The young Italian cinema was and is the product and the reflection of this aggression.

This is an extremely pertinent definition, by Borde and Bouissy, of the causes and effects that give contemporary Italian films their recognizable features. This rejection of outworn norms is reflected in almost all the significant works – those that make the names of the outstanding new directors (and their imitators).

Whatever the direction of their commitment or the extent of their talent, they all subscribe to the common fund of realism. The Italian film-makers do not invent stories in the introspective manner of the novelist. They gather them in, rather, by watching their fellow men at grips with their social or psychological problems. The legacy of neo-realism has doubtless contributed to this awareness of the human condition, which is also a response to the Italian cinema public's fondness for what De Seta calls 'a mirror in which society can recognize itself'.

This mirror for the world of the Italian economic miracle – materialistic, sceptical, estranged – has many facets. All that can be done here is to attempt to discover a few general trends and to indicate the key works.

The shared commitment of all Italian film-makers to reality, to the problems in which they are themselves involved as actors or as spectators, is the expression of a form of solidarity that is highly characteristic of the Italian mentality. Children, adults and the aged compose one human family, in the broad sense of sharing the same hopes and sorrows. The mutation that is occurring in this age-old social pattern aggravates the problems and justifies the scrutiny to which they are subjected. One problem stands out from all the others, because it is permanent and, undeniably, attractive: the problem, or problems, of the young. These problems have never been quite so dramatic as they are today, especially in Italy, where the force of tradition, with its stratified class and education systems, is particularly strong.

From Fellini's pioneering *I Vitelloni* to Francesco Maselli's *I Delfini* (1960), the story of a group of young bourgeois, the problem is posed in social terms. More corrosive, and concerned with a less privileged sector of youth, were Bolognini's *La Notte Brava* and *La Giornata Balorda*, both scripted by Pasolini, and Pasolini's own *Accattone*, a deliberately violent and at many points suspect work.

Bolognini and Pasolini worked together at the beginning of the 1960s, the former directing with undeniable yet deceptive skill to scripts by Pier Paolo Pasolini, until the latter turned to directing himself. *Accattone*, the psychological portrait of an urban proletariat of young delinquents, is marred, in the last resort, by an irritating romanticism. And, even though one can find honourable precedents for this, as Borde and Bouissy do, these precedents

Franco Citti in *Accattone* (Pasolini, 1961)

seem tiresomely literary by the standards of today: 'Accattone's mal-adjustment, his failure neurosis, his self-punishment, his infantilism, his somnambulant appearance, his brusque crises of violence or despair – all this smacks of the psychological authenticity associated with, for example, Dostoyevsky.' It was again Pasolini to whom two young directors, Paolo Heusch and Brunello Rondi, turned in 1962 for the script of *Una Vita Violenta*, another film in the same truculent, melodramatic vein. The sordid setting in the outer suburbs, the film's 'miserabilism' (a distorted variant of neo-realism), and the social approach of which the Italian cinema is so fond, here become a pretext for purely novelettish fictions quite close – though often without the poetry – to Prévert's romanticism in *Quai des Brumes* or *Portes de la Nuit*. With its sensational plot, its evident misogyny, its motto from Dante and its music from Bach, this attempt is full of pseudo-philosophical and aesthetic pretensions that are a long chalk from neo-realism as it had been known. Understandably, left-wing critics have not always been fooled by the ambivalence apparent in all Pasolini's films.

There appears to be more sincerity in the methods and aims that led a highly rated director of short films, Gian Vittorio Baldi, to make his first

195

full-length film, *Luciano*. His method was particularly conscientious and deliberate. It was the same method that he had used for his psychological documentaries. Once he has conceived the idea for his film, Baldi says, 'I try to get acquainted with it in great depth. I undertake an inquiry, a study, like a student preparing a thesis.'[5] Psychological analysis helps him to reject or occasionally to justify the novelettish side of the story, and to replace actual dramatic events by their psychological repercussions in the character affected by them.

At all events, the problems of the young studied by these directors (always from the male point of view) are first and foremost social problems, or maladjustment to social problems. The anguish of the young Italian male today is concerned less with himself than with other people, and arises from a hunger for life that is frequently stifled by a society which he has not built and which he rejects.

Girls' problems in Italy are of a different order – more personal, more intimate, but equally important in a country where moral independence comes up against social and religious prejudice. Here the conflict is both social and psychological, because the problem of the female adolescent has a direct effect on her environment, i.e. those among whom she lives; and therein lies the strength of its appeal for film directors.

Alberto Lattuada has an avowed fondness for juvenile heroines and their problems: puberty, flirtation, virginity and womanhood. After *Guendalina*, sensitive and probably less mawkish than it appears at first sight, he went a step further with *I Dolci Inganni*, whose heroine knows nothing of schoolgirl blushes or love psychology but goes after the object of her desire with the purity of a young animal.

There is less simplicity in the adventures of *La Calda Vita* (1964) by Vancini or in the heroine of Luciano Salce's *Voglia Matta*, a film in which self-consciously triumphant youth is opposed to the maturity of a man caught up in the rat race, like the hero of De Santis's *La Garçonnière*.

The problem of the young then gives way to another essential ingredient of many films in the mid-1960s: the emancipation of women, woman's position in society. From the new corrupt bourgeoisie to the archaic society of the South, from the drama of passion to comedy, from De Santis and the veterans to the very youngest directors, there was a spate of films on this question and the issues associated with it: prostitution, family life, social life, morality, conformism. *La Ragazza con la Valigia* by Zurlini, *Laura Nuda* by Ferrari, *La Cuccagna* by Luciano Salce, *L'Attico* by Puccini, *Adua e le Compagne* and *La Parmigiana* by Pietrangeli deal with the various frustrations of Italian women.

As a kind of corollary to these films on young people, Bolognini's *Agostino, o la Perdita dell'Innocenza* and *La Corruzione* (*Corruption*) and Damiani's

L'Isola di Arturo (*Arturo's Island*) portray the turpitude and weakness of the parents.

Yet few of these works can stand in their own right, as distinct from the trend which they created or followed. The literary influences behind them (Moravia was frequently involved), and their anxiety to squeeze the last drop out of a subject, tend to distort phenomena that are still too close in time to be understood correctly.

For the last part in this undertaking, which will take us up to 1969, the discussion will be centred, not on the themes (the most important of which have been stressed above), but on the directors themselves, who *are* the Italian cinema of the present day. By any standards, three names stand out: Antonioni, Fellini, Visconti. The breadth and depth of their recent works will be discussed below.

Alongside these three, other directors of skill, intelligence and talent pursue their fruitful careers with varying degrees of luck and opportunity: Lattuada, Germi, Lizzani, Castellani, Monicelli, Comencini, Risi, all belonging to the same generation. And Rossellini and De Sica may still turn up with something worthy of their gifts.

Other directors, some of whom came to the fore towards the end of the 1950s and the early 1960s, bridge the gap between the veterans and the new-comers. Many of them turned to directing or to the full-length film only in their forties, though they continue to appear young. Franco Rossi, Francesco Rosi, Pasolini, Damiani, Bolognini, De Seta, Vancini, Loy, Zurlini have been discussed above. Some of them belong to the front rank, particularly Rosi, Pasolini and Bolognini; though no older than the others, the last-named is almost in the veteran class in terms of the vast number of films he has directed. The fruits of his career are debated and still debatable, despite or because of his skill in debunking ambitions that seem more feigned than sincere. *Cahiers du Cinéma* does not spare the rod:

A few tiffs with the censor have given him the reputation of an enthusiast for social criticism. Illusion! His critique of capitalist society is superficial in the extreme. . . . His morbid world of withered or nymphomaniac women, of conquering or complex-ridden males, is a world of misogyny and homosexuality.[5]

This is in no way the opinion of Borde and Bouissy, for whom Bolognini is incontestably 'one of the best directors working today', though they do acknowledge that his career was marred, following an impeccable début, by his collaboration with Pasolini. Whatever one's opinion of him as a director, one is obliged to admit that he is not an *auteur* in the true sense, but an illustrator. All his films are transpositions of literary works, adapted not by himself but by writers such as Pasolini, Moravia or Pratolini. Hence he cannot be rated as high as other directors who, less accomplished perhaps, are more directly involved in their works. Indeed, the dubious paternity of his films may well account for their failure to give a clear impression.

The most promising member of this middle generation is Francesco Rosi. After *Salvatore Giuliano*, he directed *Le Mani sulla Città* (*Hands over the City*), a bitter and uncompromising denunciation of the housing racket. Rosi's merit is to have treated this unpromising theme with such directness and conviction that he wins the interest of his audience as completely as with the infinitely more glamorous *Salvatore Giuliano* – clear proof of his skill as a director and as a story-teller. He was less successful with *Il Momento della Verità* (*The Moment of Truth*, 1964), about bullfighting in Spain. His skill as a director is as remarkable as ever – his feeling for the image, his grasp of human truths in the most banal situations; what is wrong is the tone. Rosi shot his film in Spain, with mostly Spanish advisers and actors, notably the young *torero* Miguelin. But his actors, who were subsequently dubbed into Italian, speak with an Italian volubility that is quite foreign to the Spanish character. Rosi's entire approach is Italian, when his theme and setting are irretrievably Spanish.

With *C'Era una Volta*, a fairy tale set in the old kingdom of Naples, Francesco Rosi seems to be moving still closer to the spectacular film.

The output of Dino Risi (at over fifty, the senior member of this middle generation) is large but very uneven. He did, however, make two excellent films around 1960: *Il Sorpasso*, and *I Mostri*, a rapid succession of flashes that displays a highly developed sense of ellipsis, an occasional ferocious irony (as in the first episode), and a blend of cruelty and tenderness that makes the final episode a minor masterpiece.

These films owe much to the first-rate acting of Ugo Tognazzi and Vittorio Gassman. The black humour to which they partially subscribe is characteristic of a current trend in the Italian film: examples are the works directed by Ugo Tognazzi and (especially) the films of Marco Ferreri. The latter's *Una Storia Moderna: L'Ape Regina* (*Queen Bee*) and *La Donna Scimmia* are less subtle, however, than his early films made in Spain, for example *El Cochecito* (*The Wheelchair*).

Most of Elio Petri's films – *L'Assassino*, *Il Maestro di Vigevano*, *I Giorni Contati*, *Un Tranquillo Posto di Campagna* – are equally caustic. Petri's humour, however, is more disillusioned, though essentially human in its shrewd observation of people and manners.

Several directors from this period have still to win worldwide recognition, either because they turned to the full-length film rather late in the day or because their work has received only partial distribution outside Italy. Damiano Damiani, for instance, made documentaries for many years before

Marcello Mastroianni in *L'Assassino* (Petri, 1961)

stepping into the limelight with *Il Rossetto* (*Red Lips*, 1960; script by Zavattini), about the problems of female adolescence. Two years later, Damiani and Zavattini turned out the male counterpart of *Red Lips*, *L'Isola di Arturo* (*Arturo's Island*). Damiani went on to the almost obligatory adaptation of Moravia, in *La Noia* (*The Empty Canvas*), and with *Il Giorno della Civetta* (*Day of the Owl*) he turned to the eternal problem of the Mafia.

I have already mentioned *Le Quattro Giornate di Napoli*, Nanni Loy's major work. As for Florestano Vancini, another of this group of directors who are virtually unknown outside Italy, his qualities as a maker of documentaries persist in his feature films: *La Lunga Notte del '43*, about Ferrara under the Fascists, and *La Banda Casaroli* (1962), about wartime Bologna.

Slightly younger, Francesco Maselli brings his undeniable gifts to bear on topical themes: *I Delfini* and *Gli Indifferenti* adapted from the prolific Moravia. Yet Maselli, like Bolognini, is undoubtedly a skilful illustrator rather than an authentic creator.

Probably the best of this group of established directors is Valerio Zurlini. He made his début with an adaptation from Vasco Pratolini, the novelist, to whom he turned also for *Cronaca Familiare* (1962), an exceptionally skilful

Marcello Mastroianni in *Cronaca Familiare* (Zurlini, 1962)

transposition of an exceptional theme. The whole film exudes an incurable sadness yet is imbued with singular beauty, notably in the way some scenes are enhanced dramatically by the use of colour. The close attention to detail and the emotional restraint of this film attain to poetry and tragedy without the least striving after effect, in line with neo-realism but more profound and intimate.

What is true of Zurlini is true also of Ermanno Olmi, who has made several films of great interest. Olmi is an *auteur*, in that he devises and shapes themes expressing a personal, heightened perception of a world that we generally take for granted. His first three films, *Il Tempo si è Fermato* (1959), *Il Posto* (1961) and *I Fidanzati* (1963), recall the best of De Sica (whose influence Olmi acknowledges) in that they faithfully record the humdrum details of the life and behaviour of their heroes.

In these films realism verges on fantasy. Nothing is explicit: the characters' feelings are laid bare by the power of the image alone, without recourse to words or dramatic effects. Pierre Marcabru has called this (with reference to *Il Posto*) 'an admirable cinema of silences and glances'. It is a cinema which expresses life's sorrows (*Il Posto*), hidden warmth (*Il Tempo si è Fermato*) and patient hope (*I Fidanzati*). In this last film, Olmi contrives to express the fact of absence – something that might have seemed inexpressible in the cinema. Certain scenes here and there, such as the one with the coffee cup on the bar in *Il Posto*, say what the cinema alone can say, when it becomes the reflection of life itself – and perhaps more than a reflection – seen via the heightened perception of an artist. 'Keen observation and tender irony,' says Marcabru. 'Yet the pessimism, for all its tenderness and human kindness, is final and absolute. Olmi displays compassion for all that is fine, fragile, condemned.'

Yet scenes like the opening of *I Fidanzati* or the party sequence in *Il Posto* transcend this realism and come close to a kind of social fantasy that can be seen as the mark of an extremely original creative temperament.

Not surprisingly, the passivity of Olmi's heroes has infuriated a number of critics committed to the cinema of protest. Yet it remains to be seen whether this resignation, this silent accusation are not more convincing than the obscure symbols or ranting expostulations beloved by the specialists of alienation.

It is a pity that a director with such manifest gifts and so distinct a personality should have turned away from the style that was all his own to a biographical film which, whatever its subject, cannot help limiting the self-expression of a creative temperament. By treating the life of Pope John XXIII in *E Venne un Uomo*, Olmi abandoned what he has called 'the world of labour and the people who work'. He has also stated: 'I think I shall never tire of this extraordinary theme that summarizes a heap of others.'[6] In the cinema of today Olmi is one of the few who have remained faithful to the mission of

The office party in *Il Posto* (Olmi, 1961)

neo-realism: the representation of everyday life and the misfortunes of the less privileged members of society. That mission has become all-important since the exceptional successes of Antonioni have inaugurated a dangerous taste for the elegant narcissism of the wealthy.

Neo-realism has ceased to be a beacon in the Italian cinema, despite its persistence in the films of Olmi and one or two others. The perpetual movement which animates all art is steering the Italian cinema towards themes and forms of a different kind. As often happens, the most exacting of the directors of the previous period seem to have the most difficulty in adapting to the requirements of the renewal. Whatever Rossellini's motives may have been in abandoning the cinema – in favour of television – it is clear that his instrument was no longer sufficient to express his ideas. Whatever De Sica and Zavattini may do to revive the aims of their début (*Un Mondo Nuovo*), it is clear that their inspiration has fled. Neo-realism has become a legacy of the past; significantly, the young directors alone seem capable of carrying it through into the future.

A few older directors connected with, or formed by, the original phase of neo-realism had already shown, around the mid-1950s, the paths that would be taken after the fragmentation of the movement. The visual quality of *La Terra Trema* revealed one of the major preoccupations of Visconti, while Fellini distilled poetry from everyday life and Antonioni scrutinized the psychological background to our actions. These three directors remain the three great figures in the Italian cinema of today.

In 1963, the Venice festival recognized Visconti's mastery in *Il Gattopardo* (*The Leopard*), a classical, well-ordered work which attained a kind of perfection in the dramatic involvement of the image. This quality reappeared in *Vaghe Stelle dell'Orsa*, a classical narrative of psychological and social conflicts. Visconti's unqualified failure with his version of Albert Camus's *L'Etranger, Lo Straniero* (*The Outsider*), should not be allowed to detract from his very real qualities.

The same preoccupation with the visual aspect of the film – composition, movement, colour, psychological and social expressiveness – is found in the recent works of Antonioni and Fellini.

Much has been written about Antonioni's revolution in film style – his psychological scrutinizing of his characters and his sense of the image. *La Notte* is a profoundly pessimistic work, slightly literary at times, as befits its theme and setting. *L'Eclisse* (*The Eclipse*) is a remarkable commentary upon modern man. *Deserto Rosso* (*The Red Desert*) shows the heroine's neurosis altering her environment. These three films develop similar themes with a steadily increasing maturity of style.

Fellini, too, had been gradually working towards this freedom of expression

Alain Delon, Monica Vitti in *L'Eclisse* (*The Eclipse*, Antonioni, 1962)

founded on the impressionistic evocation of mood. The poetic fantasy of his earlier films culminated in the baroque exuberance of *Otto e Mezzo* (*8½*), in which the image is freed from reality to pursue the phantasms of the imagination, fancy and memory. (In Visconti's films, this process is reversed.) Hence the image *is* the fiction, and not merely its illustration: it becomes the expression of a creative (as distinct from representational) art.

Such, indeed, was the great revelation of Fellini's *Giulietta degli Spiriti* (*Juliet of the Spirits*) and Antonioni's *Blow-up*. Diametrically opposed as regards their style, different both in form and content, these two films resemble each other in the omnipotence of the image, which weaves the plot, reveals the theme, creates a mood – creates, in short, the work in its entirety.

Giulietta's anxieties and the photographer's obsession are conveyed by the very images to which they give rise or from which they themselves arise – a disconcerting acuteness of perception in Antonioni, a kind of oneiric delirium in Fellini, and in both a creation of the mind triggered off in its innermost recesses. Far from being gratuitous, the image here is *significant* both in its narrative function and in its aesthetic function (i.e. its power to attract, disturb, *fascinate* the spectator). 'Fascination' is indeed the word, particularly in *Juliet of the Spirits*, whose tumultuous succession of strange and beautiful images binds us in a spell as mysterious as that of a poem or a concerto.

Blow-up, which can be analysed endlessly, is both thematically and stylistically a brilliant demonstration of the essential role of the image in the world in which we live.

In this 'total' cinema, colour is obviously no mere adjunct. Like sound and music, it becomes an integral part of the audio-visual image, positive and necessary. This means that the technician – Gianni Di Venanzo, Carlo Di Palma, Armando Nannuzzi, Giovanni Fusco, Nino Rota – has an important role to play

While giving credit for these films to the Italian cinema, it is only fair to point out that their precursors were French. As regards both the blending of the real and the imaginary and the importance of the image, Alain Resnais's *L'Année Dernière à Marienbad* paved the way for *8½*. Also, though time will eventually have to tell, it is becoming increasingly apparent that Max Ophüls's much undervalued masterpiece *Lola Montès* (1955) made an important contribution to the trend that is emerging at present: with its overlapping time, its events imagined or recollected, its weird tumult of images, it did not merely herald, but actually contained, the cinema of today. Its influence on *Juliet of the Spirits* is obvious: the circus sequence in Fellini's film is an act of homage to *Lola Montès*. Not surprisingly, many critics have rejected Fellini's film as others rejected *Lola Montès*.

Other personalities have emerged in recent years. Pier Paolo Pasolini enjoys the particular distinction of being regarded as the leader of *avant-garde* directors in Italy. I have already referred to him in his capacity as Bolognini's scriptwriter. After a mere six years as a novelist, Pasolini entered the cinema as the *auteur* of a more striking form than literature. The virulence of his first offering, *Accattone*, could not have failed to attract attention, and both Catholic and Marxist critics found grounds for offence. Gratuitous contro-versiality is always suspect, yet *Mamma Roma*, Pasolini's second film, offered the same ambivalent blend of warm heart and social conscience. Then came one of the episodes in *RoGoPaG* which earned its author a suspended sentence of four months' prison for 'publicly maligning the religion of the state'. Pasolini claimed to have acted in good faith, and the following year this Marxist set out to illustrate *Il Vangelo Secondo Matteo* (*The Gospel According to Matthew*). There has been general satisfaction – even in Catholic circles – with the director's respect for his subject and with his humility in attempting to retell the story of Christ in human terms without detracting from its supernatural aspect. Much more questionable is the stress laid on a certain harshness in the character of Jesus. With regard to the form, the neo-realist style of image, while giving rise to some evocative scenes and even to a certain grandeur, occasionally lapses into mere decorativeness as conven-tional – though in a different way – as that of De Mille's *Sign of the Cross*. Emotion is also lacking, especially in the second part, where the Crucifixion is treated in a singularly offhand manner. Far from enhancing the realism, this 'dedramatization' of the theme destroys it. Finally, the accompaniment of this would-be realistic narrative by Negro spirituals and by themes borrowed from Bach, Mozart and Prokofiev – just as Bach had been used on the soundtrack of *Accattone* – completely destroys the illusion of truth and merely underlines the contradiction in the author's approach, in that the soundtrack is granted a 'sublimity' which is denied the image. Jean Renoir's use of Vivaldi in *Le Carrosse d'Or* (*The Golden Coach*) avoids this contradic-tion, since Renoir works within a theatrical aesthetic which Pasolini is trying to reject. The nature of Pasolini's images demanded the absence of any kind of musical commentary. This appeal to grandeur through the agency of music is illegitimate – as it is in the films of Bresson.

This atheist's attachment to the great themes of mythology and religion has won him the favour of numerous critics. Originality, violence, contro-versiality and a taste for (often confused) symbols – such are the charac-teristics of his resolutely contemporary films. After *Uccellacci e Uccellini*, a 'political fable', Pasolini came up with his best film to date, *Edipo Re* (*Oedipus Rex*), an adaptation of Sophocles. The tacked-on prologue and epilogue are perhaps a mistake, and out of keeping with the timeless quality which the film derives from Pasolini's respect for the spirit of the tragedy.

Shot in a totally free style in the desert landscapes of southern Morocco, directed and acted on a note of savage grandeur, this version of the ancient myth reflects the gradual, tragic revelation of the horror that the hero bears within himself, as each of us bears the burden of his hidden destiny.

The mixture of symbols is acceptable in a fiction which is itself symbolic. But it is less acceptable in Pasolini's most controversial film, *Teorema* (*Theorem*), a concoction of half-baked symbolism and the least justifiable form of realistic emphasis. Delirious interpretations based on the author's own pronouncements have been propounded for this film, which has been accused of obscenity – rightly so, if the word still has any meaning – yet has won a Catholic prize in recognition of its 'mysticism'. ('Mystification' would be a more accurate term.) Even if the obsession with sex disseminated by the hero is a revelation for all concerned, it surely cannot be regarded as the demonstration of a fundamental truth. And, while no subject is taboo in itself, it needs to be treated with tact – which is what this film fails to do. Its simultaneous exploitation of the scandalous and the miraculous is yet another example of Pasolini's clever yet questionable ambivalence.

After *Il Porcile* (*Pigsty*) Pasolini continues, with *Medea* filmed in Turkey and a planned life of Saint Paul, the ambitious series of films begun with *The Gospel According to Matthew*. Whether we like it or not, his personality has great influence in Italy, above all as a bridge between the cinema and literature.

Controversiality and aggressiveness are also the most conspicuous features of *I Pugni in Tasca* (*Fists in the Pocket*), with which Marco Bellocchio made his name in 1965. The director's qualities are beyond all doubt, but his attack on the survivors of a perished social order must be classed, not as legitimate polemic, but as what Guido Aristarco has called 'a decadent, narcissistic revolt à la D'Annunzio [which] in some respects comes close to racism'. For indeed the protest frequently looks very much like the authoritarianism that it attacks. In addition, the pathological state of the hero and his companions restricts the bearing of the facts to a particular instance, thereby depriving the film of social value.

Bellocchio's second film, *La Cina è Vicina* (*China is Near*), is much more authentic and effective. This is an ironical denunciation of the decomposition of the traditional political parties, the mellowing into 'respectability' of provincial socialism and pervasive defeatism.

Political themes are to be found also in the films of the Taviani brothers and Orsini, notably in *Un Uomo da Bruciare* and *I Sovversivi* (*The Subversives*), both of which were shown at the Venice festival. But first place in the ranks of the current social film must incontestably be ascribed to the works of Bertolucci and Mingozzi.

Bertolucci made his name with *Prima della Rivoluzione* (*Before the Revolution*), a work half way between the psychological film and the social

Terence Stamp, Anne Wiazemsky in *Teorema* (*Theorem*, Pasolini, 1968)

Lou Castel in *I Pugni in Tasca* (*Fists in the Pocket*, Bellocchio, 1965)

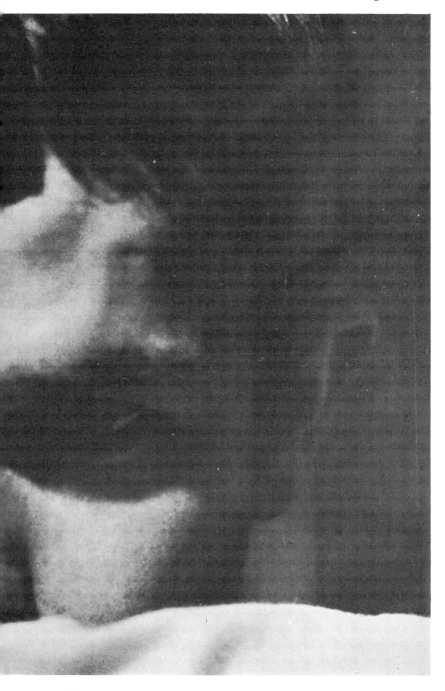

film, with a plot of unusual interest and a valid originality of style. Over and above the references to Stendhal – the film is set in Parma and the hero and heroine bear the same names as those of *La Chartreuse de Parme* – Bertolucci's discreetly accurate romanticism is also extremely modern.

Since then, Bertolucci has filmed *Partner*, adapted from Dostoyevsky, Moravia's *Il Conformista* (*The Conformist*) and several episodes for collective films, notably the parable of the barren fig-tree in *Amore e Rabbia*. Bertolucci is without doubt one of the best young Italian directors; and he has avoided – in his early films, at least – the facile conventions proclaimed in the name of liberation.

Gianfranco Mingozzi's first full-length film, *Trio*, half-way between fact and fiction, is a more than promising portrait of modern youth in search of kicks. *Sequestra di Persona* is about banditry in Sardinia.

Turning to the latest generation, we have to acknowledge the danger of a great deal of talent being nipped in the bud by an excessive and wilful attachment to pessimism, arbitrary protest and misguided imitation. Many recent newcomers wear their cinematographic or literary culture with conspicuous self-consciousness. *Una Storia Milanese* by Eriprando Visconti (Luchino's nephew), the episode in *L'Amore a Vent'Anni* by Renzo Rossellini (Roberto's son), Patroni Griffi's *Il Mare*, Vittorio Caprioli's *Leoni al Sole*, Brusati's *Il Disordine* – in all these works, influence of one kind or another is very apparent. Even more disturbing is the fact that this influence is mostly literary in its origins.

In films with social subjects the protest often seems as gratuitous and facile as the sadistic cruelty of Italian westerns or the eroticism of sex films. The sheer abundance of output is producing an incessant afflux of young directors. Time will tell what contribution has been made by this generation of young directors. What will become of Roberto Faenza (*Escalation*), Maurizio Ponzi (*I Visionari*), Luigi Magni (*Faustina*), Carmelo Bene (*Nostra Signora dei Turchi*), Andrea Frezza, Alberto Cavallone, Mauro Severina, Lamberto Benvenuti, Liliana Cavani, Salvatore Samperi, Nelo Risi (Dino's brother, who has turned to the full-length film after an important career in the social documentary and television), or Tinto Brass, whose artistic intentions are still far from obvious? Some hopes seem to be foundering already. Giuseppe Fina, whose *Pelle Viva* was a courageous denunciation of the crushing effects of industrial mechanization, is reduced to silence, for the time being at least.

Throughout its history, the Italian cinema has contrived to strike a balance between the complementary poles of realism and the baroque. At the outset, this pairing is represented by *Sperduti nel Buio* and *Cabiria*. It is continued in *Four Steps in the Clouds* and *The Iron Crown*, followed by *Open City* and

Miracle in Milan, down to *Il Posto* and *Juliet of the Spirits*. This equilibrium, or rather this adaptability, is also to be found in the economic field, in the fact that the Italian cinema has always recovered from the financial and intellectual bankruptcy to which it has periodically been exposed in the course of its seventy years of existence – proof enough of a vitality unequalled in Sweden, Germany or England. In the widespread current crisis, the Italian cinema is still keeping its head above water. Both commercially and artistically it is regaining a world audience. Neo-mythologism gave its exports a tremendous fillip, reinforced soon afterwards by the audacious invasion of that American preserve, the western. As we have seen, a thriving industry is an essential prerequisite for the emergence of a cinema concerned with art. Quality films can only be the fine flower of an abundant vegetation. If the American film has contributed so much to the world cinema, it is because it was the product of a prosperous industry.

The Italian cinema is multifarious, vigorous, expanding. In spite of its alleged defeatism and the critical broadsides fired in its direction (mainly by Italians), it may well be in the process of recapturing the position it held in 1912 – though the foundations of its success may also be as shaky now as they were then.

If directors such as De Sica, Germi, Zampa and Castellani, who formerly played an important or even capital role, seem to have abandoned their ambitions, others have contrived to adapt their talents to current problems. Some big spectacular films that are not merely spectacular have made a significant contribution: I am thinking particularly of Zeffirelli's Shakespearean films, *The Taming of the Shrew* and (still more) *Romeo and Juliet*, which represent, over and above their beauty and sumptuosity of form, a renovation of eternal themes.

Even Rossellini's sidestep into television can be seen as evidence of a desire to break new ground, although the medium to which he has turned is infinitely less subtle than the one he has deserted.

Nonetheless, these new paths extending into the future are strewn with obstacles. All originality breeds imitators. Innovation often leads to new conventions; the rebel, however good his cause, may end as a Narcissus. Fascination with the baroque image easily degenerates into 'calligraphism', gratuitous virtuosity, brilliant artifice, complete with the *dive* of our day and age. But insofar as it remains open-ended, receptive to the human kindness which even today constitutes its dominant characteristic and mainstay, the Italian cinema is certain to endure.

Jean-Louis Trintignant, Dominique Sanda in *Il Conformista* (Bertolucci, 1970)

Notes and References

1. The Early Years (1895–1908)

1. Paul Guichonnet, *L'unité italienne*. Presses Universitaires de France, Paris, 1961.
2. Carlo Lizzani, *Il cinema italiano*. Parenti, Florence, 1961.
3. Nino Frank, *Le cinéma dell'arte*. Bonne, Paris, 1951.
4. Georges Sadoul, *Louis Lumière*. Seghers, Paris, 1964.
5. Piero Regnoli, 'Le Vatican figure parmi les pionniers du cinéma', *Revue Internationale du Cinéma*, 1. 1949.
6. On Fregoli see Mario Verdone, *Leopoldo Fregoli*. Palatino, Rome, 1964.
7. Maria Adriana Prolo, *Storia del cinema muto italiano*. Poligono, Milan, 1951.
8. Henri Langlois in *Cahiers du Cinéma*, 33. March 1954.
9. Interview with Georges Sadoul, *Cinéma*. Paris, 1951.
10. Georges Sadoul, *Histoire générale du cinéma*, vol. ii. Denoël, Paris, 1947.
11. Mario Verdone, 'La littérature cinématographique', *Revue du Cinéma*, 13. May 1948.

2. The Golden Age (1909–16)

1. A complete list is given in Maria Adriana Prolo's *Storia del cinema muto italiano*. Poligono, Milan, 1951.
2. Jules Claretie, novelist and theatre director, writing in *Le Temps*; quoted by Georges Sadoul, *Histoire générale du cinéma*, vol. ii. Denoël, Paris, 1947.
3. Frederick Talbot, *Moving Pictures*, Heinemann, London, 1912.
4. L. Bianconi, 'D'Annunzio et le cinéma', *Bianco e Nero*, 11. November 1939. See also Mario Verdone, *Gabriele D'Annunzio nel cinema italiano*. Ateneo, Rome, 1963.
5. The complete text also appears in Marcel Lapierre, *Anthologie du Cinéma*. La Nouvelle Edition, Paris, 1946.
6. Talbot, listed above (3), p. 176.
7. See Henri Langlois, 'Destin du cinéma italien', *Cahiers du Cinéma*, 33. March 1954.
8. Vinicio Marinucci, *Tendenze del cinema italiano*. Unitalia Film, Rome, 1959.

9. Antonio Pietrangeli, 'Panoramique sur le cinéma italien', *Revue du cinéma*, 13. May 1948.
10. Roberto Paolella, *Storia del cinema muto*. Giannini, Napoli, 1956.
11. Georges Sadoul, *Histoire générale du cinéma*, vol. ii. Denoël, Paris, 1947.
12. Langlois, listed above (7).
13. Marinucci, listed above (8).
14. Nino Frank, *Le cinéma dell'arte*. Bonne, Paris, 1951.
15. Antonio Chiatone, *Revue du Cinéma*, 13. May 1948.
16. Langlois, listed above (7).
17. E. A. Reinhardt, *La Vie d'Eleonora Duse*. Paris, 1930.
18. Emilio Ghione, 'La parabole du cinéma italien', *L'Art Cinématographique*, vii. Alcan, Paris, 1930.
19. Mario Verdone, *Revue du Cinéma*, 13. May 1948.
20. The Société Cinématographique des Auteurs et Gens de Lettres, Pathé's production company, set up in 1906 and closed down after the First World War.

3. The Period of Decline (1917–29)

1. Robert Florey, *Cinémagazine*, 39. 1923.
2. Louis Villat, *Histoire de l'Italie*. Grand Mémento Encyclopédique Larousse, Paris, 1936.
3. Antonio Pietrangeli, 'Panoramique sur le cinéma italien', *Revue du Cinéma*, 13. May 1948.
4. Nino Frank, *Le cinéma dell'arte*. Bonne, Paris, 1951.

4. The Cinema under Fascism (1930–43)

1. Carlo Lizzani, *Il Cinema italiano*. Parenti, Florence, 1961.
2. Bardèche and Brasillach, *Histoire du cinéma*. Denoël & Steele, Paris, 1935; numerous subsequent editions.
3. Georges Sadoul, *Histoire générale du cinéma*, vol. iv. Denoël, Paris, 1954.
4. Lizzani, listed above (1).
5. De Santis, quoted by Sadoul, listed above (3).
6. Antonio Pietrangeli, 'Panoramique sur le cinéma italien', *Revue du Cinéma*, 13. May 1948.
7. De Santis, quoted by Sadoul, listed above (3).

5. The Period of Neo-Realism (1943–50)

1. Umberto Barbaro, *Servitudine e grandezza del cinema*. Riuniti, Rome, 1960.
2. *Cahiers du Cinéma*, 93. March 1959.
3. Fabio Carpi, *Cinema italiano del dopoguerra*. Schwarz, Milan, 1958.
4. *Revue du Cinéma*, 13. May 1948.
5. *Cahiers du Cinéma*, listed above (2).
6. Jean-Georges Auriol in *Revue du Cinéma*, 13. May 1948.
7. Raymond Borde and André Bouissy, *Le Néo-réalisme italien*. Cinémathèque Suisse, Lausanne, 1960.

8. Nino Frank, *Le cinéma dell'arte*. Bonne, Paris, 1951.
9. *La Table ronde*, 149. May 1960.
10. Roberto Rossellini, 'Dix ans de cinéma I', *Cahiers du Cinéma*, 50. August–September 1955.
11. François Debreczeni, 'Le Néo-réalisme italien', *Etudes cinématographiques*, 32–3.
12. Nino Frank, listed above (8).
13. Carlo Lizzani, *Il cinema italiano*. Parenti, Florence, 1961.
14. Jean-Georges Auriol, *Revue du Cinéma*, 9. January 1948.
15. Jean Queval, *Radio Cinéma*, 178. 14 June 1953.
16. Georges Sadoul, *Le galop des chevaux fit trembler la terre*. Les Lettres Françaises, 1952.
17. Willy Acher, 'Pour saluer Visconti', *Cahiers du Cinéma*, 57. March 1956.
18. Roberto Rossellini, listed above (10).
19. *L'Ecran Français*. June 1949.
20. *Cahiers du Cinéma*, 14. July-August 1952.
21. André Bazin, *Radio Cinéma*, 133. 3 August 1952.

6. The Masters of a Difficult Decade (1951–9)

1. Quoted by François Debreczeni, 'Le Néo-réalisme italien', *Etudes Cinématographiques*, 32–3.
2. Raymond Borde and André Bouissy, *Le Néo-réalisme italien*. Cinémathèque Suisse, Lausanne, 1960.
3. *Rassegna del film*. 10 January 1953; quoted by Borde and Bouissy.
4. A. J. de Baroncelli, *Le Monde*. 4 March 1955.
5. *Cinémonde*, 844. 9 October 1950.
6. 'Dix ans de Cinema II', *Cahiers du Cinéma*, 52. November 1955.
7. Maurice Schérer, *Cahiers du Cinéma*, 47. May 1955.
8. *Cinémonde*, 943. 3 October 1952.
9. *Cahiers du Cinéma*, 73. July 1957.
10. *Cinéma*. September–October 1957.
11. *Témoignage Chrétien*. September 1955.
12. Interview, *Les Lettres Francaises*. 25 May 1957.
13. J. Doniol-Valcroze, *Cahiers du Cinéma*, 56. February 1956.
14. *Cahiers du Cinéma*, 93. March 1959.
15. Yvonne Baby, *Le Monde*. 16 September 1960.

7. New and Young Cinema (1960–9)

1. *Présence du Cinéma*, 17. Spring 1963.
2. *L'Express*. 5 July 1965.
3. *Sight and Sound*, v. 19 no. 9. January 1951.
4. Raymond Borde and André Bouissy, *Le Néo-réalisme italien*. Cinémathèque Suisse, Lausanne 1960.
5. *Cahiers du Cinéma*, 131. May 1962.
6. *Film 1962*. Feltrinelli, Rome.

Biographical Dictionary

The following is a set of 150 biographies of people who have played a major part in shaping the Italian cinema. They are not necessarily the most famous or the most familiar to the modern reader. I have given pride of place to the earliest producers, directors, actors and technicians, at the expense of certain contemporary figures, notably star actors and actresses, whom I would have been happy to include. This decision has been influenced by the consideration that it is easier for the reader to fill these gaps, if he needs to do so, than to inform himself regarding the directors and *dive* of the golden age.

Alberini, Filoteo (b. Turin, 14 March 1865; d. Rome, 12 April 1937). Technical engineer at the Istituto Geografico Militare; constructed a device which he patented in Dec. 1895 as the Kinetografo. 1901, opened a cinema in Florence, followed in 1904 by one in Rome, the Moderno. The same year, he and Santoni founded a production company which in 1905/6 turned into Cines. Showman, producer, director, continued his researches with the Autosteroscopio (1911) for stereoscopic vision, and the Panoramico Alberini (1914), the first attempt at a wide film, and used in 1923 by Guazzoni in *Il Sacco di Roma*.

Aldo, G.R., pseudonym of Aldo Graziati (b. Scorze, near Treviso, 1 Jan. 1902; d. Albara di Pianiga, near Padua, 14 Nov. 1953). At 20 went to France, took up photography and became an outstanding studio cameraman, notably in films by Carné and Cocteau. After the war, made a documentary, *Couleur de Venise*. Antonioni, who had known him in Paris, introduced him to Visconti, whose director of photography he became in *La Terra Trema* (1948). Responsible for the photography in *Miracolo a Milano* (1951), *Otello*; *Umberto D* (1952), *Stazione Termini*; *La Provinciale* (1953). Killed in a car crash on the Padua–Venice autostrada while working on *Senso*.

Alessandrini, Goffredo (b. Cairo, 9 Sept. 1904). Son of an Italian contractor. Attended an English school. 1928, assistant to Blasetti. 1929, directed a documentary, *La Diga di Maghmod*, in Egypt. 1930, went to Hollywood and supervised Italian versions of M.-G.-M. films. 1931, returned to Italy, made a successful début with a remake of *La Segretaria Privata*. 1932, a spell in Berlin, then back to Italy; *Seconda B* (1934), *Don Bosco* (1935), *Cavalleria* (1936). 1936, married Anna Magnani (separated, 1940). During the Fascist era, made patriotic and colonialist propaganda films, which won him numerous prizes: *Luciano Serra, Pilota* (1937), *Abuna Messias* (1939), *Caravaggio* (1940), *Giarabub*; *Noi Vivi* (1942). 1947, resumed his career: *L'Ebreo Errante, Furia*; *Sangue sul Sagrato* (1950), *Camicie Rosse* (1952). Emigrated to Egypt in 1952, later returning to Italy. *Opinione Pubblica* (1953), *Gli Amanti del Deserto* (1956).

Almirante Manzini, Italia (b. Taranto, 1890; d. São Paulo, Oct. 1941). One of the great stars of the golden age. Went on the stage when very young, moved to the cinema c. 1911: *Cabiria* (1914), *La Figlia della Tempesta* (1916), *Ironia della Vita*; *Maternità* (1917), *Il Matrimonio di Olimpio* (1918), *Passion Tzigane*; *Zingari* (1920), *La Statua di Carne*; *La Grande Passione* (1921), *Sogno d'Amore* (1922), *L'Ombre*; *La Piccola Parrocchia* (1923). Made *Bellezza del Mondo* (1926) and *L'Ultimo dei Bergerac* (1934) with Righelli. Emigrated to Brazil, where she made a successful career in the theatre until her death during the war.

Amato, Giuseppe (b. Naples, 25 Aug. 1899). Producer and director. Of humble origins, worked as a child in several capacities till 1912, when he joined a local company as an actor. 1914, secretary in a production company in Naples. 1917, return to acting: with Lombardo Film, later with Caesar. 1922, producer, writer and cameraman for local films. 1923, assistant to Rex Ingram, who made *Mare Nostrum* in Naples. Emigrated to Hollywood, met with no success, returned to Italy with a view to importing, then began a career as producer. As Peppino, became one of the most popular producers in Italy. Directed several films: *Donne Proibite* (1953), *Gli Ultimi Cinque Minuti* (1955). Produced works by Blasetti (*Quattro Passi fra le Nuvole*, 1942), Emmer (*Parigi è sempre Parigi*, 1951), Rossellini (*Francesco, Giullare di Dio*: *St. Francis of Assisi*, 1950), De Sica, whose career as a director he sponsored (*Rose scarlatte*, 1940; *Umberto D*, 1952), Moguy (*Domani e Troppo Tardi*, 1950), etc.

Ambrosio, Arturo (b. Turin, 1869; d. Rome, 1960). Optician, dealing in photographic equipment. 1904, founded a production company in Turin, with Gandolfi as sponsor and Omegna as cameraman; built the first studio in Turin and made the first Italian films. 1906, first feature films. 1908, founded Ambrosio-Films with Gandolfi, E. M. Pasquali and Arrigo Frusta. 1911, invited to Russia by the Czar to lay the foundations of a national cinema. 1912, returned to Italy, made film versions of D'Annunzio, engaged outstanding actors and actresses (including Eleonora Duse for *Cenere*) and produced numerous films, mainly historical, up to the First World War. Joined forces with G. Reciputi, helped to form U.C.I. Abandoned the cinema for a time, but returned in 1935 to make a documentary in Palestine; 1939–43, took charge of production at Scalera. Retired after the war and died, aged 90, at his retreat at Castelli Romani.

Amidei, Sergio (b. Trieste, 30 Oct. 1904). Began with Fert in 1925; employed in a wide range of capacities: secretary, production supervisor, editor. 1926, worked in Berlin; 1928, in Paris and Nice; 1935, returned to Italy and became a scriptwriter (1938), co-scripting numerous films by Campogalliani, Gallone, Elter, Freda, Poggioli. Took an active part in the neo-realist movement as joint scriptwriter in films by Rossellini (*Roma, Città Aperta*: *Open City*, 1945; *Paisà*, 1946; *La Paura*, 1954; *Il Generale Della Rovere*, 1959; *Era Notte a Roma*; *Viva l'Italia*, 1960), De Sica (*Sciuscià*: *Shoeshine*, 1946), Castellani (*Sotto il Sole di Roma*, 1948), Lizzani (*Cronache di Poveri Amanti*, 1954; *Il Processo di Verona*, 1963; *La Vita Agra*, 1964), Zampa (*Anni Difficili*, 1948; *Anni Ruggenti*, 1962), Emmer (*Domenica d'Agosto*, 1950); several of these produced for Colonna-Film, which he had founded (1949). Still one of the most active scriptwriters in Italy.

Antonioni, Michelangelo (b. Ferrara, 29 Sept.

1912). Studied at Bologna. Difficult start in Rome, on the editorial staff of *Cinema*, short period at the Centro Sperimentale in 1942; collaborated on various scripts before being sent to Paris by Scalera for Carné's co-production *Les Visiteurs du Soir*. 1943, undertook for L.U.C.E. a documentary, *Gente del Po*, partly destroyed as a result of political events. 1947–52, scriptwriter for films by Rossellini, Visconti (not produced), De Santis (*Caccia Tragica*), Fellini (*Lo Sceicco Bianco*), and director of several shorts (*Nettezza Urbana*; *L'Amorosa Menzogna*; *Superstizione*), before making his first full-length film: *Cronaca di un Amore* (1950). The novelty of his thought and style displayed in *I Vinti* (1952), *La Signora senza Camelie* and *Tentato Suicidio* (episode in *L'Amore in Città*) (1953), *Le Amiche* (1955), *Il Grido* (1957). *L'Avventura* (1959) marked a new turning-point and linked him with Monica Vitti, henceforth his ideal interpreter. His latest works have undoubtedly made Antonioni the most modern and controversial director of his generation: *La Notte* (1960), *L'Eclisse* (1962), *Deserto Rosso* (1964), the introduction to *I Tre Volti*, with Soraya (1965), *Blow-Up* (1966), *Zabriskie Point* (U.S.A., 1969).

Arata, Ubaldo (b. Ovada, near Alessandria, 23 March 1895; d. Rome, Dec. 1947). Began as an assistant cameraman at Aquila in 1911, becoming chief cameraman in 1915. Moved to Italia, Fert, Pittaluga (1925–9) and finally to Scalera in 1939, photographing *La Tosca* and *Carmen* for Christian-Jaque. Was also the cameraman on *Roma, Città Aperta* (*Open City*, 1945) and numerous other films: *Maciste all'Inferno* (1925), *La Signora di Tutti* (1934), *Luciano Serra Pilota* (1937), *I Due Foscari* (1942), *La Vita Ricomincia* (1945), *Cagliostro* (1949), etc.

Baldi, Gian Vittorio (b. Bologna, 30 Oct. 1930). Studied law before joining the Centro Sperimentale. Directed the TV series *Cinquant'anni 1898–1948*. Acted in a film by Castellani (*I Sogni nel Cassetto*, 1957). Shorts (many prize-winners at Tours and Venice): *Il Pianto delle Zitelle* (1958), *La Vigilia di Mezza Estate*; *Via dei Canetti Spiriti* (1959), *La Casa delle Vedove*; *Juliano* (1960), *Il Bar de Gigli*; *Il Corredo di Sposa*, episode in *Le Italiane e l'Amore* (*Latin Lovers*, 1961). 1963, made his first full-length film, *Luciano* (never shown). Produced films by young directors (Mingozzi, Amico, etc.). Directed *Le Adolescenti* (1964, episode), *Fuoco* (1968), *La Notte* *dei Fiori* (1970). Producer for Idi Cinematografica since 1962.

Barattolo, Giuseppe (b. Naples, 1881; d. Rome, 20 Aug. 1949). Advocate, Deputy, founded in 1913 a production company which in 1914 became Caesar Film. Helped to inaugurate the star system by launching Francesca Bertini through a publicity campaign and founding Bertini-Film for her. Rivalry, then partnership, with the advocate Mecheri. U.C.I.'s difficulties led to production being abandoned in 1934. Company absorbed in 1938 by Scalera, where he became director of production and built the Scalera studios on the island of Giudecca at Venice. His brother Gaetano (b. Naples, 1888) was also a producer and inspector-general of E.N.I.C.

Barbaro, Umberto (b. Aci Reale, Sicily, 3 Jan. 1902; d. 1959). Writer, theoretician, scriptwriter, director. Literary beginnings: plays, novels (1927-9), journalism. Entered the cinema as director of a short (1933), followed by a full-length film (*L'Ultima Nemica*, 1937), and helped to make two art films: *Carpaccio* (1947) and *Caravaggio* (1948). Collaborated on scripts for De Santis, Alessandrini and Chiarini. Professor at the Centro Sperimentale (1937), he had translations made of the works of Balasz, Pudovkin, Eisenstein, and played a decisive role in inaugurating the neo-realist movement. His theoretical works and writings on aesthetics are authoritative: *Film: Soggetto e Sceneggiatura, Problemi del Film* (with Chiarini), *Poesia del Film, Il Film e il Risarcimento Marxista dell'Arte.* Editor of *Bianco e Nero* from 1945 to 1948.

Bava, Mario (b. San Remo, 31 July 1914). Sculptor's son, cameraman (films by Steno, Monicelli, Soldati, De Robertis, R. Z. Leonard, Emmer, Camerini, Freda, Francisci, Cottafavi). 1959, photographed for Jacques Tourneur *La Battaglia di Maratona*, then turned director: *La Maschera del Demonio* (*Revenge of the Vampire*, 1960), *Ercole al Centro della Terra; Le Meraviglie di Aladino; Gli Invasori* (*Fury of the Vikings*, all 1961), *I Tre Volti della Paura* (*Black Sabbath*, 1963), *Sei Donne per l'Assassino* (*Blood and Black Lace*, 1964), *Terrore nel Spazio* (*Planet of the Vampires*, 1965), *Diabolik* (*Danger*, 1968), *Il Rosso Segno della Follia; Cinque Bambole per la Luna d'Agosto* (1970).

Bellocchio, Marco (b. Piacenza, 1939). Made a rumbustious début in 1965 with *I Pugni in Tasca* (rejected by Venice, a prize-winner at Locarno), which took him straight into first

place in the Italian 'young cinema' establishment. Confirmed his reputation with *La Cina è Vicina* (1967); directed an episode in *Amore e Rabbia* (1967-9); *Nel Nome del Padre* (1971).

Bertini, Francesca, pseudonym of Elena Seracini Vitiello (b. Florence, 11 April 1888). Childhood in Naples, where at 15 she began her career at the Teatro Nuovo. 1904, acted in one of the first experimental films, *La Dea del Mare,* but made her real film début in 1909 with *Il Trovatore* for F.A.I. (Pathé). 1912, engaged by Celio-Film and launched by Negroni. Barattolo soon afterwards made her world-famous as the first *diva.* Numerous films, including *Per la sua Gioia* (1913), *Assunta Spina; La Signora delle Camelie* (1915), *Fedora* (1916), *Tristano e Isotta* (1920). 1920, signed a million-dollar contract with Fox of Hollywood, but broke it to marry a Swiss banker, Count Paul Cartier. After three years of luxurious retirement, resumed her career in Paris, acting in *Odette* by Luitz Morat (1927), *La Possession* by Léonce Perret, *Tu m'appartiens* by Gleize (1929), etc. A great actress in her day, she has reappeared from time to time: in 1943 in Spain; in 1957 in Italy under Simonelli.

Bertolucci, Bernardo (b. Parma, 1941). Son of a poet, and published poetry himself. Assisted Pasolini with *Accattone* (1961), was then entrusted with directing a script by the latter: *La Commare Secca* (1962). *Prima della Rivoluzione* (*Before the Revolution,* 1964), established his reputation. He directed *Agonia,* an episode in *Amore e rabbia* (1967-9) which was performed by the Living Theatre. *Partner* (1969), *Il Conformista* (1970), *La Strategia del Ragno* (for TV, 1970). Has also written scripts for westerns by Sergio Leone.

Bini, Alfredo (b. Leghorn, 1926). Studied medicine in Rome. For two years directed the university theatre, putting on plays by Betti, Calvini, Calendoli, etc. Met Pietro Germi and acted in his film *Il Brigante di Tacca di Lupo* (1952). Gave up medicine and became by turns assistant, associate producer and producer on *Il Bell'Antonio* (1960), *La Viaccia; I Nuovi Angeli; Accattone* (1961), *La Bellezza d'Ippolita; Mamma Roma* (1962), *RoGoPaG; La Corruzione* (1963), *Il Vangelo Secondo Matteo; El Greco* (1964), *La Mandragola* (1965), *Edipo Re* (1967). 1963, married the actress Rosanna Schiaffino.

Blasetti, Alessandro (b. Rome, 3 July 1900). Studied law. Wrote criticism for *L'Impero,* then edited various reviews and soon showed his polemical talents. With Vergano, Solari, Serandrei, Alessandrini and Barbaro founded a film co-operative, Augustus, and in 1929 made his first film, *Sole*, the success of which helped to revive the Italian cinema. Tried various genres with *Resurrectio*; *Nerone*; *Terra Madre* (1930), *Palio* (1931); helped to bridge gap between epochs. Made a professor of direction at C.S.C. in 1935, Blasetti survived the Fascist era, thanks to his wit and irreverence, without sinking to propaganda films. Stage productions of Pirandello, Priestley, Robert Sherwood. In the cinema, tackled every genre; in most of them, directed some works of quality, if not of genius: *1860*, precursor of historical neo-realism (1934), *Vecchia Guardia*; *Aldebaran* (1935), *Ettore Fieramosca*; *Un'avventura di Salvator Rosa* (1939), *La Corona di Ferro*, which carried historical baroque to the point of burlesque (1940), *La Cena della· Beffe* (1941), *Quattro Passi fra le Nuvole*, the product of a new kind of cinema (1942), *Un Giorno nella Vita* (1946), *Fabiola* (1948), *Prima Comunione* (1950), *Altri Tempi* (1952), *Tempi Nostri* (1953), *Peccato che sia una Canaglia* (*'Tis Pity She's a Whore*, 1954), *La Fortuna di Essere Donna* (1956), *Europa di Notte* (1958), *Io amo, tu ami* (1961), *Liolà* and an episode in *Les Quatre Vérités* (1963), *Io, Io, Io e . . . gli Altri* (1965), *La Ragazza del Bersagliere* (1966), *Simon Bolivar* (1969). For TV: *La Lunga Strada del Ritorno* (1962).

Bolognini, Mauro (b. Pistoia, 1923). Studied architecture in Florence and set design at C.S.C. (1949). Assistant to Zampa, then, in France, to Yves Allégret and Delannoy. Undistinguished début as a director with *Ci Troviamo in Galleria* (1953), *I Cavalieri della Regina* (1954) and *La Vena d'Oro* (1955), the first and third being parts of TV serials. 1955, notoriety with *Gli Innamorati*, a comedy that turned him towards a kind of optimistic neo-realism exemplified by *Marisa, la Civetta* (1957), *Giovani Mariti* (1958), then a series of films adapted from novels by Pasolini (*La Notte Brava*, 1959; *Giornata Balorda*, 1960), Brancati (*Il Bell'Antonio*, 1960), Pratesi (*La Viaccia*, 1961), Svevo (*Senilità*, 1962), Moravia (*Agostino*, 1962). *La Corruzione* (1963), *La Donna è una cosa Meravigliosa*; *La mia Signora* (1964), *Madamigella di Maupin* (1965), and episodes in *Le Bambole*; *I Tre Volti* (1965), *Le Fate* and *Le Streghe* (1966). *Arabella* (1967), *Un Bellissimo Novembre* (1968), *L'Assoluto Naturale* (1969), *Metello*

(1970), *Bubu di Montparnasse* (1971).

Bonnard, Mario (b. Rome, 21 July 1889). 1909, début as an actor, as partner to the most famous *dive*. Without abandoning acting, progressed to direction and made a number of films (some in France or Germany, including *Il Tacchino*, 1923, and *Teodoro e Socio*, 1924). 1935, resumed work in Italy. Some forty commercial films, sentimental comedies, *populiste* and historical dramas: *Il Ponte dei Sospiri*; *Marco Visconti* (1940), *Il Re si Diverte* (1941), *Rossini* and *Avanti, c'è Posto*, in which he launched Aldo Fabrizi (1942), *Campo de' Fiori*, with Magnani (1943), *Il Ratto delle Sabine* (1945), *Addio mia bella Napoli* (1946), *La Città Dolente*, where he tried his hand at neo-realism (1949), *Margherita da Cortona* (1950), *Frine, Cortigiana d'Oriente* (1953), *La Ladra* (1955), *La Venere di Cheronea* (1958), *Gli Ultimi Giorni di Pompei* (1959), *I Masnadieri* (1961), etc.

Bonzi, Count Leonardo. Davis Cup player, Olympic skiing champion and the holder of world records as a pilot before taking part in eight major expeditions in Greenland, Turkestan, Iran, the Sahara, Brazil, South-East Asia – explorations leading to films. Produced or directed *Una Lettera dall'Africa* (1952), *Magia Verde* (1953), *Continente Perduto* (1955), and, with Lizzani, *La Muraglia Cinese* (*Behind the Great Wall*, 1958).

Borelli, Lyda (b. Rivarolo Ligure, 1884; d. Rome, 2 June 1959). One of the most famous of the *dive*. 1901, worked for Francesco Pasta's company; subsequently for various other theatre groups. 1904, at Milan, played in the stage première of D'Annunzio's *La Figlia di Iorio*. 1908, first film parts. 1913, triumph with *L'Amor mio non Muore*. Took the lead in screen versions of Henri Bataille (*La Donna Nuda*, 1914; *Marcia Nuziale*, 1915; *La Vergine Folle*, 1915) and numerous other films, creating a type of woman tormented by violent passions. 1917, formed a company together with Ugo Piperno, but in July 1918 married an industrialist, Vittorio Cini, and gave up her career.

Bose, Lucia (b. Milan, 28 Jan. 1931). At 14 a typist in a lawyer's office, then a shop-assistant in a cake-shop. Miss Italy, 1947. 1949, acted in De Santis's *Non c'è Pace tra gli Ulivi*. 1950, Antonioni's *Cronaca di un Amore* guarantees her career. Acted in *Parigi è sempre Parigi* (1951), *Roma, Ore II* (1952), *La Signora senza Camelie* (1953), Bardem's *Muerte di un Ciclista*; *Gli Sbandati* (1954), Buñuel's *Cela s'appelle l'Aurore* (1955).

Married the famous *torero* Miguel Dominguin and for many years deprived the Italian cinema of one of its best actresses, though she appeared in Cocteau's *Le Testament d'Orphée* (1959). Later resumed her career in Italy: *Sotto il Segno dello Scorpione* (1968), *Satyricon* (1969), *Ciao, Gulliver* (1970), *L'Ospite* (1971).

Brass, Tinto (b. Milan, 1933). Followed his father into law, then went to Paris, where he worked at the Cinémathèque and met the members of the *nouvelle vague*. Collaborated with Rossellini (*India*, 1958) and Joris Ivens. First film in 1963: *Chi Lavoro è Perduto*; followed by an episode in *La Mia Signora* and *Il Fiume della Rivolta* (1964), a documentary on contemporary rebellions. Has tried various genres, including the short film (*Il Disco Volante: The Flying Saucer*, 1965) and the western (*Yankee*, 1966). *Col Cuore in Gola* (1967). In London, made *L'Urlo* (1968) and *Nero su Bianco* (on the racial problem, 1969). *Dropout* (1970), *La Vacanza* (1971).

Calamai, Clara (b. Prato, 7 Sept. 1915). Début in 1938. Made a reputation in dramatic roles, notably in Blasetti's *Ettore Fieramosca* (1939). Appeared also in *Caravaggio* (1940), *Luce nelle Tenebre*; *La Regina di Navarra* (1941), *Le Capitaine Fracasse* (1942). Visconti's *Ossessione* (1942) showed her in a new light and won her a more lasting fame. Later films mostly of second rank. Visconti gave her a part in *Le Notti Bianche* (1957).

Camerini, Mario (b. Rome, 6 Feb. 1895). Studied law; 1914–18, officer in light infantry. 1920, scriptwriter and assistant to his cousin, Augusto Genina. His first silent films were *Jolly, Clown da Circo* (1923) and *Kiff Tebbi* (1927). *Rotaie* (1929) showed a feeling for truth rare at that period. After a brief spell at Paramount's St.-Maurice studios (1930) confirmed his gifts with *Gli Uomini, che Mascalzoni!* (1932), *T'Amerò Sempre* (1933), *Il Cappello a tre Punte* (1934), *Darò un Millione* (1935), *Il Signor Max* (1937), pleasant comedies which established Vittorio De Sica as a leading young actor. There followed *Batticuore* (1938), *Grandi Magazzini* (1939), *Una Romantica Avventura* (1940), *I Promessi Sposi* (1941), *Una Storia d'Amore* (1942). *Due Lettere Anonime* (1945) tackles the theme of the Resistance. After the war Camerini was content to direct a variety of commercial films: *La Figlia del Capitano* (1947), *Il Brigante Musolino* (1950), *Ulisse* (1954), *La Bella Mugnaia* (1955), *Suor Letizia* (1956), *Vacanze a Ischia* (*One Week with Love*, 1957),

Crimen (*Killing in Monte Carlo*), *Via Margutta* (*Run with the Devil*, 1960), *I Briganti Italiani* (*Seduction of the South*, 1961), *Kali Yug la Dea della Vendetta* (1963), *Il Misterio del Tempio Indiano* (1964), *Delitto quasi Perfetto* (*Imperfect Crime*, 1966).

Campogalliani, Carlo (b. Concordia, near Modena, 10 Oct. 1885). Self-educated, attracted by decoration and the theatre. Joined a company and made his screen début as an actor in 1910: *Re Lear*, by De Liguoro. 1913, Ambrosio let him direct his first film. Directed and acted in numerous films, often with Letizia Quaranta, whom he married. An athletic and fearless actor, he left Italy during the crisis in the 1920s for Brazil and the Argentine where, a pioneer in an embryonic cinema, he made several films (1925–6). The advent of sound brought him back to Europe: to Germany (one film in Berlin), then Italy, where he resumed his career, making, notably, *Montevergine* (*La Grande Luce*, 1938), and, in recent years, numerous costume films, e.g. *Capitan Fuoco* (1958), *Il Terrore dei Barbari* (*Goliath and the Barbarians*, 1959), *Il Ponte dei Sospiri* and several films featuring Maciste, whom in 1918–19 he had helped to create.

Canudo, Ricciotto (b. Gioia del Colle, near Bari, 2 Jan. 1879; d. Paris, 10 Nov. 1923). Critic and aesthetician, writing in French. 1902, arrived Paris, wrote essays, published three novels (1910–12), was an intimate of Picasso, Paul Adam, Ravel, Rodin, Dufy, Max Jacob, Romain Rolland, Carco and Apollinaire; his famous Montjoie garret was an active centre of *avant-garde* art and literature. During the war, fought in Argonne, was wounded in Macedonia, wrote war poetry and prose. Presently the cinema fired his imagination, and he became the leading aesthetician of what he christened 'the seventh art'. Founded the Club des Amis du Septième Art. Writings on the cinema were collected posthumously in 1927 by Fernand Divoire in *L'Usine aux Images*. 1922, published a novel, *L'Autre Aile*. Henri Fescourt has given a vivid picture of Canudo in *La Foi et les Montagnes*.

Cardinale, Claudia (b. Tunis, 15 April 1939). A beauty competition elected her 'the most beautiful Italian girl in Tunis' and enabled her to arrive in Venice during the Festival. Back in Tunis, acted in Jacques Baratier's *Goha* (1957), then signed a contract with Franco Cristaldi, who got her a part in an American co-production, *I Soliti Ignoti* (*Big Deal on Madonna Street*, 1958). An international star whose numerous films include *La Prima Notte*; *Un Maledetto Imbroglio* (*A Sordid Affair*, 1959), *Il Bell'Antonio*; *Austerlitz*; *I Delfini*; *La Ragazza con la Valigia*; *Rocco e i suoi Fratelli* (1960), *La Viaccia*; *Cartouche* (in France, 1961), *Senilità* (1962), *Otto e Mezzo*; *Il Gattopardo*; *La Ragazza di Bube* (*Bebo's Girl*, 1963), *The Pink Panther* (U.S.A.), *The Magnificent Showman* (in Spain), *Gli Indifferenti*; *Il Cornuto Magnifico* (1964), *Vaghe stelle dell'Orsa* (1965), *Le Fate* (1966), *Una Rosa per Tutto*; *Il Giorno della Civetta* (1967), *The Adventures of Gerard*; *L'Udienza* (1970).

Caserini, Mario (b. Rome, 1874; d. Rome, 17 Nov. 1920). Originally a painter who attempted every genre; became one of the most prolific directors of the golden age. Between 1908 and 1920 made for Cines and Ambrosio some 73 films, of which several added considerable lustre to the Italian cinema: *Romeo e Giulietta* (1908), *Giovanna d'Arco*; *Macbeth* (sold to U.S.A. for 10,000 dollars), *Beatrice Cenci*; *I Tre Moschettieri* (50 copies in U.K., 1909), *Amleto*; *Anita Garibaldi*; *Il Cid*; *Catilina*; *Lucrezia Borgia* (1910), *Santarellina* (*Mam'zelle Nitouche*), *L'Ultimo dei Frontignac*; *Mademoiselle de Scudéry* (1911), *I Cavalieri di Rodi*; *I Mille*; *Dante e Beatrice*; *Parsifal*; *Siegfried*; *Infamia Araba* (1912), *Gli Ultimi Giorni di Pompei*; *Il Treno degli Spettri*; *Nerone e Agrippina*; *L'Amor mio non Muore* (1913), *La Gorgona* (1914), *Resurrezione*; *Capitan Fracassa* (1917), *Anima Tormentata* (1919), *Fiori d'Arancio* (1920).

Castellani, Renato (b. Finale Ligure, 4 Sept. 1913). Spent part of his childhood in the Argentine where his parents were settled; studied architecture at Milan but presently entered the cinema as a scriptwriter with Camerini, Soldati and Blasetti (*La Corona di Ferro*, 1940). His first film, *Un Colpo di Pistola* (1941), and still more *Zaza* (1943), placed him among the 'calligraphers'. There followed *La Donna della Montagna* (1943), *Mio Figlio Professore* (1946), both marking a step forward, and finally three dynamic films, full of humour and observation, which made him world-famous: *Sotto il Sole di Roma* (1948), *E Primavera* (*Springtime*, 1949), and *Due Soldi di Speranza* (1952), his most original works. *Giulietta e Romeo* (1954) confirmed his position, but despite some excellent qualities he never recovered the wit and vigour of style which inspired his neo-realist films. *I Sogni nel Cassetto* (1957), *Nella Città l'Inferno* (1959),

Il Brigante (1961), *Mare Matto* (1962), episodes in *Tre Notti d'Amore* and *Controsesso* (1964), *Questi Fantasmi* (1967), *Una Breva Stagione* (1969).

Cecchi d'Amico, Suso (b. Rome, 21 July 1914). Daughter of Emilio Cecchi, author and scriptwriter. Herself a translator and journalist, entered the cinema by working with the novelist Flaiano on the script of Castellani's *Mio Figlio Professore* (1946), then on that of *Vivere in Pace* (1947). Was soon helping the best scriptwriters and directors in adaptations of a wide range of works, including many outstanding Italian films: *Il Delitto di Giovanni Episcopo* (1947), *Ladri di Biciclette* (1948), *E Primavera* (1949), *Miracolo a Milano*; *Bellissima* (1951), *I Vinti* (1952), *La Signora senza Camelie* (1953), *Senso* (1954), *Le Amiche* (1955), *Le Notti Bianche*; *La Sfida* (1957), *Rocco e i suoi Fratelli* (1960), *Boccaccio '70*; *Salvatore Giuliano* (1962), *Il Gattopardo*; *Les Quatre Vérités* (1963), *Gli Indifferenti* (1964), *Vaghe Stelle dell'Orsa* (1965), etc.

Cervi, Gino (b. Bologna, 3 May 1901). Son of a theatre critic, entered the theatrical profession as a member of Alda Borelli's troupe, joining the Pirandello Company two years later. 1932, film début. 1933, *T'Amerò Sempre*. 1935, first major success: *Aldebaran*. Became Blasetti's favourite actor: *Ettore Fieramosca*; *Un'Avventura di Salvator Rosa* (1939), *La Corona di Ferro* (1940), above all *Quattro Passi fra le Nuvole* (1942). Alternating between theatre and cinema, equally at home with historic figures and ordinary characters, Cervi has acted in numerous films, including *Senza Famiglia* (1944), *Daniele Cortis* (1947), *Donne senza Nome* (1950), *Il Cristo Proibito* (1951), the *Don Camillo* series (as the famous militant communist Peppone), *La Signora senza Camelie*; *Stazione Termini* (1953), *La Maja Desnuda* (1958). Has also made films in France (*Quelle Joie de Vivre!*, 1961; *Le Crime ne paie pas*, 1962) and England (*Becket*, 1964).

Checchi, Andrea (b. Florence, 21 Oct. 1916). Accademia di Belle Arti, drama course under Blasetti, in whose *1860* (1934) and *Vecchia Guardia* (1935) she began her career. Established her popularity with *L'Assedio dell'Alcazar* (1940), followed by numerous films: *Via delle Cinque Lune* (1941), *Malombra*; *Giacomo l'Idealista* (1942), *Due Lettere Anonime* (1945), *Roma, Città Libera* (1946), *Caccia Tragica*; *I Fratelli Karamazoff* (1947), *Au-delà des Grilles* (*Le Mura di Malapaga*, 1948), *Achtung! Banditi!* (1952), *La Signora* *senza Camelie* (1953), *Casa Ricordi* (1954), specializing in suspect or equivocal characters. Later films include *La Lunga Notte del '43*; *La Ciociara* (*Two Women*, 1960), *L'Assassino*; *L'Oro di Roma* (1961), *Il Processo di Verona* (1963), *Italiani Brava Gente* (1964).

Chiarini, Luigi (b. Rome, 20 June 1900). Studied law. Literary critic. 1935, appointed director of Centro Sperimentale di Cinematografia, holding this post till 1943; founded *Bianco e Nero* (1937) and edited it till 1951. Vice-president of C.S.C., 1947–50. In 1959, appointed to a chair in film history and criticism at Pisa. 1963–9, director of the Venice film festival to whose character and objects he gave new life. A theoretician, Chiarini has co-scripted various films, e.g. *Stazione Termini* (1953), and directed several others, including *Via delle Cinque Lune* (1941), *La Bella Addormentata* (*The Sleeping Beauty*, 1942), *La Locandiera* (adapted from Goldoni, 1944), *Ultimo Amore* (1946), *Patto col Diavolo* (1948). Principal writings: *Problemi del film* (with Umberto Barbaro, 1939), *Cinque capitoli sul film* (1941), *Il film nei problemi dell'Arte* (1949), *Il film nella battaglia delle idee* (1954), *Arte e tecnica del film* (1962).

Cicognini, Alessandro (b. Pescara, 25 Jan. 1906). Composer, began working for the cinema in 1936 with Palermi's *Il Corsaro Nero*. Became De Sica's accredited collaborator during his neo-realist period: *Sciuscià* (*Shoe-shine*, 1946), *Ladri di Biciclette* (1948), *Miracolo a Milano* (1951), *Umberto D* (1952), *Stazione Termini* (1953), *L'Oro di Napoli* (1954). Other scores: *Due Soldi di Speranza* (1952), *Ulisse*; *Peccato che sia una Canaglia* (1954).

Comencini, Luigi (b. Salo, near Brescia, 8 June 1916). Studied architecture in France. With Lattuada, laid the foundations of the Cineteca Italiana in Milan. Journalist and scriptwriter, turned director with a short documentary, *Bambini in Città* (1946). The theme of youth recurred in his first major film, *Proibito Rubare* (1948), followed by more commercial works: *L'Imperatore di Capri* (1949), *Heidi* (in Switzerland, 1952), *Pane, Amore e Fantasia* (1953), which made him famous, *Pane, Amore e Gelosia* (1954), *La Bella di Roma* (1955), *La Finestra sul Luna Park* (1957), *Tutti a Casa* (1960), *La Ragazza di Bube* (1963), episodes in *Tre Notti d'Amore*; *La mia Signora* (1964) and *Le Bambole*; *La Bugiarda* (1965), *Incompreso* (1966), *Italian Secret Service* (1967), *Casanova* (1969), *Senza Sapere Niente di Lei* (1969)

Cottafavi, Vittorio (b. Modena, 30 Jan. 1914). Studied law, literature and philosophy in Rome. 1938, C.S.C. diploma. Scriptwriter and assistant to Vergano, De Sica and Blasetti. Directed as his first film an adaptation of an Ugo Betti play, *I Nostri Sogni* (1943). Moved from drama to the cloak-and-dagger film (*Il Boia di Lilla*, or *La Vita Avventuriosa di Milady*: *Milady and the Musketeers*, 1952), from documentary (*Fiesta Brava*, 1955) to the mythological film, which he often managed to endow with his own virtues. Was one of the champions of 'neo-mythologism'. 1956, after a course in Paris with R.T.F. (now O.R.T.F.), broadcast literary and theatrical adaptations on Italian radio. Main films: *La Fiamma che non si Spegne* (1949), *Una Donna ha Ucciso* (1951), *Il Cavaliere di Maison Rouge*; *Traviata '53* (1953), *Una Donna Libera* (1954), *La Rivolta dei Gladiatori* (*The Revolt of the Gladiators*, 1958), *Le Legioni di Cleopatra* (1959), *Messalina, Venere Imperatrice*; *La Vendetta di Ercole* (1960), *Ercole alla conquista di Atlantide* (*Hercules Conquers Atlantis*, 1961), *I Cento Cavalieri* (*The Hundred Horsemen*, 1964). Switched to television and directed a number of classics.

Cristaldi, Franco (b. Turin, 3 Oct. 1924). Studied law. Produced documentaries, then (1953) full-length films. President of Vides. *La Pattuglia Sperduta* (1954), *Un Eroe dei Nostri Tempi* (1955), *Kean*; *Le Notti Bianche*; *La Sfida*; *L'Uomo di Paglia* (1957), *Un Ettaro di Cielo*; *La Legge è Legge* (1958), *I Delfini*; *Kapò* (1960), *L'Assassino*; *Divorzio all'Italiana* (1961), *Salvatore Giuliano*; *Mare Matto* (1962), *I Compagni* (*The Organizer*); *Omicron*; *La Ragazza di Bube*; *Sedotta e Abbandonata* (1963), *Gli Indifferenti* (1964), *Vaghe Stelle dell'Orsa* (1965). 1966, president of the Italian film producers' union.

D'Ambra, Lucio, pseudonym of Renato Eduardo Manganella (b. Rome, 1 Nov. 1880; d. Rome, 31 Dec. 1939). Teacher, author, playwright, journalist; then became a script-writer for F.A.I. with films directed by Gallone and Genina. Success enabled him to turn director: *Il Re, le Torri, gli Alfieri* (1916). 'The Goldoni of the Italian cinema', he excelled in light comedy, whether as scriptwriter or director: *Napoleoncina*; *Carnavalesca* (1917), *Il Girotondo degli Undici Lancieri* (1918), *Il Bacio di Cirano* (1919), *I Sette Peccati Capitali* (series, 1919–20), *La Falsa Amante* (1920), *Tragedia su Tre Carte*; *Nemesis* (1921). Theatre critic; and in 1920 inaugurated 'the book of the film' with his Romanzo Film series, and gave up the cinema, returning in 1935 as scriptwriter and supervisor of several films.

Damiani, Damiano (b. Pasiano, near Udine, 23 July 1922). Accademia di Belle Arti, Milan. 1946–56, short documentaries. Co-scripted *Cronache di Poveri Amanti* (1954), *I Misteri di Parigi* (1957), *Erode il Grande* (1959); worked with Zavattini. Moved on to direction: *Il Rossetto* (1960), *Il Sicario* (1961), *L'Isola di Arturo* (1962), *La Rimpatriata*; *La Noia* (*The Empty Canvas*, 1963), *Le Ho Amate Tutte* (1965), *La Strega in Amore* (1966), *Il Giorno della Civetta* (1967), *Una Ragazza piuttosto Complicata* (1969), *La Moglie più bella* (1970), *Confessione di un Commissario di Polizia al Procuratore della Republica* (1971).

D'Annunzio, Gabriele (b. Pescara, 12 March 1863; d. Gardone Riviera, 1 March 1938). Poet, dramatist (*La Città Morta*; *Francesca da Rimini*; *La Nave*; *Le Martyre de Saint Sébastien*; *La Figlia di Iorio*), novelist (*Il Piacere*; *Le Vergini delle Rocce*; *Il Fuoco*; *La Leda senza Cigno*). From 1911, most of his works were adapted for the screen by Arrigo Frusta for Ambrosio. At Pastrone's request he put his name to the script and edited the sub-titles for *Cabiria* (1914); Pastrone also made *Il Fuoco* (1915). But D'Annunzio took little interest in these adaptations. 1914–18, action in the Navy and Air Force. 1919, Sept., seized Fiume in protest against Allied decisions. 1920, retired to his property of Vittoriale near Lake Garda, where he continued to write. His influence on the cinema of his age, rather than the screen adaptation of his own works, earned D'Annunzio an important place in the history of the golden age of the Italian cinema.

De Bosio, Gianfranco (b. Verona, 16 Sept. 1923). Studied at Padua, where he directed the university theatre. 1954, with Diego Fabbri, founded the Nuovo Teatro company, putting on plays in Trieste, Asti, Ferrara, even Paris during the international festival. Now director of the Teatro Stabile di Torino. 1963, at Venice, showed his first film, *Il Terrorista*.

De Filippo, Eduardo, pseudonym of Eduardo Pasarelli (b. Naples, 24 May 1900). Son of a famous Neapolitan actor, lived in the theatre from childhood, as did his sister Titina and his brother Peppino. At 13 joined the famous dialect company of Eduardo Scarpetta. 1932, with his brother and sister, founded an enormously successful company. Pride of

Naples, actor, dramatist, theatrical producer who staged the plays of his master Scarpetta, with traditional Neapolitan masks. Stage successes led him to the cinema with *In Campagna è Caduta una Stella* (1942). *Napoli Milionaria* (1950), adapted from one of his plays, was an international hit. Other films: *Filumena Marturano* (1951), two episodes in *I Sette Peccati Capitali* (1952), *Napolitani a Milano* (1953), *Questi Fantasmi* (1954), *Fortunella* (1958), in most of which he acted as well as directing. Acted also in numerous other films, notably *Villa Borghese* (1953), *L'Oro di Napoli* (1954), *Tutti a Casa* (1960), *Ieri, Oggi, Domani*; *Matrimonio all'Italiana* (1964).

De Laurentiis, Dino (b. Tore Annunziata, near Naples, 8 August 1919). C.S.C. Began as an actor. 1938–9, associate producer. 1946–9, produced for Lux *Il Bandito* (1946), *La Figlia del Capitano* (1947), *Riso Amaro* (1948), *Il Lupo della Sila* (1950), and on his own account *Napoli Milionaria* (1950) and several others. 1950, joined Carlo Ponti in founding under their names a company that produced several major films: *Guardie e Ladri* (*Cops and Robbers*, 1951), *Europa 51* (1952), *Ulisse*; *L'Oro di Napoli* (1954), *War and Peace*; *Le Notti di Cabiria* (*Cabiria*, both 1956), *Fortunella* (1958). The company broke up in 1957, but De Laurentiis continued producing films in collaboration with other international firms: *La Diga sul Pacifico* (*The Sea-Wall*, 1957), *La Tempesta* (1958), *La Grande Guerra* (1959), *Il Gobbo* (*The Hunchback of Rome*, 1960), *Barabbas*; *Il Giudizio Universale* (*The Last Judgement*, 1961), *Il Mafioso* (1962), *L'Immortale*; *Il Boom* (1963), the monumental film version of the Bible, and *Waterloo* (1970). He remains one of the giants of the Italian film industry.

Del Duca, Cino (b. Montedinove, 25 July 1899). Came to France around 1932 and made his name as a publisher of books and sentimental magazines, launching numerous series and periodicals before turning in 1953 to film production. Financed films by Becker (*Touchez pas au Grisbi*, 1954), Carné (*L'Air de Paris*, 1954), Autant-Lara (*Marguerite de la Nuit*, 1955), and took over the production of *L'Avventura* (1959), enabling it to be completed. Other Italian productions include *Accattone* (1961). Founded the Milan daily *Il Giorno*.

De Liguoro, Giuseppe (b. Naples, 10 Jan. 1869; d. Rome, 19 March 1944). Stage and film actor and director: *Il Conte Ugolino*;

L'Inferno (1909), based on Dante, with De Liguoro playing a number of parts. Specialized in historical and similar films: *Marin Faliero, Doge di Venezia* (1909), *Sardanapolo Re dell'Assiria*; *Re Lear*; *Charles X*; *La Cena dei Borgia*; *Edipo Re* (1910), *L'Odissea*; *Burgos*; *San Sebastiano* (1911), *Giuseppe Verdi nella Vita e nella Gloria* (1913), *Fedora* (1916), *Lorenzaccio* (1918). Retired in 1924, except for a short documentary in 1931.

De Robertis, Francesco (b. San Marco in Lamis, near Foggia, 16 Oct. 1902; d. Rome, 3 Feb. 1959). Naval academy at Leghorn. Naval officer, playwright and theatrical producer; appointed head of the naval cinematographic service. 1939, directed a documentary, *Mine in Vista*, followed by *Uomini sul Fondo* (*S.O.S. 103*, 1941), played by a submarine crew and directed with an austerity that opened one of the paths to a new cinema. Supervised Rossellini's first film, *La Nave Bianca* (*The Hospital Ship*, 1941) and directed in the same vein *Alfa-tau* (1942), *Marinai senza Stelle* and *Uomini e Cieli* (1943). 1943–5, in Venice, organizing the cinema of the Fascist Republic. Later directed some films with conventional plots: *La Vita Semplice* (*I Figli della Laguna*, 1945), *Il Mulatto* (1949), *Gli Amanti di Ravello* (1951), *Carica Eroica* (1952), *Mizar* (1953), *La Donna che venne del Mare* (1957).

De Santis, Giuseppe (b. Fondi, 11 Feb. 1917). Studied literature and philosophy. Contributor to *Cinema*, denouncing the shortcomings of the contemporary Italian cinema and demanding a new realism. C.S.C.: began as a scriptwriter with Visconti (*Ossessione*, 1942), then as assistant to Vergano. Directed *Caccia Tragica* (1947), *Riso Amaro* (1948), *Non c'è Pace tra gli Ulivi* (1949), *Roma, Ore 11* (1952), *Un Marito per Anna Zaccheo* (1953), in all of which he dealt with social problems, his treatment somewhat marred by the demands of the plot. There followed *Giorni d'Amore* (1954), *Uomini e Lupi* (1956), *La Strada da Lunga un Anno* (in Jugoslavia, 1958), *La Garconnière* (1960), *Italiani Brava Gente* (Russian co-production, 1964).

De Seta, Vittorio (b. Palermo, 15 Oct. 1923). Studied architecture. Co-scriptwriter and assistant to Le Chanois in *Vacanze d'Amore* (1953). 1954–9, nine short documentaries, including *Isole di Fuoco* (1954), *Contadini del Mare* (1955), *Pastori di Orgosolo* (1958), *I Dimenticati* (1959). Spent several months in Sardinia and used the shepherds in making the truthful *Banditi a Orgosolo* (1961). Co-scripted

Vacanze a Ischia (1957). Latest films: *Un Uomo a Metà* (1965), *L'Invitata* (1969).

De Sica, Vittorio (b. Sora, 7 July 1901). Neapolitan on father's side; childhood in Naples. Impoverished bourgeois, worked in an office, but soon took off for the theatre. Acted in musical comedy, vaudeville, music-hall; success everywhere allowed him, from 1928, a brilliant career in films as a juvenile lead, his popularity dating from Camerini's *Gli Uomini, che Mascalzoni!* (1932). Turned director with *Rose Scarlatte* (1940) and made several successful comedies in which he also acted: *Maddalena Zero in Condotta* (1940), *Teresa Venerdì* (1941), *Un Garibaldino al Convento* (1942). Meeting with Zavattini turned him towards more serious subjects: *I Bambini ci Guardano* (1943), *La Porta del Cielo* (1945), and finally his great neo-realist works: *Sciuscià* (*Shoeshine*, 1946), *Ladri di Biciclette* (*Bicycle Thieves*, 1948), *Miracolo a Milano* (1951), *Umberto D* (1952), *Stazione Termini* (*Indiscretion of an American Wife*, 1953), *L'Oro di Napoli* (1954), *Il Tetto* (1956), marking a wide range of preoccupations. The 150 or so films in which he has acted include *Roma, Città Libera* (1946), *Madame de . . .* (1953), the *Pane, Amore . . .* series (1953–5) and *Il Generale Della Rovere* (1959). After a break of several years De Sica returned to directing in collaboration with Zavattini: *La Ciociara* (*Two Women*, 1960), *Il Giudizio Universale* (*The Last Judgement*, 1961), an episode in *Boccaccio '70*; *I Sequestrati di Altona* (*The Condemned of Altona*, 1962); often mediocre. The remarkable commercial success of *Ieri, Oggi, Domani* (*Yesterday, Today and Tomorrow*) and *Matrimonio all'Italiana* (*Marriage Italian Style*, 1964) have not deterred their creators from returning to something more like their former interests in *Un Mondo Nuovo* (1965) and *Le Streghe* (1966). Later films: *Caccia alla Volpe* (*After the Fox*, 1966), *Amanti* (*A Place for Lovers*, 1968), *Il Girasoli* (*Sunflower*, 1969), *Il Giardino dei Finzi-Contini* (1970), and an episode in *Le Coppie*.

Di Venanzo, Gianni (b. Teramo, 18 Dec. 1920; d. Feb. 1966). One of the outstanding Italian cameramen. Began as assistant to Arata, Martelli, Tonti. Responsible for the photography in *Achtung! Banditi!*; *Ai Margini della Metropoli* (1952), *Cronache di Poveri Amanti*; *Le Ragazze di San Frediano*; *Gli Sbandati* (1954), *Lo Scapolo* (1956), *Kean* (1957), *La Legge è Legge* (1958), *I Delfini* (1960), Losey's *Eva* (*Eve*, 1962), *La Ragazza di Bube* (1963),

Gli Indifferenti (1964); and above all in the films of Antonioni – episode in *L'Amore in Città* (1953), *Le Amiche* (1955), *Il Grido* (1957), *La Notte* (1960), *L'Eclisse* (1962); of Rosi – *La Sfida* (1957), *Salvatore Giuliano* (1962), *Le Mani sulla Città* (1963), *Il Momento della Verità* (1964); and of Fellini – *Otto e Mezzo* (1963), *Giulietta degli Spiriti* (1965). Died prematurely, aged 45.

Emmer, Luciano (b. Milan, 19 Jan. 1918). Law studies abandoned in favour of the cinema, beginning with Enrico Gras on the art documentary, a formula which he completely renovated: *Racconto da un Fresco* (on Giotto, 1941), *Il Cantico delle Creature* (1943), *Il Paradiso Terrestre* (on Bosch, 1946), *Leonardo da Vinci* (1952); also a remarkable documentary on the Allied cemeteries in Italy, *Bianchi Pascoli*; *Romantici a Venezia* (1948), *Isole nella Laguna* (1949). First full-length film, *Domenica d'Agosto* (1950) showed that neorealism could embrace humour. Subsequent films show a falling off: *Parigi è sempre Parigi* (1951), *Le Ragazze di Piazza di Spagna* (*Three Girls from Rome*, 1952), *Terza Liceo* (*High School*, 1953), *Camilla* (1954), *Il Bigamo* (1956), *Il Momento più Bello* (1957), *Paradiso terrestre* (*Ritual of Love*, 1959; a mediocre montage of 16 mm. exotic films), *La Ragazza in Vetrina* (*The Girl in the Window*, 1960). Also a film on ˌPicasso (1954).

Fabrizi, Aldo (b. Rome, 1 Nov. 1905). Variety actor, originally in suburban Roman music-halls, where he rapidly became popular. After a spell in radio, in 1942 made his film début in character parts. The part of the priest in *Roma, Città Aperta* (*Open City*, 1945) opened up his career, and he acted in numerous films, specializing in demotic characters, truculent or good-natured: *Vivere in Pace* (1947), *Prima Comunione*; *Francesco, Giullare di Dio* (*St. Francis of Assisi*, 1950), *Guardie e Ladri* (*Cops and Robbers*, 1951), *Altri Tempi* (*Times Gone By*, 1952), *Cento Anni d'Amore* (1954). In the Argentine, directed *Emigrantes* (1949), and made a dozen or so further films of average quality, including *Il Maestro* (1958). Recently appeared in guest role in *Cose di 'Cosa Nostra'* (1971).

Fellini, Federico (b. Rimini, 20 Jan. 1920). Wrote and drew strip cartoons in Florence, then became a cartoonist in Rome. Engaged by Aldo Fabrizi to write lyrics and sketches for a touring variety show. On returning to Rome, wrote his first script for Mario Bonnard. 1942, met Giulietta Masina through a radio programme, and married her the following year. Rossellini discovered him drawing silhouettes of American soldiers and offered him work. Co-scripted *Roma, Città Aperta* (*Open City*, 1945), *Paisà* (1946) and *Il Miracolo* (1948), in which he also acted. Joined the neorealists, working with Germi and Lattuada, whose assistant he became, and presently co-director: *Luci del Varietà* (1950). *Lo Sceicco Bianco* (1952), which he based on an idea of Antonioni's, recalls the cartoon strips of his youth. After contributing an episode to *L'Amore in Città* (1953), attracted worldwide attention with *I Vitelloni* (1953), *La Strada* (1954) and *Il Bidone* (1955). These films trace not only the experiences of their creator, but also the development of his thought. *Le Notti di Cabiria* (*Cabiria*, 1956) confirmed this revelation, as, still more, did *La Dolce Vita* (1960), which employed a new style. An episode in *Boccaccio '70* added nothing to his stature, but *Otto e Mezzo* (1963) and *Giulietta degli Spiriti* (1965), original in conception, exuberant in style, are among the most representative films of the cinema of today. Latest films: episode in *Histoires Extraordinaires* (1967), *Satyricon* (1969), *I Clowns* (for TV, 1970),

Ferreri, Marco (b. Milan, 11 May 1928). Entered the cinema via advertising shorts. With Riccardo Ghione, tried to launch a series of films entitled *Documento Mensile*, whose contributors included Visconti, Fellini, Moravia, De Sica and Zavattini. Only two numbers appeared and achieved only limited showings. Joined with Messina industrialists in financing Lattuada's *Il Cappotto* (1952). Returned to Rome as an associate producer, and renewed his attempt at a kind of film chronicle with *L'Amore in Città* (1953), an investigation in six episodes, directed by Antonioni, Fellini, Lizzani, Lattuada, Maselli and Risi. 1956, went to Spain, where he directed two films of savage humour: *El Pisito* (1958) and *El Cochecito* (*The Wheelchair*, 1959). Returned to Italy and directed *Una Storia Moderna: l'Ape Regina* (*Queen Bee*, 1963), *La Donna Scimmia*; *L'Uomo a Cinque Palloni*; episode in *Controsesso* (1964), *Marcia Nuziale* (1965), *L'Harem* (1967), *Dillinger è Morto* (*Dillinger is Dead*, 1968), *Il Seme dell'Uomo* (1969), *L'Udienza* (1970).

Flaiano, Ennio (b. Pescara, 5 March 1910). Studied architecture, theatre critic of *Oggi*, author of a novel, stories and plays. Artistic adviser for *Pastor Angelicus* (1942), then co-scripted *La Freccia nel Fianco* (1943), *Roma, Città Libera* (1946). Worked for Soldati, Emmer, Blasetti, Castellani, Franciolini: *Fuga in Francia* (1948), *Villa Borghese* (1953), *Peccato che sia una Canaglia* (1954), *La Donna del Fiume*; *Il Segno di Venere* (1955), *Fortunella*; *Un Ettaro di Cielo* (1958), *La Ragazza in Vetrino* (*The Girl in the Window*), Antonioni's *La Notte* (1960). In particular he worked with Fellini, from *Luci del Varietà* (1950) to *Giulietta degli Spiriti* (1965).

Fosco, Piero, *see* **Pastrone, Giovanni.**

Franciolini, Gianni (b. Florence, 1 June 1910; d. Rome, May 1960). Technical institute, course in 'syndical and corporative studies'. 1929, attended the Ecole de Journalisme in Paris. Interested in the cinema, with *avant-garde* tendencies shown in collaboration with Eugène Deslaw; assistant director to Lacombe. 1939, returned to Italy, made his début as a director with a documentary, followed by full-length films, *L'Ispettore Vargas* (1940) and more notably *Fari nella Nebbia* (1941), which showed qualities and a temperament that reappeared in *Buongiorno Elefante!*(1952). His other films, of various genres, are less personal: *Giorni Felici* (1942), *Addio Amore* (1943), *Notte di Tempesta* (1945), *Gli Amanti senza Amore* (1947), *Siamo Donne* (*We, the Women*); *Villa Borghese* (1953), *Il Letto* (1954), *Racconti Romani* (1955), *Racconti d'Estate* (1958), *Ferdinand I Re di Napoli* (1959).

Francisci, Pietro (b. Rome, 9 Sept. 1906). Studied law, music, painting. Amateur filmmaker; 1934, made his first 35 mm. documentary, *Rapsodia in Roma*, and for ten years made documentaries for L.U.C.E. before becoming artistic director of Incom. 1946, first full-length film, *Io t'ho Incontrato a Napoli*, followed by *Natale al Campo 119* (1948), *Antonio di Padova* (1949), *Il Leone di Amalfi* (1950), *La Regina di Saba* (*The Queen of Sheba*, 1952), *Attila* (1954). Specialized in costume films and launched Hercules: *Le Fatiche di Ercole* (1957), *Ercole e la Regina di Lidia* (*Hercules Unchained*, 1958), *L'Assedio di Siracusa* (1959), *Safo, Venere di Lesbos* (1960).

Freda, Riccardo (b. Alexandria, 24 Feb. 1909). Studied in Milan: university, then school of sculpture. Art critic for *Il Popolo di Lombardia*. 1939, head of the technical and artistic department of Tirrenia Film; 1940, founder-director of Elica Film. 1938–42, co-scriptwriter in several films. 1942, produced and

directed *Don Cesare di Bazan*. 1943, *Buongiorno, Madrid!* (Italian version of Max Neufeld's film). Soon became a specialist in elaborate period films: *Aquila Nera* (1946), *I Miserabili* (1947), *Il Cavaliere Misterioso* (1948), *La Vendetta di Aquila Nera* (1951), *Spartaco* (1952), *Teodora* (1953), *Beatrice Cenci*; *I Vampiri* (1956), *Agguato a Tanger* (1957), *La Carica dei Cossacchi* (1957–8), *Nel Segno di Roma* (1958), *Caltiki, il Mostro Immortale* (*The Immortal Monster*, 1959), *I Mongoli* (1960), *I Giganti della Tessaglia* (1961), *Solo contro Roma* (*Vengeance of the Gladiators*); *Le Sette Spade del Vendicatore*; *Oro di Cesari* (1962), *Il Magnifico Avventurioso* (1963), *Giulietta e Romeo* (1964); also several Maciste films, melodramas (including *Veni Napoli e poi Muori*, 1951, and *I Due Orfanelli*, 1965), and miscellaneous films: *Caccia all' Uomo* (*Man Hunt*, 1961), *L'Orribile Segreto del Dr. Hichcock* (1962), *Lo Spettro* (1963), *Agente Coplan: Missione Spionaggio* (1965), *A Doppia Faccia* (1969).

Frusta, Arrigo, pseudonym of Augusto Ferrari (b. Turin, 26 Nov. 1875; d. 12 July 1965). Studied law; journalist, poet. 1908, head of the scenario department at Ambrosio, writing on numerous subjects and in every genre. 1910, with Vitrotti, made three documentaries on Mont Blanc, shot at altitudes around 13,000 feet. 1909–23, wrote 300 scripts, often based on literary works including (1911) those of D'Annunzio. Also scripted *Il Granatiere Rolland* (1910) and *Nozze d'Oro* (1911), two of the best films of the period.

Fusco, Giovanni (b. Sant'Agata dei Goti, 10 Oct. 1906). Studied music in Rome at the Accademia di Santa Cecilia. 1936, began working for the cinema. A regular member of Antonioni's team following the short *L'Amorosa Menzogna* (1949), he is notable for the intelligence of his tactful, evocative scores: *Cronaca di un Amore* (1950), *I Vinti* (1952), *Il Grido* (1957), *L'Avventura* (1959), *L'Eclisse* (1962), *Deserto Rosso* (1964). Also wrote the music for *I Pirati della Malesia* (1941), *Rocambole* (1947–8), *Traviata* (1953), *Gli Sbandati* (1954), *Hiroshima, mon Amour* (with Georges Delerue, 1959), *L'Oro di Roma* (1961), *Lo Sceicco Rosso*; *La Corruzione* (1963).

Gallone, Carmine (b. Taggia, near Imperia, 18 Sept. 1886). Poet and dramatist; came to the cinema as a scriptwriter at Cines, then directed *Il Bacio di Cirano* (1913). *La Donna Nuda* (1914), adapted from Henri Bataille,

229

with Lyda Borelli, assured his future. Directed some twenty silent films, mainly on high-society subjects – *Redenzione*; *Marcia Nuziale*; *Avatar* (1915), *La Falena* (1916) – together with a number of costume films: *Storia dei Tredici* (1917), *La Cavalcata Ardente* (1923). After ensuring completion of *Gli Ultimi Giorni di Pompei* (1926), left for Germany. Ten years working in Berlin, Poland (*L'Inferno dell' Amore*, 1928; *Terra senza Donne*, 1929), London (*The City of Song*, 1931), Paris: many successful films in the early days of sound, e.g. *Ma Cousine de Varsovie*; *Un Soir de Rafle*; *Le Chant du Marin* (1932), *Mon Cœur t'Appelle* (1936). Back in Italy, films included *Casta Diva* (1935), *Scipione l'Africano* (1937), *Giuseppe Verdi* (1938), *Il Sogno di Butterfly*; *Manon Lescaut* (1939), *La Regina di Navarra* (1941), *Le Due Orfanelle*; *Odessa in Fiamme* (1942), *Davanti a lui Tremava tutta Roma* (1946), *Rigoletto*; *La Signora delle Camelie* (1947), *Il Trovatore* (1949), *Messalina* (1951), *Cavalleria Rusticana* (1953), *Casa Ricordi* (1954), *Madama Butterfly* (1955), *Tosca*; *Michel Strogoff* (1956), *Cartagine in Fiamme* (1960), *Don Camillo Monsignore ma non troppo* (1961), *Carmen di Trastevere* (1962). Specialized in musical films.

Gassman, Vittorio (b. Genoa, 1 Sept. 1922). Studied law in Rome; did a drama course under Silvio D'Amico. Stage actor and producer; foreign tours. Screen début: *Preludio d'Amore* (1946). Dramatic parts in *Daniele Cortis*; *La Figlia del Capitano* (1947), *Riso Amaro* (1948), *Anna* (1951), *La Donna più Bella del Mondo* (*Beautiful but Dangerous*, 1955), *War and Peace* (1956), but only really made his name in comedy: *I Soliti Ignoti* (1958), *Audace Colpo dei Soliti Ignoti*; *La Grande Guerra* (1959), and above all *Il Sorpasso* (1962) and *I Mostri* (1963). Other films include *Il Giudizio Universale* (*The Last Judgement*), *Barabbas* (1961), *La Marcia su Roma* (1962), *Frenesia dell'Estate* (1963), *Il Gaucho*; *La Congiuntura*; *Se Permette Parliamo di Donne* (1964), *La Guerra Segreta* (1965), *Il Tigre*; *Questi Fantasmi* (*Ghosts – Italian Style*); *Il Profeta* (1967), *L'Arcangelo*; *Una su 13* (1969), *Contestazione generale*; *Il Divorzio* (1970), *Brancaleone alle Crociate* (1971). Directed *Kean* (1957).

Genina, Augusto (b. Rome, 28 Jan. 1892; d. Rome, 28 Sept. 1957). Directed some 150 films over 40 years. 1913, début as Negroni's scriptwriter. Early films include *Addio Giovinezza!* (1918, sound version 1927), *La*

Maschera e il Votto (1919), *Cirano de Bergerac* (1922), *Il Focolare Spento* (*Il più Grande Amore*, 1925), starring Carmen Boni whom he later married, and *L'Ultimo Lord* (*La Femme en Homme*, 1926). 1927, a Franco-German film (*Sprung ins Glück*), followed by a highly successful period in France: *Quartier Latin* (1928), *Prix de Beauté* (1930), *Les Amours de Minuit* (1931), *Ne sois pas Jalouse*; *Paris-Béguin* (1932), *Nous ne sommes plus des Enfants* (1934), *La Gondole aux Chimères* (1935), *Naples au Baiser de Feu* (1937). Later Italian films include *Squadrone Bianco* (1936), two Fascist propaganda films, *L'Assedio dell'Alcazar* (1940) and *Bengasi* (1942), *Cielo sulla Palude* (1949), *Tre Storie Proibite* (1952), *Maddalena* (1953). *Frou-Frou* (1955) was a co-production made in France.

Gentilomo, Giacomo (b. Trieste, 5 April 1909). Studied classics in Rome. Successively script-boy, assistant to Bragaglia and Mattoli, editor, adapter. Début as director with a colour documentary, *Sinfonie di Roma* (1937), followed by *Il Carnavale di Venezia* (1940), *La Granduchessa si Diverte* (1941), *Mater Dolorosa* (1942), *O Sole Mio* (1945, on the Resistance in Naples), *I Fratelli Karamazoff* (1947), *Enrico Caruso, Leggenda di una Voce* (1951), *Le Due Orfanelle* (1955), *Sigfrido* (1957), *L'Ultimo dei Vichinghi* (1960), *I Lancieri Neri*; *Maciste contro il Vampiro* (1961), *Maciste e la Regina di Samar* (1964).

Germi, Pietro (b. Colombo, Liguria, 14 Sept. 1914). Modest origins and beginnings: job as errand-boy, course at nautical school abandoned in order to try his chance in Rome at the C.S.C.; two-year course in acting, third year studying direction. Earned his living in various capacities, as an extra, co-scriptwriter, assistant (not the easiest person to work with), actor (*Fuga in Francia*, 1948). Wrote script for his own first film, *Il Testimone* (1945). Following films established him as one of the best neo-realist directors: *Gioventù Perduta* (1947), *In Nome della Legge* (1949), *Il Cammino della Speranza* (1950), *Il Brigante di Tacca del Lupo*; *La Presidentessa* (1952), *Gelosia* (1953), episode in *Amori di Mezzo Secolo* (1954), *Il Ferroviere* (*Man of Iron*, 1956), *L'Uomo di Paglia* (1957), with admirable performances of his own in these two last. Somewhat underrated as a director, he achieved commercial success in satirical comedy: *Un Maledetto Imbroglio* (*A Sordid Affair*, 1959), *Divorzio all'Italiana* (1961), *Sedotta e Abbandonata* (1963); his earlier films, however, though less smooth, are more sensitive and richer in content. 1965, with L. Vincenzoni, founded a production company, R.P.A., and made *Signore e Signori (The Birds, the Bees and the Italians)*. Recently: *L'Immorale* (1966), *Serafino* (1968), *Le Castagne sono buone* (1970).

Ghione, Emilio (b. 1880; d. Rome, 7 Jan. 1930). Son of a painter, himself a miniaturist at Turin. Started as an extra and began acting along with Francesca Bertini, whose frequent partner he became under Negroni. Soon became a director, while continuing to act, often in his own films: *L'Amazzone Mascherata*; *Nelly la Gigolette (La Danzatrice della Taverna Nera)*; *La Mia Vita per la Tua* (1914), *Ciceruacchio*; *Guglielmo Oberdan* (1915), *La Grande Vergogna* (1916), *L'Ultima Impresa*; *Don Pietro Caruso* (1917), *Il Quadrante d'Oro* (1921), *Ultissime di Notte* (1922). Launched detective films in Italy with series based on French models: *Za la Mort* (1914), *I Topi Grigi* (1917–18); he himself created the part of Za la Mort, a romantic apache. Migrated to Paris, where he failed to establish himself, fell ill, and returned to die in Rome. He wrote the *Cinéma italien* volume in the series 'L'Art Cinématographique', published by Alcan.

Giannini, Ettore (b. Naples, 15 Oct. 1912). Lawyer by training, hesitated between diplomatic and artistic careers. 1935, successful experimental films, radio plays. Accademia d'Arte Drammatica in Rome. Double career in the cinema (scriptwriter, dialogue-writer, in *Europa 51* actor) and the theatre, producing plays by Pirandello, Shaw, Goldoni, Labiche, Salacrou, Tolstoy, etc., and bringing new life to the Italian stage. Script or dialogue for *Addio Giovinezza!* (1941), *Processo alla Città* (1952), etc. Replacement director in *Gli Uomini sono Nemici* (1948–50), he revealed his original qualities in an interesting choreographic film, *Carosello Napoletano* (1954). Was on the board of directors of C.S.C., and later directed the dubbing of films.

Girotti, Massimo (b. Mogliano, 18 May 1918). Studied engineering. A polo and swimming champion, with a fine physique that caught Blasetti's eye and earned him a small part in *Dora Nelson* (1939) and the lead in *La Corona di Ferro* (1940). Visconti, whom he got to know in *La Tosca* (1940) gave him the lead in *Ossessione* (1942). These two parts placed him on the top rung of the ladder for many years: *La Porta del Cielo* (1945), *Un Giorno nella Vita* (1946), *Caccia Tragica*; *Gioventù Perduta*; *Souvenir d'Italie* (1947), *Natale al Camp 119*; *Fabiola*; *Anni Difficili* (1948), *In Nome della Legge* (1949), *Cronaca di un Amore* (1950), *Naso di Cuoio*; *Roma, Ore 11*; *Spartaco*; *Ai Margini della Metropoli*; *Sul Ponte dei Sospiri* (1952), *L'Amour d'une Femme* (Grémillon, 1953), *Senso* (1954), *Marguerite de la Nuit* (Autant-Lara, 1955), *La Strada da lunga un Anno*; *Giuditta e Oloferne* (1958), *Erode il Grande* (1959), *Lettere di una Novizia* (1960), *I Giganti della Tessaglia* (1961), *Vénus Impériale*; *Oro di Cesari* (1962).

Gregoretti, Ugo (b. Rome, 1930). Journalist. Directed a number of successful television plays. Films: *I Nuovi Angeli* (1961), episodes in *RoGoPaG* (1962) and *Les Plus Belles Escroqueries du Monde*; *Omicron* (1963), *Le belle Famiglie* (1964). An author and director of caustic humour.

Guarini, Alfredo (b. Sestri Ponente, near Genoa, 23 May 1901). Vienna, 1928, assistant to Korda and Engel. Made documentaries in Berlin and Paris. 1933, returned to Italy as associate producer, Tirrenia Film: *La Signora Paradiso* (1934), *Passaporto Rosso* (1935). 1936, director with Alfa Film, where he organized co-production. 1937, went to Hollywood (Paramount), worked on the script of *Hotel Imperial* (1939), and in the same year married Isa Miranda. After the war, helped in the organization of *La Terra Trema* (1948), and also supported Rossellini's *Germania, Anno Zero* (1947) and *Viaggio in Italia* (1953), as well as various foreign co-productions: *Au-delà des Grilles (Le Mura di Malapaga*, 1948), *La Beauté du Diable* (1949), *Rasputin* (1954), *Goubbiah* (1955). Chosen as vice-president of E.N.I.C. 1950, returned to independent production, films including *I Colpevoli* (1956), *Esterina* (1959) and *Meravigliosa* (1960). Has directed several films: *Senza Cielo* (1940), *E Caduta una Donna* (1941), *Senza una Donna* (1943) and an episode in *Siamo Donne (We, the Women*, 1953).

Guazzoni, Enrico (b. Rome, 18 Sept. 1876; d. Rome, 24 Sept. 1949). Painter, diploma of the Istituto di Belle Arti. Technical adviser for a film on *Raphaël* (1907), and remained one of the masters of historical spectacle: *Brutus*; *Agrippina*; *I Maccabei* (1910), *La Gerusalemme Liberata* (1911 and two later versions, one in sound), *Quo Vadis?* (1912), *Marcantonio e Cleopatra* (1913), *Caius Julius Caesar* (1914), *Ivan il Terribile*; *Alma Mater* (1915), *Madame*

Tallien (1916), *Fabiola* (1917), *Lady Macbeth* (1918), *Il Sacco di Roma* (1923, experimenting with a wide screen), *Messalina* (1923). Marked feeling for composition and crowd movements. Sound films include *I Due Sergenti*; *Re di Denari*; *Ho Perduto mio Marito* (1936), *Il dottore Antonio* (1938), *Il suo Destino*; *Ho visto Brillare le Stelle* (1939), *La Figlia del Corsaro Verde*; *I Pirati della Malesia*; *Oro Nero* (1941), *La Fornarina* (1943–4).

Jacobini, Maria (b. Rome, 17 Feb. 1890; d. 20 Nov. 1944). 'The most cultured and intelligent of the *dive*', according to Maria Adriana Prolo. Well-born, stage actress, screen début in 1910 with F.A.I. Heroine of numerous historical and society films: *Giovanna d'Arco* (1913), *Resurrezione* (1917), *La Vergine Folle*; *I Borgia* (1919), *Beatrice Cenci*; *Il Carnavale di Venezia* (1926). Invited to Germany in late 1920s and acted in *Fünf bange Tage*; *Unfug der Liebe*; *Villa Falconieri* (1928), *Der lebende Leichnam*; *Vera Mirzewa* (*The Crime of Vera Mirzewa*), and (in France, under Duvivier) *Maman Colibri*. Married Alexander Korda and lectured on his art at the C.S.C. from 1938 to 1943. Last film: Castellani's *La Donna della Montagna* (1942).

Lattuada, Alberto (b. Milan, 13 Nov. 1914). Son of the composer Felice Lattuada. University studies, intellectual activities (articles, stories, novels), qualified architect at 23. A devotee of the cinema, joined with Mario Ferrari and Luigi Comencini to set up the Cineteca Italiana in Milan. 1940, as part of the Milan Triennale, organized a retrospective film festival. 1941, published two volumes of photographs. Political events brought him to Rome. Worked with Soldati as assistant scriptwriter on *Piccolo Mondo Antico* (*Old-fashioned World*, 1941). Directed *Giacomo l'idealista* (*James the Idealist*, 1942), adapted from De Marchi, and revealing a somewhat precious style which earned him the label of 'calligrapher'. After *La Freccia nel Fianco* (1943), adopted the neo-realist style (*Il Bandito*, 1946), and confirmed his quality with *Il Delitto di Giovanni Episcopo* (1947), *Senza Pietà* (1948), *Il Mulino del Po* (1949). *Luci del Varietà* (with Fellini, 1950), *Anna* (a considerable commercial success, 1951), *Il Cappotto* (1952), one of his best films, and an episode in *I 'amore in Città* (1953). A dynamic director, accomplished in every genre, moving from the study of manners to adventure films, from psychological problems to costume films: *La Lupa* (1953), *La Spiaggia* (1954), *Scuola Elementare*

(1955), *Guendalina* (1957), *La Tempesta* (1958), *I Dolci Inganni*; *Lettere di una Novizia* (1960), *L'Imprevista* (*Unexpected*, 1961, made in France), *La Steppa*; *Il Mafioso* (1962), *La Mandragola* (after Machiavelli, 1965), *Matchless* (1966), *Don Giovanni in Sicilia* (1967), *L'Amica* (1969), *Venga a Prendere il Caffè da Noi* (1970).

Leone, Sergio. The best-known director of Italian westerns: *Per un Pugno di Dollari* (*A Fistful of Dollars*, 1964), *Per qualche dollaro in più* (*For a Few Dollars More*, 1965), *Il buono, il brutto, il cattivo* (*The Good, the Bad, and the Ugly*, 1966), *C'era una volta il West* (*Once Upon a Time in the West*, 1968, made in U.S.A.), *Giù la Testa* (1971). Had previously helped in making 58 films by major Italian and American directors (Wyler, Zinnemann, Walsh, Wise), and made his début with a remake of Mario Bonnard's *Gli Ultimi Giorni di Pompei* (1959), followed by *Il Colosso di Rodi* (1960).

Lizzani, Carlo (b. Rome, 30 April 1922). One of the young critics who, in *Cinema* and *Bianco e Nero*, prepared the way for neorealism. 1946, took part in Vergano's *Il Sole Sorge Ancora* as co-scriptwriter, assistant and actor (the Resistance priest). Contributed to scripts of films by De Santis (*Caccia Tragica*, 1947; *Riso Amaro*, 1948; *Non c'è Pace tra gli Ulivi*, 1949), Rossellini (*Germania, Anno Zero*, 1947) and Lattuada (*Il Mulino del Po*, 1949). Made various social documentaries (*Nel Mezzogiorno Qualcosa è Cambiato*, etc., 1950). *Achtung! Banditi!* made on a co-operative basis (1951), *Ai Margini della Metropoli* (1952), episode in *L'Amore in Città* (1953), *Cronache di Poveri Amanti* (1954), *Lo Svitato* (1956), *La Muraglia Cinese* (full-length documentary, produced by Count Leonardo Bonzi, 1958), *Esterina* (1959). Several successful war films: *Il Gobbo* (*The Hunchback of Rome*, 1960), *L'Oro di Roma* (1961), *Il Processo di Verona* (1963). Also *Il Carabinieri a Cavallo* (1961), *La Vita Agra*; *La Celestina* (1964), episodes in *La Guerra Segreta* and *Amori Pericolosi* (1965), *Svegliati e Uccidi*; *Un Fiume di Dollari*; *Requiescant* (1966), *Banditi a Milano*; *L'Amante di Gramigna* (1968), *Barbagia* (1969). Lizzani has published a well-documented book, *Il Cinema Italiano* (1953).

Lollobrigida, Gina (b. Subiaco, 4 July 1927). Father an industrialist ruined by the war; family left Subiaco. Course at an arts school. Small parts in *Aquila Nera* (1946), *Il Delitto di Giovanni Episcopo* (1947). Posed for romantic picture-story magazines under the pseudonym of Diana Loris. 1947, won a beauty contest. 1948–9, first real acting parts. 1949, married Milko Scozfic. Physical attractiveness and talent led to an international career: *Enrico Caruso* (1951), *Achtung! Banditi!*; *Fanfan la Tulipe* (Christian-Jaque), *Altri Tempi*; *Les Belles de Nuit* (René Clair, 1952), *La Provinciale*; *Le Infedeli*; *Pane, Amore e Fantasia* (1953), *Le Grand Jeu*; *Pane, Amore e Gelosia* (1954), *La Bella di Roma*; *La Donna più Bella del Mondo* (*Beautiful but Dangerous*, 1955), *Trapeze*; *Notre-Dame de Paris* (Jean Delannoy, 1956), *Anna di Brooklyn* (1958), *La Loi* (Jules Dassin), *Solomon and Sheba* (Spain), *Never So Few* (U.S.A., 1959), *Come September* (U.S.A., 1961), *La Bellezza d'Ippolita*; *Vénus impériale*; *Mare matto* (1962), *Woman of Straw* (U.K., 1964), *Strange Bedfellows* (U.S.A.), *Le Bambole*; *Les Sultans* (France, 1965), *Cervantes* (1967), *Un Bellissimo Novembre* (1968).

Lombardo, Goffredo (b. Naples, 15 May 1920). Son of the producer Gustavo Lombardo and the *diva* Leda Gys. Various activities in production and dubbing. Succeeded his father as director of Titanus. President of the national union of film producers until 1966.

Loren, Sophia, pseudonym of Sofia Scicolone (b. Rome, 20 Sept. 1934). Childhood at Pozzuoli, near Naples. Miss Elegance, Miss Italy. Small parts in *Aïda*; *Tempi Nostri* (1953), *Carosello Napoletano* (1954). De Sica gave her the part (in *L'Oro di Napoli*, 1954) that launched her; soon became, with Lollobrigida, one of the two most popular Italian actresses. *Peccato che sia una Canaglia* (1954), *La Donna del Fiume*; *Pane, Amore e . . .* (1955), *La Fortuna di essere Donna* (1956). In U.S.A.: *The Pride and the Passion*; *Boy on a Dolphin*; *Legend of the Lost* (1957), *Desire under the Elms* (1958), *The Black Orchid*; *That Kind of Woman* (1959), *Heller in Pink Tights* (1960). In U.K.: *The Key* (1958), *The Millionairess* (1960). *La Ciociara* (*Two Women*, 1960), *El Cid* (Spain), *Madame Sans-Gêne* (1961), *Boccaccio '70*; *Le Couteau dans la Plaie*; *I Sequestrati di Altona* (*The Condemned of Altona*, 1962), *Ieri, Oggi, Domani*; *Matrimonio all'Italiana* (1964), *The Fall of the Roman Empire* (1964), *Lady L.* (1965), *A Countess from Hong Kong* (Chaplin), *Arabesque* (1966), *C'era una Volta* (1966), *Questi Fantasmi* (*Ghosts – Italian Style*, 1967), *La Moglie del Prete* (1970). Married to producer Carlo Ponti.

Loy, Nanni (Giovanni) (b. Cagliari, 23 Oct. 1925). Course in documentary at C.S.C.

Assistant to Alessandrini, Zampa, Genina. 1955, directed the second unit in *Tam Tam Mayumbe* (in the Congo). Co-directed with Puccini *Parola di Ladro*; *Il Marito* (1957). Directed *Audace Colpo dei Soliti Ignoti* (*Fiasco in Milan*, 1959), *Un Giorno da Leoni* (1961), *Le Quattro Giornate di Napoli* (1962), *Il Padre di Famiglia* (1967), *L'Inferno del Deserto* (1969), *Rosolino Paternò, Soldato* (1970). Acted in *Le Belle Famiglie* (1964), *Made in Italy* (1965). Television: *Specchio Segreto* (1964).

Lualdi, Antonella, pseudonym of Antonietta De Pascale (b. Beirut, 6 July 1931). Italian father, Greek mother. 1949, began career as actress. Films, made in Italy and France, include *Tre Storie Proibite*; *Adorables Créatures*; *Il Cappotto* (1952), *Cronache di Poveri Amanti*; *Le Rouge et le Noir* (1954), *Gli Innamorati* (*Les Amoureux*), *Goubbiah* (1955), *Padri e Figli*; *Mon Coquin de Père* (1956), *Une Vie*; *Giovani Mariti* (1958), *A Double Tour*; *Match contre la Mort*; *La Notte Brava* (1959), *I Mongoli*; *I Delfini* (1960), *Il Disordine* (1962), *Le Repas des Fauves*; *Un Monsieur de Compagnie* (1964), *I Cento Cavalieri* (1965), *Il Massacro della Foresta Nera* (1966), *Il Grande Colpo di Surcouf* (1967), *100 Ragazze per un Playboy* (1968). 1955, married the actor Franco Interlenghi.

Maciste, character in *Cabiria*, created by Giovanni Pastrone (1914) and played by a Genoese docker, Bartolomeo Pagano (1878–1947), who, taking as a pseudonym the name of his part, had a long career in the role of this mythological creature: *Maciste Alpino*; *Maciste Bersagliere* (1916), *Maciste contro Maciste*; *Maciste supera Maciste* (1917), *Maciste Atleta* (1918), *Maciste in Vacanza* (1920), *Maciste Detective* (1923–4), *Maciste Imperatore* (1924), *Maciste all'Inferno* (1925), *Maciste e la Regina dell'Argento*; *Maciste nella Gabbia dei Leoni*; *Il Gigante delle Dolomiti*; *Maciste contro lo Sceicco* (1926), *Il Vetturale del Moncenisio* (1927), *Gli Ultimi Zar* (1928). The man whom Delluc called 'the Guitry with the biceps' had to give up his career, not because of the advent of sound, but for reasons of health. The character he created survived the avatars of Italian production and with the arrival of 'neo-mythologism' in 1960 found a new vitality which did not seem unduly threatened by his rivals, Hercules and Ursus.

Maggi, Luigi (b. Turin, 21 Dec. 1867; d. Turin, 22 Aug. 1946). Printer, then actor and director in a Piedmontese dialect company. Engaged by Ambrosio, directed and acted in numerous films, moving to Film d'Arte, Milano Film, etc. *Gli Ultimi Giorni di Pompei* (1908), *Spergiura!*; *Il Figlio delle Selve*; *Luigi XI, Re di Francia* (1909), *Il Granatiere Rolland* (1910), *Nozze d'Oro*; *La Gioconda*; *La Nave*; *Thomas Chatterton*; *Il Danaro di Giuda* (1911), *Satana* (1912), *La Lampada della Nonna*; *Notturno di Chopin*; *Il Barbiere di Siviglia*; *Il Matrimonio di Figaro* (1913), *Per un'Ora d'Amore*; *Le Rose della Madonna*; *Il Fornaretto di Venezia* (1914). In 1927, after a new *Teodora*, abandoned the cinema. 1939–40, Radio Turin, television productions and experiments.

Magnani, Anna (b. Alexandria, 7 March 1908). Italian mother, Egyptian father. Academy of Dramatic Art under Silvio D'Amico. 1926, stage début. Toured in the Argentine. 1927, first small screen part, in *Scampolo*. 1935, married Goffredo Alessandrini (marriage annulled, 1950), who considered her unsuited to the cinema. Brilliant music-hall career in Totò's company. Some small screen parts. 1941, *Mademoiselle Vendredi*. 1945, *Roma, Città Aperta* (*Open City*), revealing an unsuspected dramatic talent and leading to a magnificent career: *Il Bandito*; *Davanti a lui Tremava tutta Roma* (1946), *Abasso la Ricchezza*; *L'Onorevole Angelina* (1947), *L'Amore* (1948), *Vulcano* (1950), *Bellissima* (1951), *Le Carrosse d'Or* (Renoir), *Siamo Donne* (*We, the Women*, 1953), *The Rose Tattoo* (U.S.A., 1955), *Suor Letizia* (1956), *Wild is the Wind* (U.S.A., 1957), *Nella Città l'Inferno*; *The Fugitive Kind* (U.S.A., 1959), *Risate di Gioia* (1960), *Mamma Roma* (1962), *Le Magot de Joséfa* (Autant-Lara, 1963), *Made in Italy* (1965), *Il Segreto di Santa Vittoria* (1968).

Malaparte, Curzio, pseudonym of Kurt Suckert (b. Prato, 9 June 1898; d. Rome, 19 July 1957). 1921, began writing; published numerous works: *L'Europa Vivente* (1923), *L'Italia Barbara* (1926), *Intelligenza di Lenin* (1930), *Sangue* (1938), *Il Volga nasce in Europa* (1943) and above all *Kaputt* (1944) and *La Pelle* (*The Skin*, 1949), which established his reputation outside Italy. Contributed to various periodicals; edited *L'Italia Letteraria* and, from 1928 to 1931, the newspaper *La Stampa*. For the theatre: *Du côté de chez Proust* (1948), *Das Kapital* (1949). His activity in the cinema was confined to a singular and powerful work: *Il Cristo Proibito* (1951), for which he wrote the script and supervised the sets and the musical commentary. His death interrupted another project, finally completed

by Monicelli in 1963 as *I Compagni* (*The Organizer*).

Mangano, Silvana (b. Rome, 21 April 1930). Mother English. Studied dancing with Zhia Ruskaya. Miss Rome, 1946. Small parts in *L'Elisir d'Amore* (1946), *Il Delitto di Giovanni Episcopo* (1947). *Riso Amaro* (1948) made her world-famous. 1949, married Dino De Laurentiis. Pursued her chosen career and confirmed her position as a great actress: *Il Lupo della Sila*; *Il Brigante Musolino* (1950), *Anna* (1951), *Ulisse*; *Mambo*; *L'Oro di Napoli* (1954), *Uomini e Lupi* (1956), *La Diga sul Pacifico* (*The Sea-Wall*, 1957), *La Tempesta* (1958), *La Grande Guerra*; *Jovanka e l'Altri* (*Five Branded Women*, 1959), *Il Giudizio Universale* (*The Last Judgement*); *Barabbas*; *Una Vita Difficile* (1961), *Il Processo di Verona* (1963), *La Mia Signora* (1964), *Il Disco Volante* (1965), *Le Streghe* (1966), *Edipo Re* (1967), *Teorema* (1968), *Medea* (1969), *Scipione detto anche l'Africano* (1971).

Martelli, Otello (b. Rome, 19 May 1902). Began in the silent era, working for Caesar. 1928, photographer with the Nobile expedition to the North Pole. Chief cameraman at Scalera, making numerous fine films, from neo-realism to the present day: *Paisà* (1946), *Caccia Tragica* (1947), *Riso Amaro* (1948), *Luci del Varietà*; *Francesco, Giullare di Dio* (*St. Francis of Assisi*, 1950), *Stromboli* (1951); *Roma, Ore 11* (1952), *I Vitelloni* (1953), *La Strada* (1954), *Il Bidone* (1955), *La Diga sul Pacifico* (*The Sea-Wall*, 1957), *La Dolce Vita* (1960), *Cyrano et d'Artagnan* (1963), *La Mia Signora* (1964), *I Tre Volti* (with Di Carla, 1965).

Martoglio, Nino (b. Catania, 3 Dec. 1870; d. Catania, 15 Sept. 1921). Journalist, poet, playwright, director of a dialect theatre company. 1913, in Rome, directed *Il Romanzo* for Cines. 1914, in Catania, founded Morgana Film and made *Capitano Blanco* and, more notably, *Sperduti nel Buio* (1914) and *Teresa Raquin* (1915), ancestors of neo-realism.

Maselli, Francesco (b. Rome, 9 Dec. 1930). 1944, amateur film-making. 1946, entered C.S.C. 1947, assisted Antonioni and Chiarini with shorts. 1949, first short documentary. 1950, assistant scriptwriter, *Cronaca di un Amore*. 1950–3, a dozen shorts, and assistance to Antonioni, Visconti. An episode (*Storia di Caterina*) in *Amore in Città* (1953), *Gli Sbandati* (1954), *La Donna del Giorno* (1957), *I Delfini* (1960), episode in *Le Italiane e l'Amore* (*Latin Lovers*, 1961), *Gli Indifferenti*

(1964), *Fai in Fretta ed Uccidermi . . . ho Freddo!* (1966), *Ruba al Prossimo Tua* (1968), *Lettera Aperta a un Giornale della Sera* (1970).

Masina, Giulietta (Giulia-Anna) (b. Giorgio di Piano, near Bologna, 22 Feb. 1920). Daughter of a teacher; faculty of literature at Rome and university theatre. 1942, Teatro delle Arti, radio series, *Cico e Pallina*, written by Fellini, whom she married in 1943. A remarkable little part in *Senza Pietà* (1948), *Luci del Varietà* (1950), *Lo Sceicco Bianco*; *Europa 51*; *Ai Margini della Metropoli* (1952), *La Strada* (1954), in which the character of Gelsomina won her universal acclaim; *Il Bidone* (1955), *Le Notti di Cabiria* (*Cabiria*, 1956), *Fortunella* (1958), *Nella Città l'Inferno* (1959), *La Grande Vie* (Duvivier, 1960), *Giulietta degli Spiriti* (1965), *Scusi lei è Favorevole o Contrario?* (1966), *Non Stuzzicate la Zanzara* (1967), *The Madwoman of Chaillot* (G.B., 1968).

Mastroianni, Marcello (b. Fontana Liri, near Rome, 28 Sept. 1923). A slow start; acted with amateur groups. 1947, screen début (*I Miserabili*). 1948–9, engaged by Visconti to play Alfieri and Shakespeare on the stage. Theatrical success; film career developed more slowly: *Domenica d'Agosto* (1950), *Parigi è sempre Parigi* (1951), *Le Ragazze di Piazza di Spagna* (*Three Girls from Rome*, 1952), *Cronache di Poveri Amanti*; *Peccato che sia una Canaglia* (1954), *Il Bigamo*; *La Fortuna di Essere Donna*; *Padri e Figli* (1956), *Le Notti Bianche* (1957), *La Loi* (1959), *Il bell'Antonio*; *La Dolce Vita*; *Adua e le Compagne*; *La Notte* (1960), *Fantasmi a Roma*; *L'Assassino*; *Divorzio all'Italiana*; *Vie Privée* (1961), *Cronaca Familiare* (1962), *Otto e Mezzo*; *I Compagni* (*The Organiser*, 1963), *Ieri, Oggi, Domani*; *Matrimonio all'Italiana*; *L'Uomini a Cinque Palloncini* (1964), *Casanova '70*; *La Decima Vittima* (1965), *Lo Straniero* (The *Outsider*, 1967), *Amanti* (*A Place for Lovers*, 1968), *Dramma della Gelosia* (*Jealousy Italian Style*), *Leo the Last* (in Britain, 1969), *La Moglie del Prete*; *Giuochi Particolari* (1970), *Scipione detto anche l'Africano* (1971).

Mattoli, Mario (b. Tolentino, 30 Nov. 1898). Studied law. Directed in succession eleven theatrical companies, including the 'Za Boum' show which had a great success. 1933, début as a film producer: *La Segretaria per Tutti*. 1934, turned to direction, launched Alida Valli, brought into the cinema the comedians Macario, Totò and Fabrizi. By 1961 had made over eighty films, and attempted every genre: *Gli Ultimi Giorni di Pompei* (1937), *Luce nelle*

Tenebre; *Ore 9 Lezione di Chimica* (1941), *Catene Invisibili* (1942), *L'Intruse*; *L'Ultima Carrozzella* (1943), *La Vita Ricomincia* (1945), *I due Orfanelli* (1947), *I Giorni più Belli* (1956), *Signori si Nasce* (1960), *Obiettivo Ragazze* (1963), *Cadavere per Signora* (1964).

Menichelli, Pina (Giuseppina) (b. Sicily, 1893). *Femme fatale* of the golden age, outstandingly successful in films of high society: *Il Fuoco* (1915), *Tigre Reale* (1916), *La Passagera* (1917), *Il Giardino della Voluttà*; *Il Padrone delle Ferriere* (1918), *Una Pagina d'Amore* (1919), *Il Romanzo di un Giovane Povero*; *La Disfatta delle Erinni* (1920). Married a producer, Baron Carlo Amato, and retired in 1924.

Mingozzi, Gianfranco (b. Bologna, 3 April 1932). Remarkable début in the social documentary: *La Tarenta*; *Con il Cuore ferma, Sicilia* (1966), *Note su una Minoranza* (on Italian Canadians), *Tre Minuti e non più*, which formed an episode in his first full-length film, *Trio* (1966). *Sequestro di Persona* (1968).

Miranda, Isa, pseudonym of Inès Isabella Sampietro (b. Milan, 5 July 1909). Manual and clerical work, mannequin, course in drama, stage début in Milan. Rome: an extra at Cines. 1934, Ophüls gave her the lead in *La Signora di Tutti* and determined her career. Made films in Italy, France, Germany and America: *Passaporto Rosso* (1935), *L'Homme de Nulle Part*; *Scipione l'Africano*; *Le Mensonge de Nina Petrovna* (1937), *Hotel Imperial* (1939), *Malombra* (1942), *Zazà* (1943), *Audelà des Grilles* (*Le Mura di Malapaga*, 1948), *La Ronde* (1950), *I Sette Peccati Capitali* (1952), *Siamo Donne* (*We, the Women*); *Avant le Déluge*; *Le Secret d'Hélène Marimon* (1953), *Rasputin* (1954), *Il Tesoro di Rommel* (1956), *Une Manche et la Belle* (*La Febbre del Possesso*, 1957), *Le Secret du Chevalier d'Eon* (1958), *La Noia*; *La Coruzione* (1963), *Un'Estate con Sentimento* (1970).

Monaco, Eitel (b. Montazzoli, near Chieti, 16 March 1903). Barrister. 1926–36, Secretary, then Director, National Association of Independent Film-Makers. 1941–3, Director-General, Italian Cinematography. 1944, organized A.N.I.C.A. (President, 1950–1), created Unitalia. Permanent representative, International Cinema Bureau.

Monicelli, Mario (b. Rome, 15 May 1915). Studied literature and philosophy. Amateur film-making at the Milan G.U.F. 1935, an experiment with reduced format presented at Venice. Assistant to Machaty, Genina and others. Scriptwriting and direction in association with Steno; eight comedies, including *Al Diavolo la Celebrità*; *Totò Cerca Casa* (1949), *Guardie e Ladri* (*Cops and Robbers*, 1951), *Le Infedeli* (1953). 1953, partnership dissolved. Monicelli made on his own *Proibito* (*Du Sang dans le Soleil*, 1954), *Un Eroe dei Nostri Tempi* (1955), *Donatella*; *Padri e Figli* (1956), *Il Medico e lo Stregone* (*The Doctor and the Quack*, 1957). His later films have confirmed his gift for satiric comedy: *I Soliti Ignoti* (1958), *La Grande Guerra* (1959), *Risate di Gioia* (1960), *Casanova '70*; *L'Armata Brancaleone* (1965), *Le Fate* (1966), *La Ragazza colla Pistole* (1968), *To'è Morta la Nonna* (1969), *Brancaleone alle Crociate* (1971). Has also contributed episodes to *Boccaccio '70* (1962) and *Alta Infedeltà* (1964), *Le Coppie* (1971), and made a social film, *I Compagni* (*The Organiser*, 1963).

Moravia, Alberto, pseudonym of Alberto Pincherle (b. Rome, 22 Nov. 1907). Fiction includes *Gli Indifferenti* (1929), *Le Ambizioni Sbagliate* (1935), *Agostino* (1945), *La Romana* (1947), *Il Conformista* (1951), *Racconti Romani* (1954), most of which have been filmed. 1951, directed and acted in an episode in *Documento Mensile* (celluloid magazine). From 1950, co-scripted, e.g. *Racconti Romani* (1955), *I Delfini*; *La Ciociara* (*Two Women*, 1960). Film criticism in *La Nuova Europa* (1944–6), *L'Espresso* (since 1955).

Nazzari, Amedeo, pseudonym of Salvatore Amedeo Buffa (b. Cagliari, 10 Dec. 1907). At 20, abandoned engineering studies for the theatre. Acted with several companies. 1935, screen début. 1936, *Cavalleria*, a success which allowed him a fruitful and varied career. Cast as a romantic juvenile lead: *Luciano Serra, Pilota* (1937), *Montevergine* (*La Grande Luce*, 1938), *Il Cavaliere senza Nome*; *Caravaggio* (1940), *Scampolo* (1941), *Bengasi* (1942), *La Donna della Montagna*; *Il Romanzo di un Giovane Povero* (1943). Played partisan roles in neo-realist films (*Il Bandito*; *Un Giorno nella Vita*, 1946) before returning to the parts that have made him famous: *La Figlia del Capitano* (1947), *Il Lupo della Sila* (1950), *Il Brigante di Tacca del Lupo*; *Sensualità*; *Processo alla Città* (1952), *Un Marito per Anna Zaccheo* (1953), *Anna di Brooklyn* (1958). Acted for Cayatte (*Nous Sommes Tous des Assassins*) and Fellini (*Le Notti di Cabiria*: *Cabiria*, 1956). The revival of the costume film allowed him to maintain his popularity un-diminished after 30 years: *Antinea, l'Amante della Città Sepolta*; *Nefertiti, Regina del Nilo*;

I Fratelli Corsi (1961), *La Leggenda di Fra Diavolo* (1962).

Negroni, Count Baldassare (b. Rome, 21 Jan. 1877; d. 1948). Barrister, joined Cines where he was cameraman and director of comedies by Ferdinando Guillaume. 1912, moved to Celio-Film: *Idillio Tragico* and *Lagrime e Sorrisi* (with Francesca Bertini and Emilio Ghione), *Il Pappagallo della Zia Berta* (1912), *Histoire d'un Pierrot* (with Bertini), based on a pantomine by Fernand Beissier, *L'Ultima Carta*, and Genina's first scripts: *L'Anima del Demi-monde*; *La Gloria* (1913). With Genina, moved to Milano-Film in order to direct Hesperia, whom he followed to Tiber and later (1923) married. He then made numerous films for the famous *diva*: *L'Ereditiera*; *L'Ostacolo* (1914), *Vizio Atavico* (1915), *La Cuccagna*; *La Principessa di Bagdad* (1916), *La Donna Abbandonata* (1917), *Madame Flirt* (1918), *Vertigine* (1919), *Madame Sans-Gêne* (1921), *Beatrice Cenci* (1926), *Il Vetturale del Moncenisio* (1927), *Giuditta e Oloferne* (1928). Continued his career into the era of sound (*Due Cuori Felici*, 1932). 1937–46 as an associate producer.

Nelli, Piero (b. Pisa, 1926). Assisted De Santis. Short documentaries: *Cavatori di Marmo* (1950), *Patto d'Amicizia* (1952), *La Montagna Muore* (1953), *Crepusculo di un Mondo* (1953), all on social and historical themes. *La Pattuglia Sperduta* (1954), a remarkable feat of historical reconstruction. Returned to short documentaries with *Vita di Chioggia* (1956), *La Valle dell'Inferno*; *Gramsci* (1958), *Ricordate Mathausen* (1959).

Olmi, Ermanno (b. Bergamo, 24 July 1931). Studied at drama school. Actor, producer, stage comedies and musicals. 1953, some thirty documentaries for Edison-Volta, which also gave him the chance to make his first full-length film: *Il Tempo si è Fermato* (1959). In the direct line of neo-realism, Olmi confirmed his qualities with *Il Posto* (1961), *I Fidanzati* (1963), *E Venne un Uomo* (on Pope John XXIII, 1965), *Un Certo Giorno* (*One Fine Day*, 1968). *I Recuperanti* (*The Scavengers*) and *Durante L'Estate* (1970, both for TV). Acted in *Una Storia Milanese*, by Eriprando Visconti (1962).

Omegna, Roberto (b. Turin, 28 May 1876; d. Turin, 19 Nov. 1948). First Italian camera-man. Began with newsreels for Ambrosio, then became Maggi's cameraman. 1907, began making scientific films, including *La Neuro-patologia* (1908) and *La Vita delle Farfalle* (1911), which won first prize at an international congress in Turin. Travelled in Abyssinia (*Caccia a Leopardo*, 1908), Russia, South America, the Indies, Burma, China (1910–11). 1926, joined L.U.C.E. and devoted himself to educational films. Made over 150 films, the last in 1942.

Oxilia, Nino (Angelo Agostino Adolfo) (b. Turin, 13 Nov. 1889; d. Grappa, 18 Nov. 1917). Journalist, poet, playwright (*La Donna e lo Specchio*). Led to the cinema by the success of his play *Addio Giovinezza!* (1911), written in collaboration with Sandro Camasio, whom he himself imported into the cinema (Turin, 1913), together with the *diva* Lydia Quaranta. Was drawn to the historical film: *Giovanna d'Arco*, with Maria Jacobini, *Redenzione*; *In hoc Signo Vinces* (1913); then shared in the success of the *dive* with films that had aesthetic pretensions: *Il Cadavere vivente* (1913), *Sangue azzurro* (with Francesca Bertini, 1914), *Rapsodia satanica* (with Lyda Borelli, 1915). Killed in action at 28, before he could fulfil the brilliant promise of his youth.

Pagano, Bartolomeo, see **Maciste.**

Pagliero, Marcello (b. London, 15 Jan. 1907). Father Genoese, mother French. Studied law in Italy. Art and literary critic. 1941–3, translated the dialogue of American films and wrote original scripts. First film as director: *07, Tassi* (*Taxi*, 1943). *Roma, Città Aperta* (*Open City*, 1945) offered him an unexpected chance as an actor, but directing interested him more. Collaborated on various films: *Giorni di Gloria* (with Visconti and De Santis, 1945), *Desiderio* (with Rossellini, 1946), *Fosse Ardeatine*, a documentary allegedly seized by the Americans. *Roma, Città Libera* (1946), his best film. 1947, invited to France as an actor (*Les Jeux sont Faits*; *Dédée d'Anvers*, 1947; also *Le Bel Age*, 1959), he directed several films there: *Un Homme Marche dans la Ville*; *La Rose Rouge* (1950), *Les Amants de Bras-Mort* (1951), *La P . . . Respectueuse* (1952). Subsequently divided his activities between France and Italy: *Vergine Moderna*; *Chéri-Bibi* (1954), *Il Tesoro Nero* (1956) and a great Franco-Soviet documentary, *Vingt Mille Lieues sur la Terre* (1960). From 1964 onwards has taken part in French television programmes.

Palermi, Amleto (b. Rome, 11 June 1889; d. Rome, 20 April 1941). Journalist, playwright (in Sicily). Between 1914 and 1928 made twenty-one silent films; 1929–37, sixteen in sound, some of them in Germany. Then *Partire*; *Napoli d'Altri Tempi* (1938), *Le Due*

Madri, and above all *Cavalleria Rusticana*, based on Verga (1939), *La Peccatrice*; *San Giovanni Decollato* (1941), films with which Chiarini, Barbaro, Pasinetti, Zavattini and Vergano were also associated. A forerunner of the new cinema, Palermi returned to more commercial films: *Il Signore della Taverna* (1940), *L'Allegro Fantasma* (*Totò, Allegro Fantasma*, 1941).

Pasinetti, Francesco (b. Venice, 1 June 1911; d. Rome, 2 April 1949). Film critic and cinema historian. 1934, directed *Il Canale degli Angeli*, a fictionalized documentary, followed later by other films on Venice: *La Gondola*; *Venezia Minore*; *I Piccioni di Venezia* (1942), *Palazzo dei Dogi* (1947), *Città sull'Acqua* (1948–9), etc. Collaborated on various scripts. 1939, published his famous *Storia del Cinema dalle Origini al Oggi*, and edited a montage film on the history of the cinema: *Cinema di Tutti i Tempi*. Other books: *La Regia cinematografica* (1945), *Mezzo Secolo di Cinema* (1946). 1948, director of C.S.C., where he saw the *Filmlexicon* (1948) through the press.

Pasolini, Pier Paolo (b. Bologna, 5 March 1922). University. 1942, published a volume of verse: *Poesia a Casarsa*. Novelist, polemicist, published *Il Sogno di una Cosa*; *Ragazzi di Vita* (1955), *Le Ceneri di Gramsci* (1957), *L'Usignolo della Chiesa Cattolica* (1958), *Una Vita Violenta* (1959), *La Religione del Mio Tempo* (1961), *L'Odore dell'India* (1962). Equally interested in language and literature, published an anthology of dialect poetry, *Canzoniere Italiano* (1955), and a volume of essays, *Passione e Ideologia, 1948–1958* (1960). Wrote the scripts for several of Bolognini's films: *La Notte Brava* (1959), *Giornata Balorda* (1960), etc. Worked on adaptations of some of his novels, and himself directed *Accattone* (1961), *Mamma Roma* (1962), an episode in *RoGoPaG* (1963), *Comizi d'Amore*; *Il Vangelo secondo Matteo* (1964), *Uccellacci e Uccellini* (1966), *Edipo Re* (1967), *Teorema* (1968), *Porcile*; *Medea* (1969), *Il Decamerone* (1971). Acted in Lizzani's *Il Gobbo* (1960) and *Requiescant* (1966). The leading figure of his generation.

Pasquali, Ernesto Maria (b. Pavia, 1883; d. Turin, 9 May 1919). Journalist in Turin. 1908, founded Pasquali Film, for which he himself directed some of the earliest costume films: *I Due Sergenti* (1908), *Teodora, Imperatrice di Bisanzio*; *Capitan Fracassa*; *Cirano de Bergerac*; *Ettore Fieramosca* (1909), *Goetz-Mano-di-Ferro* (1910), *Il Carabiniere*; *Spartaco* (*Il*

Biographical Dictionary

Gladiatore della Tracia); *I Promessi Sposi* (1913); as well as films with modern themes – *Il Delitto della Brughiera* (1909), *L'Innocente* (1911), *Passione Tzigana* (1916) – in which he launched many stars. 1912, opened a branch in Rome, and remained active until the creation of U.C.I.

Pastrone, Giovanni, or Piero Fosco, the pseudonym under which he directed certain of his films (b. Asti, 11 Sept. 1883; d. Turin, 27 June 1959). Studied engineering. At 20, entered the firm of Carlo Rossi in Turin, and rapidly became a key figure, working on the administrative and technical sides, and directing the productions of what had become Itala-Film. Produced or directed *Giordano Bruno*; *L'Eroe di Valmy* (1908), *La Caduta di Troia* (1910), *Cabiria* (1914; 4,500 m.), the most important film of the epoch; *Il Fuoco* (1915), *Tigre Reale* (1916), *Hedda Gabler* (1919). Retired from the cinema after Itala was incorporated in U.C.I. (1920).

Perilli, Ivo (b. Rome, 10 April 1902). Qualified architect. Sets and costumes in films by Brignone, Camerini, etc. 1933, assistant script-writer and director under Camerini: *T'Amerò Sempre* (1933), *Il Cappello a Tre Punte* (1934), *Darò un Millione* (1935). 1942, directed *Margherita fra i Tre*; 1943, *La Primadonna*. Co-scripted *Europa 51* (1952), *Attila*; *Mambo* (1954), *War and Peace* (1956), *La Diga sul Pacifico* (*The Sea-Wall*, 1957), *La Tempesta* (1958), *Barabbas* (1961), *The Bible* (1966).

Petri, Elio (b. Rome, 29 Jan. 1929). Critic, scriptwriter, assistant director of documentaries. 1961, début as director with *L'Assassino*. *I Giorni Contati* (1962), *Il Maestro di Vigevano* (1963), episode in *Alta Infedeltà* (1964), *La Decima Vittima* (1965), *A Ciascuno il suo* (1966), *Un Tranquillo Posto di Campagna* (1968), *Indagine su un Cittadino al di sopra di Ogni Sospetto* (*Investigation of a Citizen above Suspicion*, 1970), *La Classe Operaia va in Paradiso* (1971).

Petrucci, Antonio (b. Rome, 1 Jan. 1907). Journalist. 1931, assistant scriptwriter. 1934, directed *Cinema, che Passione!* 1942, deported to Germany; after the war, devoted himself to documentary. 1949–53, directed the Venice festival. Documentaries: *Mestieri Veneziani* (1952–3), *Concerto d'Autunno*; *Elegie Romane* (1955), *Parma, Città d'Oro* (1957), *Il Sogno dei Gonzaga* (1958). Feature films: *Il Matrimonio* (1953), *Il Cortile* (for children, 1955). Co-edited a montage film for C.S.C., in three parts: *Antologia del Cinema* (1957). Secretary of the Associazione del Sindicato Nazionale dei Giornalisti Cinematografici.

Pietrangeli, Antonio (b. Rome, 19 Jan. 1919; d. 1968). Film critic; originally doctor of medicine. President of the Circoli del Cinema. Co-scripted *Ossessione* (1942), *Europa 51* (1952). Directed *Il Sole negli Occhi* (1953), episode in *Amori di Mezzo Secolo* (1954), *Lo Scapolo* (1956), *Souvenir d'Italie* (1957), *Nata di Marzo* (1958), *Adua e le Compagne* (1960), *Fantasmi a Roma* (1961), *La Parmigiana*; *La Visita* (1963), *Il Cornuto Magnifico* (1964), *Io la Conoscevo Bene* (1965), *Come, Quando, Perche* (1968).

Pinelli, Tullio (b. Turin, 24 June 1908). Studied law and political science. Barrister until 1942. Wrote for the theatre (*Lotta con l'Angelo*; *I Padri Etruschi*; *Gorgonio*) and radio. Film scripts: *La Figlia del Capitano* (1947), *L'Amore* (1948), *Il Mulino del Po*; *In Nome della Legge* (1949), *Il Cammino della Speranza* (1950), *Europa 51* (1952), *Il Gaucho* (1964), and, with Flaiano, all Fellini's films from *Lo Sceicco Bianco* (1952) to *Giulietta degli Spiriti* (1965). Active simultaneously in the cinema, theatre and radio.

Pittaluga, Stefano (b. Campomorone, near Genoa, 2 Feb. 1887; d. Rome, 5 April 1931). 1913, début as cinema proprietor. 1914, organized a pool for the marketing of raw film (S.A.S.P.). 1920, directed or controlled 300 cinemas, increased his capital from 50 to 150 million lire, bought up bankrupt firms. 1927, interview with Mussolini, who entrusted him with reorganizing Cines and distributing L.U.C.E. documentaries. 1930, equipped studios for sound. Initiated recovery in the Italian film industry.

Poggioli, Ferdinando Maria (b. Bologna, 15 Dec. 1897; d. Rome, 2 Feb. 1945). Commercial school. Edited short documentaries: *Presepi*; *Paestum* (1932), *Impressioni Siciliane* (1933). Feature films: *Arma Bianca* (1936), *Ricchezza senza Domani* (1939), *Addio Giovinezza!*; *L'Amore Canta* (1941), *Sissignora*; *La Bisbetica Domata* (*The Taming of the Shrew*); *Gelosia* (1942), *Il Capello da Prete* (1943). A director with a gift for narrative, who held an honourable place immediately before the period of neo-realism.

Pontecorvo, Gillo (Gilberto) (b. Pisa, 19 Nov. 1919). Degree in chemistry; course in musical composition. Journalism: Paris correspondent of Italian journals. Assistant to Yves Allégret, Mario Monicelli. 1956, directed for D.E.F.A. (East Berlin) the Giovanna episode in *De Vind Rose* (*La Rosa dei Venti*; principal director Joris Ivens), recalling women's struggle for social progress. *La Grande Strada Azzurra* (1958), *Kapò* (1960), *La Battaglia di Algeri* (*Battle of Algiers*, 1965), *Queimada!* (1968).

Ponti, Carlo (b. Magenta, near Milan, 11 Dec. 1910). Doctor of Law. 1941, associate producer, *Piccolo Mondo Antico* (*Old-Fashioned World*). Produced at Lux films by Comencini, Lattuada, Zampa. 1950, partnership with De Laurentiis (*q.v.*), resulting in major films. 1957, went to Hollywood; involved in production of films featuring Sophia Loren (*Heller in Pink Tights*, etc.), then returned to Italy. 1961 onwards, numerous Franco-Italian co-productions: *Lettere di una Novizia*; *La Ciociara* (*Two Women*, 1960), *Madame Sans-Gêne*; *Cléo de 5 à 7*; *L'Œil du Malin*; *Léon Morin, Prêtre* (1961), *Le Doulos*; *Landru*; *Boccaccio '70*; *I Sequestrati di Altona* (1962), *Les Carabiniers*; *Le Mépris* (1963), *Ieri, Oggi, Domani* (1964), *La Belva di Düsseldorf* (1965). 1964, became French citizen. 1966, married Sophia Loren.

Puccini, Gianni (b. Milan, 9 Nov. 1914; d. 1968). Studied in Copenhagen and Rome (literature and philosophy), then C.S.C. From 1938 to 1942 worked for *Cinema*, becoming editor in 1943. Scripts and adaptations: *Don Pasquale* (1940), *Soltanto un Bacio*; *Ossessione* (1942). 1946, with Pasinetti, published a work on direction. Co-scripted *Il Sole Sorge Ancora*; *Caccia Tragica* (1947), *Riso Amaro* (1948), *Non c'è Pace tra gli Ulivi* (1949), *Roma, Ore 11* (1952), *Donne Proibite* (1953), *Giorni d'Amore* (1954), *Uomini e Lupi* (1956). Assistant director on films by De Santis. Directed *Il Capitano di Venezia* (1952), *Parola di Ladro*; *Il Marito* (both with Nanni Loy, 1957), *Carmela è una Bambola* (1958), *Il Nemico di mia Moglie*; *L'Impiegato* (1959), *Carro Armato dell'Otto Settembre* (1960), an episode (*L'Idea Fissa*) in *L'Amore in Quattro Dimensioni* (1964), *I 7 Fratelli Cervi* (1967).

Quilici, Folco (b. Ferrara, 9 April 1930). 1950–2, course at C.S.C. 1952, directed a short, *Pinne e Arpioni*. 1952–3, took part in a deep-sea expedition in the Red Sea, directed *Sesto Continente* (1954) and wrote *Avventura nel Sesto Continente* and *Mala Kebir*. Journey to Belgian Congo resulted in three shorts (*Trofei d'Africa*; *Brazza*; *Storia d'un Elefante*, 1954) and the hunting scenes in *Tam Tam Mayumbe* (1955). Expedition to the South Seas: *L'Ultimo Paradiso* (1957), and numerous shorter documentaries. *Dagli Appennini alle Ande* (1959), *Ti-kojo e il suo Pescecane* (1962). Collaborated on *Le Schiave Esistono Ancora* (1964). Reporter, contributing to *Epoca, Europeo, Life, Paris-Match, L'Illustré*, etc.

Righelli, Gennaro Salvatore (b. Salerno, 12 Dec. 1886; d. Rome, 6 Jan. 1949). 1911, entered Cines, directing numerous films starring Maria Righelli. 1916, moved to Tiber, where he directed Maria Jacobini: *La Regina del Carbone* (1918), *La Casa sotto la Neve*; *Amore Rosso* (1921), etc. 1926, went to Berlin: *Heimweh* (*Homesickness*, 1927), *Der Praesident*; *Fünf bange Tage*; *Der geheime Kurier* (*Le Rouge et le Noir*, 1928). 1929, returned to Italy and made three versions of the first Italian sound film, *La Canzone dell'Amore* (1930). Directed numerous films, including *Patatrac* (1931), *L'Armata Azzurra* (1932), *L'Ultimo dei Bergerac* (1934), *La Luce del Mondo* (1935), *Amazzoni Bianche* (1936), *L'Allegro Cantante*; *Fuochi d'Artificio* (1938), *Manovre d'Amore* (1940), *Colpi di Timone* (1942), *Tempesta sul Golfo* (1943), *Abbasso la Miseria!* (1945), *Abbasso la Ricchezza!* (1947), *Il Corriere del Re* (*Le Rouge et le Noir*, 1948).

Risi, Dino (b. Milan, 23 Dec. 1917). Doctor's son, himself a psychiatrist, came to the cinema thanks to Lattuada (trainee assistant on Soldati's *Piccolo mondo antico* (*Old-fashioned World*); assistant on *Giacomo l'Idealista* (1942). Critic, scriptwriter, story-writer. Interned in Switzerland during the war, attended Jacques Feyder's courses in Geneva. Returned to Milan, directed documentaries: *Barboni* (1946), *Cortili*; *Strade di Napoli* (1947). *Vacanze col Gangster* (1952), *Il Viale della Speranza*; *L'Amore in Città* (1953), *Il Segno di Venere*; *Pane, Amore . . .* (1955), *Poveri ma Belli* (1956), *La Nonna Sabella*; *Belle ma Povere* (1957), *Venezia, la Luna e Tu* (1958), *Poveri Milionari*; *Il Vedovo* (1959), *Il Mattatore* (*Love and Larceny*); *Un Amore a Roma* (*L'Inassouvie*, 1960); *A Porte Chiuse* (*Behind Closed Doors*); *Una Vita Difficile* (1961), *Il Sorpasso* (1962), *Il Giovedì*; *I Mostri* (1963), *Il Gaucho* (1964); episode in *Le Bambole*; *L'Ombrellone* (*Weekend Italian Style*, 1965), episode in *I Nostri Mariti* (1966), *Il Tigre*; *Il Profeta* (1967), *Straziami ma di Baci Saziami* (1968), *Vedo Nudo*; *Il Giovane Normale* (1969), *La Moglie del Prete* (1970).

Rizzoli, Angelo (b. Milan, 31 Oct. 1889; d. 1970). Founder-director of a publishing group. 1934, founded Novella Film and produced Max Ophüls's *La Signora di Tutti*. 1935, *Darò*

Biographical Dictionary

un Millione. After the war, resumed production with D.E.A.R. Film: *Francesco, Giullare di Dio* (*St Francis of Assisi*), 1950. Chairman of Cineriz, responsible for the *Don Camillo* series as well as more difficult films: *Umberto D* (1952) and, more recently, *La Dolce Vita* (1960), *L'Eclisse* (1962), *Otto e Mezzo* (1963), *Il Momento della Verità* (1964), *Giulietta degli Spiriti* (1965).

Rosi, Francesco (b. Naples, 15 Nov. 1922). Studied law at university. Producer, Radio Napoli. 1946, moved to Rome. Assistant to Giannini (in the theatre), then to Visconti (*La Terra Trema*, 1948) and, for ten years, to Emmer, Giannini, Visconti, Antonioni, Monicelli. Co-scripted *Bellissima* (1951), *Racconti Romani* (1955). Technical adviser to Gassman on *Kean* (1957). Directed *La Sfida* (1957), *I Magliari* (1959), *Sicilia 43/60* (documentary short, 1960), *Salvatore Giuliano* (1962), *Le Mani sulla città* (1963), *Il Momento della Verità* (1964), *C'era una Volta* (*Cinderella Italian Style*, 1967), *Uomini Contro* (1970).

Rossellini, Roberto (b. Rome, 8 May 1906). Farmer's son. University studies; interest in cinema dates only from 1934. Dubbing, set designing, editing. L.U.C.E., making documentary shorts: *Daphne* (1936), *Prélude à l'Après-midi d'un Faune* (1938), *Fantasia Sottomarina* (1939). Co-scripted *Luciano Serra, Pilota* (1937). Directed *La Nave Bianca* (*The Hospital Ship*; under supervision of De Robertis, 1941), *Un Pilota Ritorna* (1942), *L'Uomo della Croce* (1943). *Roma, Città Aperta* (*Open City*, 1945), an intended short which grew into a full-length film, made Rossellini world-famous and opened the way to neo-realism. *Paisà*; *Desiderio* (with Pagliero; 1946), *Germania, Anno Zero* (1947), *L'Amore* (comprising *Una Voce Umana* and *Il Miracolo*), *La Macchina Ammazzacattivi* (1948), *Francesco, Giullare di Dio* (*St Francis of Assisi*), 1950. 1950, married Ingrid Bergman, who acted in *Stromboli, Terra di Dio* (1951), *Europa 51* (1952), an episode in *Siamo Donne* (*We, the Women*), *Viaggia in Italia* (1953), *Giovanna d'Arco al Rogo*; *La Paura* (1954). Also contributed Envy episode in *Les Sept Péchés Capitaux* (1952), and one in *Amori di Mezzo Secolo* (1954), and made *Dov'è la Libertà?* (1952–4). 1957, went to India and made *India* (1958), later shown on French television as a series of shorts. *Il Generale Della Rovere* (1959), *Era Notte a Roma*; *Viva l'Italia* (1960), *Vanina Vanini* (1961), *Anima Nera* (1962), episode in *RoGoPaG* (1963). For

television: *L'Era del Ferro* (1964), *La Prise de Pouvoir par Louis XIV* (1966), *Atti degli Apostoli* (1968), *Socrate* (1970). All-round director who shows psychological conflicts in a social or mystical perspective. Rossellini now proposes limiting himself to cultural shorts and television films.

Rossi, Franco (b. Florence, 28 April 1919). University, student theatricals; degree in literature. Dubbing, assistant to Comencini, Castellani, Trenker, Vergano. Radio productions. Films: *I Falsari* (1950), *Solo per Te, Lucia* (1952), *Il Seduttore* (1954), *Amici per la Pelle* (1955, his best film), *Amore a Prima Vista* (1957), *Calypso* (exotic documentary, 1958), *Tutti Innamorati* (in supervisory capacity, 1959), *Morte di un Amico* (1960), *Odissea Nuda* (1961), *Smog* (1962), *Una Rosa per Tutti* (*Everyman's Woman*, 1965). Episodes in such films as *Alta Infedeltà*; *Controsesso*; *Tre Notti d'Amore* (1964), *Le Bambole* (1965), *Le Streghe* (1966). Also *Le Avventure di Ulisse* (1968), *Giovinezza Giovinezza* (1969).

Rota, Nino (b. Milan, 3 Dec. 1911). Degree in literature; also studied music. Composed oratorio, *opéra bouffe*, songs, musical comedy. Much sought after as a composer of film music, having written scores for Castellani, Soldati, Zampa, Germi (*In Nome della Legge*, 1949), not to mention *War and Peace* (1956) and *Rocco e i Suoi Fratelli* (1960). Above all, he is Fellini's accredited musical collaborator; he has composed the scores of all his films, often repeating themes from one to another. The tunes in *I Vitelloni* (1953) and *La Strada* (1954) have been particularly popular.

Sala, Vittorio (b. Palermo, 1 July 1918). Studied law; amateur film-making. Journalist in Sicily, then Rome. Entered C.S.C., posted to the Army Cinema Centre, moved to Radio Bari (1943), returned to Rome after the liberation and wrote film criticism for a daily newspaper for five years. Assistant to De Robertis, and directed some fifty shorts. Feature films: *Donne Sole* (1956), *Costa Azzurra* (1959), *La Regina delle Amazzoni* (1960, a skit on neo-mythologism), *L'Intrigo*; *Il Treno del Sabato* (1964), *Ischia, Operazione amore* (1966).

Salce, Luciano (b. Rome, 25 Sept. 1922). Diploma in production at the Accademia d'Arte Drammatica. 1947–9, stage productions. 1949, put on a sketch at the Rose Rouge in Paris, with Bonucci and Capriolo. 1950–4, in Brazil, as a lecturer in drama, artistic director of the Teatro Brasileiro de Comédia; produced various plays. 1955, returned to

Italy, worked in the theatre and in radio. Films: *Le Pillole di Ercole* (1960), *La Voglia Matta* (*This Crazy Urge*, 1962), *Le Ore dell'Amore*; *Le Monachine* (*The Little Nuns*, 1963), episode in *Alta Infedeltà*; *El Greco* (1964), *Come Imparai ad Amare le Donne* (1966), *Ti ho Sposato per Allegria* (1967), *Colpo di Stato* (1967), episode in *La Pecora Nera* (1968), *Basta Guardaria* (1970).

Salvatori, Renato (b. Forte dei Marmi, 20 March 1933). Discovered by chance at Viareggio and engaged for *Le Ragazze di Piazza di Spagna* (*Three Girls from Rome*, 1952); success determined an unpremeditated career. *Poveri ma Belli* (1956), *Marisa la Civetta* (1957), *I Soliti Ignoti* (1958), *Audace Colpo dei Soliti Ignoti* (*Fiasco in Milan*, 1959), *Era Notte a Roma* and above all *Rocco e i Suoi Fratelli* (1960) made him an actor of international stature. Two films made in France: *Le Glaive et la Balance* (1962) and *Les Grands Chemins* (1963). Other films: *Il Disordine* (1962), *Omicron*; *I Compagni* (*The Organiser*, 1963), *Tre Notti d'Amore* (1964), *Una Bella Grinta* (1965), *La Ragazza del Bersagliere* (1966), *L'Harem* (1967), *Z* (in France), *Queimada!* (1968). Married Annie Girardot.

Serandrei, Mario (b. Naples, 23 May 1907). The most famous editor in the Italian film industry. Responsible for the cutting in *Ossessione* (1942), *Il Bidone* (1955), *La Ragazza con la Valigia* (1960), *Salvatore Giuliano* (1962), *Il Momento della Verità* (1964), *Vaghe Stelle dell'Orsa* (1965) and many other films. Co-directed *Giorni di Gloria* (1945) and directed a documentary: *Campane d'Italia*.

Soldati, Mario (b. Turin, 17 Nov. 1906). Studied literature in Turin, art history in Rome. Studied and lectured at Columbia University, N.Y. 1931, returned to Italy. Scriptwriter, editor, assistant, working mainly with Camerini (wrote script for *Gli Uomini, che Mascalzoni!*, 1932); also had a brilliant career as an author, publishing novels and *reportages* (*America Primo Amore*, 1945). Collaborated with Ozep: *La Principessa Tarakanova* (1937). Directed *Dora Nelson* (1939), *Piccolo Mondo Antico* (*Old-fashioned World*, 1941), *Malombra* (1942), thereby becoming the leading 'calligrapher'. His work is uneven, but the following deserve mention: *Eugenia Grandet* (1946), *Daniele Cortis* (1947), *Fuga in Francia* (1948), *Donne e Briganti* (1950), *La Provinciale* (1953, his best film), *La Donna del Fiume* (1955), *Italia Piccola* (1957), *Policarpo, Ufficiale di Scrittura* (1959). Also acted in *Mio*

Figlio Professore (1946) and *Napoli Milionaria* (1950).

Sordi, Alberto (b. Rome, 15 June 1919). At 13, won an M.-G.-M. competition for dubbing the voice of Oliver Hardy. Music-hall and theatre. Became popular through radio sketches. 1936, joined Ermete Zacconi's company. 1938 onwards, acted regularly in films, but only made his mark around 1952: *Lo Sceicco Bianco* (1952), *I Vitelloni*; *Tempi Nostri* (1953), *La Bella di Roma* (1955), *Lo Scapolo* (1956), *A Farewell to Arms* (1957), *Fortunella* (1958), *Nella Città l'Inferno*; *I Magliari*; *Policarpo, Ufficiale di Scrittura* (1959), *Tutti a Casa* (1960), *Il Mafioso* (1962), *Il Boom*; *Il Maestro di Vigevano*; *Il Diavolo* (*To Bed or not to Bed*, 1963), *I Tre Volti* (1965), *Un Italiano in America* (1967), *Amore Mio, Aiutami* (1969), *Contestazione Generale*; *Il Presidente del Borgorosso Football Club* (1970), *Le Coppie* (1971). The most popular Italian actor, in 1965 Sordi directed: *Fumo di Londra*, and in 1969, *Amore Mio, Aiutami*. Also an episode in *Le Coppie* (1971).

Steno, Stefano Vanzina (b. Rome, 19 Jan. 1915). University. 1938, C.S.C., editor and cartoonist of a humorous journal. 1939, qualified lawyer. Assistant to Mattoli, Bragaglia, Freda. Scripts for Soldati, Blasetti. After the war, scriptwriting and direction, mainly of comedies, in association with Monicelli (*q.v.*). Partnership broke up in 1953; Steno continued making films in the same vein: *Cinema d'Altri Tempi* (1953), *Le Avventure di Giacomo Casanova* (1954), *Mio Figlio Nerone* (1956), *Gli Eroi del West* (1964), *Il Trapianto* (1970).

Stoppa, Paolo (b. Rome, 16 June 1906). A specialist in secondary parts in films, he has enjoyed a full career, both in the cinema and on the stage, where he began around 1930. With Rina Morelli he directed a theatrical company for which Visconti produced several plays. His first screen parts date from about 1935. Without becoming a star, he showed considerable inventiveness, and was featured in numerous Italian and French films: *La Corona di Ferro* (1940), *I Cavalieri della Maschera Nera* (1947), *Miracolo a Milano* (1951), *Les Belles de Nuit*, where he played a colourful operatic director; *Roma, Ore 11* (1952), *Le Retour de Don Camillo*; *L'Amour d'une Femme* (1953), *L'Oro di Napoli* (1954), *La Bella Mugnaia*; *La Bella di Roma* (1955), *La Legge* (1959), *Giornata Balorda*; *Rocco e i Suoi Fratelli*; *Quelle Joie de Vivre* (1960), *Il*

Giudizio Universale (*The Last Judgement*), *Vanina Vanini* (1961), *Boccaccio '70* (1962), *Il Gattopardo* (1963), *Becket* (1964), *Caccia alla Volpe* (1966), *C'era una Volta il West* (*Once Upon a Time in the West*), *La Matriarca* (1968).

Taviani, Paolo and **Vittorio.** (Paolo b. San Miniato, 1931; Vittorio b. San Miniato, 1929). Starting in the theatre, they joined V. Orsini in organizing a cycle of popular yet *avant-garde* performances at the Teatro della Cronaca, Livorno. Made their cinema début with a short, *San Miniato, Giulio 1944*, on the theme of the Resistance. After moving to Rome, collaborated with Joris Ivens (1959–60) and directed *Un Uomo da Bruciare* (1962), on the struggle against the Mafia in Sicily. 1963, *I Fuorilegge del Matrimonio*. Parted company with Orsini and made *Sotto il Segno dello Scorpione* and *I Sovversivi* (1968).

Tognazzi, Ugo (b. Cremona, 23 March 1922). Lower-middle-class origins. Accountant. Took part in a competition for young actors, joined various minor companies. 1950, first screen part: *I Cadetti di Guascogna*. During the 1950s, minor parts only, achieving success after 1960: *Quelle Joie de Vivre!*; *Il Federale* (*The Fascist*, 1961), *La Marcia su Roma*; *La Voglia Matta* (*This Crazy Urge,* 1962), *RoGoPaG*; *Una Storia Moderna*; *l'Ape Regina* (*Queen Bee*); *Liolà*; *I Mostri* (1963; a dazzling demonstration, with Gassman, of inventive gifts), *Alta Infedeltà*; *La donna Scimmia*; *Il Cornuto Magnifico*; *La Vita Agra* (1964), *Il Fischio al Naso* (1967), *Sissignora* (1968), *La Califfa* (1970). Directed *Il Mantenuto* (1961).

Tonti, Aldo (b. Rome, 2 March 1910). An outstanding cameraman in numerous outstanding films: *Fari nella Nebbia* (1941), *Ossessione* (1942), *Il Sole Sorge Ancora*; *Il Delitto di Giovanni Episcopo* (1947), *Il Mulino del Po* (1949), *Il Lupo della Sila* (1950), *Europa 51* (1952), *War and Peace* (working with Jack Cardiff, 1956), *L'Uomo a Cinque Palloni* (1964), *Casanova '70* (1965), *Citta Violentà* (1970). Has acted in a number of character parts.

Totò, pseudonym of Antonio De Curtis (b. Naples, 15 Feb. 1901; d. Rome, 15 April 1967). Impoverished family, hard childhood. Haunted suburban theatres. Began acting in obscure variety theatres, gradually gained popularity, but was late in making his film début (1936). Success came only after the war, when eventually Totò became one of the most popular comic actors of the Italian cinema: *Napoli Milionaria* (1950), *Guardie e Ladri*

(*Cops and Robbers*, 1951), *Dov'è la Libertà?*; *L'Oro di Napoli* (1954), *La Legge è Legge* (1956), *I Soliti Ignoti* (1958), *I Tartassati* (1959), *Risate di Gioia* (1960), *Tempo di Roma* (*Esame di Guida*, 1963), and the Totò series: *Totò a Parigi*; *Totò e Marcellino* (1958), *Totò, Peppino e . . . la dolce vita* (1961), *Totò contro Maciste* (1962), in which he created a comic type. Starred for Pasolini in *Uccellacci e Uccellini* (1966).

Valli, Alida, pseudonym of Alida Maria Altemburger (b. Pola, 31 May 1921). Daughter of a journalist of Austrian origin. 1928, school at Como. 1936, entered C.S.C., but was immediately engaged and began her career at 15, playing ingénues. Her ability and charm rapidly established her as the representative of a new school opposed to the sophisticated extravagance of the *dive*: *Manon Lescaut* (1939), *Luce nelle Tenebre*; *Piccolo Mondo Antico* (*Old-fashioned World*; prize for acting), *Ore 9 Lezione di Chimica* (1941), *Catene Invisibili*; *Le Due Orfanelle*; *Stasera Niente di Nuovo* (1942). After *Noi Vivi* (*Addio, Kira!*, 1942), refused parts in Fascist films and announced abandonment of career. Three years later, reappeared in *La Vita Ricomincia* (1945) and *Eugenia Grandet* (1946). Was engaged by Hollywood and became an international star, acting in *The Paradine Case* (in U.S.A., 1947), *The Third Man* (in Vienna, 1949), *La Torre Bianca*; *Les Miracles n'ont Lieu qu'une Fois* (in France, 1950), *Les Amants de Tolède* (in Spain, 1953). Each of her performances added to her stature: *Senso* (1954), *Il Grido*; *La Diga sul Pacifico* (*The Seawall*, 1957). More films in France: *Les Bijoutiers du Clair de Lune* (1957), *Les Yeux sans Visage* (1959), *Le Dialogue des Carmélites* (1960), *Une Aussi Longue Absence* (1961), *Ophélia* (1962), *L'Autre Femme* (1963). Stayed for some time in Mexico; returned to Italy and acted in *Edipo Re* (1967), *La Strategia del Ragno* (1970).

Vallone, Raf (b. Tropea, Calabria, 17 Feb. 1916). Studied in Turin. 1945, journalist specializing in the cinema. Began career with a major part in *Riso Amaro* (1948). His success and physical attributes determined his future as an actor: *Non c'è Pace tra gli Ulivi* (1949), *Il Cammino della Speranza* (1950), *Il Cristo Proibito* (1951). His performance in Carné's *Thérèse Raquin* (1953) consolidated his international renown. His films include: made in France, *Obsession* (1954), *Le Secret de Sœur Angèle* (1955); in Italy, *La Spiaggia* (1954),

Guendalina (1957), *La Garçonnière* (1960); in Germany, *Bernd* (1956); in Spain, *La Venganza* (1957), *El Cid* (1961); in Greece, *Phaedra* (1962); in America, *A View from the Bridge* (1962), *The Cardinal* (1963), *Secret Invasion* (1964). Also a stage actor and producer, he has staged in France, most notably, *A View from the Bridge* and *Le Repos du Guerrier*, which he himself had dramatized from Christine Rochefort's novel. He made his début as a scriptwriter in a film featuring Shirley MacLaine.

Vancini, Florestano (b. Ferrara, 24 August 1926). Directed some forty documentaries. Feature films: *La Lunga Notte del '43* (1960), based on Bassani's *Cinque Storie Ferraresi*; episode in *Le Italiane e l'Amore* (*Latin Lovers*, 1961), *La Calda Vita* (1964), *Le Stagioni del Nostro Amore*; *I Lunghi Giorni della Vendetta* (1966), *L'Isola* (1968), *I Fatti di Bronte* (1970).

Vergano, Aldo (b. Rome, 27 August 1891; d. Rome, 21 Sept. 1957). Various occupations in Sardinia. Journalist; 1921–3, Balkan correspondent. Advent of Fascism decided him to abandon journalism. Returned to Italy, as street hawker, head waiter, decorator. Returned to journalism on the opposition paper *La Voce Republicana*, soon suppressed, and Vergano castigated for 'infamous political behaviour'. Returned to Sardinia, then to the South. Blasetti invited him to collaborate on his first film: *Sole* (1929). Moved in anti-Fascist circles, had to retire again to Sardinia. Returned, worked on various scripts. Helped Alessandrini to direct *Cavalleria* (1936). Became an associate producer and director: *Pietro Micca* (1938), *Quelli della Montagna* (1943). Joined the Action Party, fought in Latium, was arrested, escaped and joined the partisans. Took an active part in forming the 'Syndicate of Cinema Workers'. His *Il Sole Sorge Ancora* (1947) remains a classic among Resistance films. Directed *Il Passo del Diavolo* (in Poland, 1949), *I Fuorilegge* (1950), *La Grande Rinuncia* (1951), *Amore Rosso* (1953). Had previously helped in the making of L'Herbier's *Gli Ultimi Giorni di Pompei* (1950). Unjustly neglected, badly treated by life and the difficulties of his career, Vergano gave vent to his bitterness in a book, *Cronaca degli Anni Sperduti*.

Visconti, Luchino, Duke of Modrone (b. Milan, 2 Nov. 1906). Old, aristocratic Lombard family. Maintained stables and devoted ten years to horses and racing. 1935, via set-designing, became interested in the cinema.

Gabriel Pascal suggested he should make a film with Korda, but nothing came of this. London, then Paris; assistant to Jean Renoir (*Les Bas-Fonds*; *Une Partie de Campagne*, 1936). Returned to Italy, designed sets. Joined forces again with Renoir for *Tosca* (completed by Carl Koch, with Visconti's help, 1940). Made contact with the *Cinema* team, wrote a script on a Verga theme which was turned down, but made *Ossessione* (1942). Took up a stance with the Communists in the country's political and cultural life. Worked with Antonioni on various abortive projects, then collaborated with Pagliero, De Santis and Serandrei on *Giorni di Gloria* (1945), a montage film about the liberation. 1945, staged several plays (*Les Parents Terribles*; *Antigone*; *Huis Clos*) at the Eliseo in Rome, winning world renown for his daring productions. 1947, returned to a Verga theme and made *La Terra Trema* (1948), intended as the first film in a Sicilian trilogy. Returning to the theatre, Visconti staged Shakespeare with sets by Dali and Provençal choruses. Next film, three years later, was *Bellissima* (1951), followed by two episodes, one in *Siamo Donne* (*We, the Women*, 1953), and *Senso* (1954). Continued his stage work in Italy and abroad. 1957, at Venice, presented a new film, *Le Notti Bianche*, based on a story by Dostoyevsky. *Rocco e i suoi Fratelli* (1960), episode in *Boccaccio '70* (1962), *Il Gattopardo* (1963), *Vaghe stelle dell'Orsa* (1965), episode in *Le Streghe* (1966), *Lo Straniero* (based on Camus, 1967), *La Caduta degli Dei* (*The Damned*, 1969), *Morte a Venezia* (*Death in Venice*, 1970).

Vitti, Monica, pseudonym of Maria Luisa Ceciarelli (b. Rome, 3 Nov. 1933). Stage début around 1953. Three years of touring and small theatres. 1955, radio and television. 1957, met Antonioni in connection with *Il Grido* (in which she dubbed the voice of Dorian Gray), and became the star of the theatrical company which he then assembled (1958). Had already appeared in small film parts. Antonioni revealed her gifts in *L'Avventura* (1959), after which she became his leading actress: *La Notte* (1960), *L'Eclisse* (1962), *Deserto Rosso* (1964). Has also acted in *Alta Infedeltà* (1964), *Le Bambole* (1965), *La Cintura da Castità; La Moglie del Prete* (1969); in France, *Les Quatre Vérités* (1963), *Château en Suède; Dragées au Poivre* (1963), *La Femme Ecarlate* (1968), *Dramma della Gelosia; Amore Mio Aiutami* (1969), *Nini*

Biographical Dictionary

Tirabusciò la Donna che Invento la Mossa (1970); in U.K. *Modesty Blaise* (1966).

Zampa, Luigi (b. Rome, 2 Jan. 1904). Studied engineering. 1928, wrote three plays, all of which were performed. 1935–8, course at C.S.C. 1938–41, wrote a dozen scripts. 1941, directed *L'Attore Scomparso*, followed by other films. Success established with *Un Americano in Vacanza* (1946), *Vivere in Pace*; *L'Onorevole Angelina* (1947) and *Anni Difficili* (1948), a satirical comedy and the prototype of *Anni Facili* (1953) and *Anni Ruggenti* (1962). His later films show less verve than the earlier ones. They include *Processo alla Città* (*City on Trial*, 1952), an episode in *Siamo Donne* (*We, the Women*, 1953), *La Ragazza del Palio* (*The Love Specialist*, 1957), *Il Magistrato* (1959), *Frenesia dell'Estate* (1963), an episode in *I Nostri Mariti* (1966), *Le Dolci Signore* (*Anyone can Play*, 1967), *Il Medico della Mutua* (1968), *Contestazione Generale* (1969).

Zavattini, Cesare (b. Luzzara, Emilia, 20 Sept. 1902). 1927, began writing journalism. 1931–40, edited reviews, wrote for children's magazines, published novels and stories, wrote his first scripts, including *Darò un Millione* (1935). From 1940, became one of Italy's most prolific scriptwriters, and played a key part as a writer on neo-realist themes, especially in collaboration with De Sica. Remained the most intransigent defender of primitive neo-realism. Principal scriptwriter in some hundred films: *Quattro Passi fra le Nuvole* (1942), *I Bambini ci Guardano* (1943), *Un Giorno nella Vita*, *Sciuscià* (*Shoeshine*, 1946), *Ladri di Biciclette*; *Au-delà des Grilles* (*Le Mura di Malapaga*, 1948), *E Primavera* (*Springtime*, 1949), *Prima Comunione*; *Domenica d'Agosto* (1950), *Miracolo a Milano* (1951), *Umberto D*; *Buongiorno Elefante!* (1952), *L'Amore in Città* (1953), *L'Oro di Napoli* (1954), *Il Tetto* (1956), *La Ciociara* (*Two Women*, 1960), *Il Giudizio Universale* (*The Last Judgement*), *Le Italiane e l'Amore* (*Latin Lovers*, 1961), *Boccaccio '70* (1962), *Ieri, Oggi, Domani* (1964), *Un Mondo Nuovo* (1965).

Zeffirelli, Franco (b. Florence, 12 Feb. 1923). Began as an actor and painter of sets. 1948–53, assisted Visconti for *La Terra Trema* (1948), *Bellissima* (1951), *Senso* (1954) and his stage productions: *A Streetcar named Desire*; *The Three Sisters*, etc. He himself graduated to production, and scored a success at the Scala, Milan, with Rossini's *Cenerentola*. Pursued this career with verve, in Italy, France, the U.K. and U.S.A. Made an episode film, *Camping* (1957), and, in 1966, a version of *The Taming of the Shrew*, with Elizabeth Taylor and Richard Burton. Confirmed his mastery with *Romeo and Juliet* (1968), which in 1961 he had produced at the Old Vic.

Zurlini, Valerio (b. Bologna, 19 March 1926). Studied law; active in university theatre. 1948, began making shorts (fifteen documentaries). Feature films: *Le Ragazze di San Frediano* (1954, based on Pratolini), *Estate Violenta* (1959), *La Ragazza con la Valigia* (1960), *Cronaca Familiare* (1962), *Le Soldatesse* (*The Camp-followers*, 1964, based on Ugo Piero), *Seduta alla sua Destra* (*Out of Darkness*, 1968).

Select Bibliography

ARMES, Roy: *Patterns of realism: a study of Italian neo-realist cinema.* London, Tantivy Press; New York, A. S. Barnes, 1971.

BIANCHI, Pietro: *La Bertini e le dive del cinema muto.* Turin, U.T.E.T., 1969.

GILI, Jean A., *editor*: *Fascisme et résistance dans le cinéma italien.* Paris, Lettres Modernes, 1970. (Etudes Cinématographiques no. 82/83)

HOVALD, Patrice G.: *Le néo-réalisme italien et ses créateurs.* Paris, Editions du Cerf, 1959.

HUACO, George A.: *The sociology of film art.* New York, London, Basic Books, 1965. [Includes a section on Italian neo-realism.]

JARRATT, Vernon: *The Italian cinema.* London, Falcon Press, 1951.

MALERBA, Luigi, *and* SINISCALO, Carmine, *editors*: *Fifty years of Italian cinema.* Rome, Carlo Bestetti, 1954. [Heavily illustrated.]

MALERBA, Luigi, *editor*: *Italian cinema 1945–1951.* Rome, Carlo Bestetti, 1951.

MARINUCCI, Vinicio: *Tendencies of the Italian cinema.* Rome, Unitalia Film, 1959.

RONDI, Brunello: *Cinema e realtà.* Rome, Edizione Cinque Lune, 1957.

RONDI, Gian Luigi: *Italian cinema today, 1952–1965.* London, Dennis Dobson, 1966. [Heavily illustrated.]

RONDOLINI, Gianni: *Dizionario del cinema italiano, 1945–1969.* Turin, Giulio Einaudi, 1969.

Individual Studies

CAMERON, Ian, *and* WOOD, Robin: *Antonioni.* London, Studio Vista, 1969; New York, Praeger, 1969.

LEPROHON, Pierre: *Michelangelo Antonioni: an introduction*; translated from the French by Scott Sullivan. New York, Simon and Schuster, 1963.

BUDGEN, Suzanne: *Fellini.* London, British Film Institute, 1966.

SALACHAS, Gilbert: *Federico Fellini*; translated from the French by Rosalie Siegel. New York, Crown, 1969.

SOLMI, Angelo: *Fellini*; translated from the Italian by Elizabeth Greenwood. London, Merlin Press; 1967; New York, Humanities Press, 1968.

STACK, Oswald: *Pasolini on Pasolini: interviews.* London, Thames and Hudson, 1969; Bloomington, Indiana University Press, 1970.

GUARNER, José Luis: *Roberto Rossellini*; translated by Elisabeth Cameron. London, Studio Vista; New York, Praeger, 1970.

NOWELL-SMITH, Geoffrey: *Luchino Visconti.* London, Secker and Warburg, 1967; Garden City (N.Y.), Doubleday, 1968.

ZAVATTINI, Cesare: *Zavattini: sequences from a cinematic life*; translated from the Italian by William Weaver. Englewood Cliffs, Prentice-Hall, 1970.

Federico Fellini directing *Satyricon*, 1969

Index

Index

Inferno (Giuseppe De Liguoro, 1909), 21
In Nome della Legge [*In the Name of the Law*] (Pietro Germi, 1949), 118–19
Iron Crown, The see *Corona di Ferro, La*
Itala-Film, 14
Italiani Brava Gente (Giuseppe De Santis, 1964), 189

Jacobini, Diomira, 55
Jacobini, Maria, 232
Jacoby, Georg, 54
Jannings, Emil, 54
Jason and the Golden Fleece see *Giganti della Tessaglia, I*
Jester's Supper, The see *Cena delle Beffe, La*
Juliet of the Spirits see *Giulietta degli Spiriti*

Kanzler, Baron, 10
Kapò (Gillo Pontecorvo, 1960), 188
Korda, Maria, 58

Labours of Hercules, The see *Fatiche di Ercole, Le*
Ladri di Biciclette [*Bicycle Thieves*] (Vittorio De Sica, 1948), 109–10, 114, 116, 128
Last Days of Pompeii, The see *Ultimi Giorni di Pompei, Gli*
Latium, 14
Lattuada, Alberto, 73, 77–9, 98, 103–4, 120, 162–3, 196, 232
Laurentiis, Dino De see De Laurentiis, Dino
Leda senza Cigno, La (Giulio Cesare Antamoro, 1917), 23
Legenda della Passiflora, La (1911?), 39
Lelieur, Mme, 10
Lenghi, Otto, 14
Leone, Sergio, 232
Leopard, The see *Gattopardo, Il*
Lépine, Charles, 13
L'Herbier, Marcel, 97
Liguoro, Giuseppe De see De Liguoro, Giuseppe
Linder, Max, 24
Lisi, Virna, 182
Lizzani, Carlo, 100, 109, 116, 157–8, 188, 232

Lola Montès (Max Ophuls, 1955), 206
Lollobrigida, Gina, 109, 182, 232–3
Lombardo, Goffredo, 233
Long Night of 1943, The see *Lunga Notte del '43, La*
Loren, Sophia, 233
Lo Savio, Gerolamo, 17
Lost Youth see *Gioventù Perduta*
Love in the City see *Amore in Città, L'*
Loy, Nanni, 189, 233
Lualdi, Antonella, 233
L.U.C.E. (L'Unione Cinematografica Educativa), 58
Luciano (Gian Vittotio Baldi, 1963), 196
Luciano Serra, Pilota (Goffredo Alessandrini, 1937), 72
Luci del Varietà (Alberto Lattuada, Federico Fellini, 1950), 141–2
Lumière, Auguste and Louis, 10
Lunga Notte del '43, La (Florestano Vancini, 1960), 189
Luzzati, Emmanuelle, 186

Macchina Ammazzacattivi, La (Roberto Rossellini, 1948), 133
Maciste, 31, 55, 233
Maciste nella Valle dei Re (Carlo Campogalliani, 1960), 175
Mafioso (Alberto Lattuada, 1962), 191
Maggi, Luigi, 13, 17, 22, 233–4
Magliari, I (Francesco Rosi, 1959), 190
Magnani, Anna, 72, 116, 134, 234
Ma L'Amor Mio non Muore (Mario Caserini, 1913), 34
Malaparte, Curzio, 162, 234
Malia dell'Oro (Gaston Velle, 1906), 12
Mamma Roma (Pier Paolo Pasolini, 1962), 207
Mangano, Silvana, 234
Mani sulla Città, Le [*Hands over the City*] (Francesco Rosi, 1963), 198
Man of Iron see *Ferroviere, Il*
Man of Straw see *Uomo di Paglia, L'*
Manzini, Italia Almirante see Almirante Manzini, Italia
Marcia su Roma, La (Dino Risi, 1962), 189
Mari, Febo, 38, 42, 44
Marinetti, F. T., 45
Martelli, Otello, 234
Martoglio, Nino, 40–2, 234

252

Index